Moving Mountains

Edited by Jean Michaud and Tim Forsyth

Moving Mountains
Ethnicity and Livelihoods in Highland China, Vietnam, and Laos

UBCPress · Vancouver · Toronto

© UBC Press 2011

All rights reserved. No part of this publication may be reproduced, stored in a retrieval system, or transmitted, in any form or by any means, without prior written permission of the publisher, or, in Canada, in the case of photocopying or other reprographic copying, a licence from Access Copyright, www.accesscopyright.ca.

21 20 19 18 17 16 15 14 13 12 11   5 4 3 2 1

Printed in Canada on FSC-certified ancient-forest-free paper
(100% post-consumer recycled) that is processed chlorine- and acid-free.

Library and Archives Canada Cataloguing in Publication

Moving mountains : ethnicity and livelihoods in highland China, Vietnam, and Laos / edited by Jean Michaud and Tim Forsyth.

Includes bibliographical references and index.
ISBN 978-0-7748-1837-7

1. Mountain people – Southeast Asia – Social conditions. 2. Mountain people – Southeast Asia – Economic conditions. I. Michaud, Jean II. Forsyth, Tim

GN635.S58M69 2010   305.800959   C2010-904720-6

Canada

UBC Press gratefully acknowledges the financial support for our publishing program of the Government of Canada (through the Canada Book Fund), the Canada Council for the Arts, and the British Columbia Arts Council.

This book has been published with the help of a grant from the Canadian Federation for the Humanities and Social Sciences, through the Aid to Scholarly Publications Programme, using funds provided by the Social Sciences and Humanities Research Council of Canada.

UBC Press
The University of British Columbia
2029 West Mall
Vancouver, BC V6T 1Z2
www.ubcpress.ca

Contents

Illustrations / vii

Foreword / ix
Terry McGee

Acknowledgments / xvii

1 Rethinking the Relationships between Livelihoods and Ethnicity in Highland China, Vietnam, and Laos / 1
Tim Forsyth and Jean Michaud

2 Economic Marginalization and Social Identity among the Drung People of Northwest Yunnan / 28
Stéphane Gros

3 Integration of a Lineage Society on the Laos-Vietnam Border / 50
Steeve Daviau

4 Oral Histories of Livelihoods and Migration under Socialism and Post-Socialism among the Khmu of Northern Laos / 76
Olivier Évrard

5 Of Rice and Spice: Hmong Livelihoods and Diversification in the Northern Vietnam Uplands / 100
Claire Tugault-Lafleur and Sarah Turner

6 Hani Agency and Ways of Seeing Environmental Change on the China-Vietnam Border / 123
John McKinnon

7 Land Reform and Changing Identities in Two Tai-Speaking Districts in Northern Vietnam / 146
Marie Mellac

8 Commoditized Ethnicity for Tourism Development in Yunnan / 173
Margaret Byrne Swain

9 Rubber Transformations: Post-Socialist Livelihoods and Identities for Akha and Tai Lue Farmers in Xishuangbanna, China / 193
Janet C. Sturgeon

10 Conclusion: Lesson for the Future / 215
Jean Michaud

Contributors / 228

Index / 231

Illustrations

1.1 The Southeast Asian Massif and the eight case study chapters / 4
2.1 Nujiang Lisu Nationality Autonomous Prefecture and Gongshan Dulong and Nu Nationalities Autonomous County / 29
2.2 Distribution of the Dulong population in Gongshan County / 30
2.3 Main political spheres in northwestern Yunnan (c. 1900) / 32
3.1 Tarieng area in the Annam Range / 51
3.2 Original Tarieng village setting / 53
3.3 Resettled Tarieng village / 57
3.4 Village development cluster, Xieng Louang, Dakcheung district / 59
3.5 Free-roaming buffaloes typical of Tarieng husbandry / 63
3.6 Customary buffalo sacrifice ritual among the Tarieng / 63
3.7 Educational board by German Agro Action / 64
4.1 Mon-Khmer populations in northwest Laos / 78
4.2 Khmu subgroups' areas *(tmoys)* / 82
4.3 Resettlement of highland villages in Nalae district / 86
4.4 Mokkoud and Konkoud villages / 88
4.5 "Strengthen friendship between all the ethnic groups to unify the [Lao] society" / 89
4.6 "The army needs the people like the fish needs water" / 93
5.1 Sa Pa district in Lào Cai province, northern Vietnam / 103
5.2 Sa Pa District and Hoàng Liên National Park / 105
5.3 Typical Hmong household labour calendar in Sa Pa district / 107
5.4 A Hmong household's fuel wood collection in San Sả Hồ commune / 109
5.5 A Hmong healer in her medicinal plant garden / 111
5.6 Livelihood portfolio for Hoa's household, Lào Chải commune / 114
5.7 Livelihood portfolio for Tao's household, Bản Khoang commune / 114

6.1 Study area / 127
6.2 Land use in Shapu sector of Badong sub-catchment, 1990 / 137
6.3 Land use in Shapu sector of Badong sub-catchment, 1999 / 138
7.1 Fieldwork location in Northern Vietnam / 149
7.2 Overlapping influences of land-based institutions' models / 150
7.3 Land management and administration, situation at the national and local level / 151
7.4 An upper view of Ban Luot village, Than Uyên district / 160
7.5 Phong Huan commune, Cho Don district / 162
7.6 Behind the differences: two apparently opposite cases generated by similar processes / 164
9.1 Yunnan province, China / 194
9.2 Xishuangbanna, Yunnan province and Muang Sing, in Laos / 195
9.3 Rubber plantations in Xishuangbanna / 203
9.4 Modern young Akha women in Xishuangbanna / 210

Foreword
Terry McGee

> *It is much easier to move mountains than to change minds.*
> – Mien saying

It is a little surprising to find myself as an avowed urbanist writing a foreword for a book that focuses on the ethnic minorities in the eastern part of the Southeast Asian Massif, and in particular, on the highland borderlands of socialist China, Vietnam, and Laos – an area that is not characterized by high levels of urbanization. Fifty years of research on urbanization in Southeast Asia and China rarely took me beyond the metropoles of the region. The closest I got to the Massif was in the 1980s when I conceived the idea of what I believed to be a cunningly devised project to carry out research on the "colonial origins" of the "hill stations" of Southeast Asia, where history and liveability would combine to enable "comfortable fieldwork" in the pleasant temperatures of the highlands. Unfortunately, the project had to be aborted. Someone more clever than I had already mined the field and published it in a rather obscure press that my far from thorough research had failed to unearth.

However, in the process of doing preliminary work for that project, I spent a month in Dalat, the summer residence of the Emperor Bao Dai and the former French colonial administration. With the help of Vietnamese colleagues, a visit to an "ethnic minority village" was organized. At first, this appeared to be unlikely. Many permits had to be obtained from officials at different levels of the administration. But eventually we set forth in heavy rain; the macadam road ceased three kilometres outside Dalat and became a dirt road, which seemed to have temporarily become a major watercourse. Eventually, we stopped at a village that consisted of what appeared to be rather comfortable government-like housing. Not at all my image of a so-called ethnic minority village. It was in fact the commune headquarters, where, after meeting the chairman of the People's Committee who, along with everyone else, appeared to be Kinh, we were entertained to a lengthy and quite alcoholic lunch. This seemed to break the ice, and around about 4 p.m. we set off for the ethnic minority village, where we met our first ethnic minority representative. He spoke English with a marked American accent (somewhere in the South), and it turned out he had spent the last twenty-five years in the United States after arriving there as a refugee with his family. His family had originally come from this village, and he had returned to try to develop the village as a tourist site, working with tourist operators in Dalat. Members of the village staged a program featuring cheerful presentations of the local culture, dances, and goods – for example, woven baskets, food, and rice wine – which involved ample opportunity for the participation of the tourist that I had become instead of the researcher I had been. Far from the grassroots entrepreneurs of Yunnan of whom Margaret Byrne Swain writes in Chapter 8, the organizer was engaged in manipulating the authentic, in what seemed to me a reflection of American marketing practices. Having filled in the comments form with fulsome praise, we left at about 9 p.m. for the rather arduous journey back to Dalat.

I have engaged in this lengthy anecdote as a perhaps irreverent way to find an intersection between the world of cities that has been my research focus and this study of the ethnic minorities of the Southeast Asian Massif. A world remote and isolated from the large lowland cities, or so I believed. But as the Dalat experience reveals, this idea of remoteness and isolation and separation from urban areas needs to be carefully evaluated.

This observation leads me to the central issue I would like to explore in this brief foreword, which is how the processes of change among upland ethnic minorities resonate with the changes occurring in the urban areas of Southeast Asia. On the face of it, this is a very provocative proposition, for it challenges the conventional wisdoms that rural and urban areas are sharply differentiated, that urbanites are somehow more entrepreneurial and cosmopolitan than people who live outside urban areas, and that urban dwellers are less resistant to change. This, like much of the conventional wisdoms that influence research and policies in developing countries, is mostly derived from the experience of developed countries, as Forsyth and Michaud emphasize in Chapter 1 with their statement that "clearly, we should be careful in transferring concepts developed in settings such as modern industrial societies or post-industrial cities to locations such as the Southeast Asian Massif."

Expanding the Knowledge of Southeast Asia

The three specific questions, paraphrased from Chapter 1, that this book seeks to answer in the study of these upland ethnic minorities are, I suggest, also echoed in the current rethinking about the urbanization process in Southeast Asia:

1 How do local populations on the margins of centralized states make a living and maintain their identity in terms of external forces – the state and, the market – and their own agency?
2 Why does the understanding of highland livelihoods need a more nuanced frame of transnationalism rather than simply proceeding by country analysis?
3 How can a more complex stance about assumptions of the region as a predictable social space be adopted?

These questions reflect a wider set of underlying themes that relate to the way knowledge is being generated about the processes of social and economic change in developing countries. But my interest in the book is the way it contributes to expanding our understandings of what I have called elsewhere the many "knowledge(s)" of Southeast Asia (McGee 2007). In this piece, I identify three types of knowledge as they are being used to interpret Southeast Asia. The first is "above ground knowledge," which is what I would call globally applied theories that rely on hegemonic paradigms. The second is what I call "grounded knowledge," which is a form of knowledge embedded in the practices of people and culture that inform these practices. Third, the idea of "underground knowledge," which is influenced by James C. Scott's formulations of everyday forms of resistance and the hidden transcripts of local people (Scott 1985, 1990).

In focusing on these issues, I of course realize that I am leaving aside important issues such as culture, kin systems, and identity that are an important part of the intellectual underpinning of the book. The editors and the other authors are certainly aware of the debates about the meaning of these terms that have been generated in the literature. I will leave it for reviewers to engage the issue of how important culture and identity are to an understanding of the way ethnic minorities survive in the Southeast Asian Massif.

Utilizing the framework of many knowledge(s), I would suggest three ways in which the book intersects with the formation of knowledge about Southeast Asian urban areas and contributes to our understanding of Southeast Asia as a whole. These are emphasizing the need to (1) (re)conceptualize hegemonic paradigms that are applied at a global level to interpret social, economic, and political change at national and local levels (above ground); (2) stress the importance of long-term grounded research into the practices and knowledge of local people that empower the role of local knowledge (grounded knowledge); and (3) recognize that there is also a form of underground knowledge and action that informs these practices, that is not understood or in many cases even known by policy makers, and that rarely informs global theories. In the next section, I explore these ideas in greater detail in a suggestive way rather than a prescriptive one.

(Re)conceptualizing Global Hegemonic Paradigms (Above Ground Knowledge)

Three hegemonic paradigms have influenced thinking about processes of change in Southeast Asia.

The Domination of the Idea of Urban and Rural Difference

First is the spatially embedded idea that rural and urban spaces are sharply divided and that within these spaces, rural and urban life are sharply different. This is a powerful hegemonic belief that effects assumptions about research and policy. Thus, urban areas (particularly the metropoles) are thought of as dynamic centres of political, economic, and social change. Rural areas are portrayed as increasingly marginalized – places where socio-economic change is slow and people are poor and resistant to change.

Much of the research reported in this book refutes this idea of the rural as static and marginalized. This is particularly important given that ethnic minorities are widely portrayed in popular perceptions as being at the extreme end of some rural-urban continuum. What we find is the stories of people of the Massif who are actively engaged in livelihood strategies that are, again in the words of Forsyth and Michaud, "experiments in finding solutions to basic needs, while at the same time asserting identity in accordance with their economic potential *and* the moral dimensions of local cultures." This is occurring within the context of the modernization projects implemented by what many label the post-socialist state but which I prefer to call a form of hybrid socialism in the sense that the political control of the state still remains from the previous socialist period.

The Role of Globalization

A second hegemonic paradigm that influences thinking about social and economic change is the idea of the dominant role of international forces on the economy of Southeast Asia, which is often summed up with the term "globalization" in an attempt to capture the major components of economic and technical change that have characterized the world over the last fifty years. It is argued that globalization embodies three main elements. First, it is a process whereby the global economy is becoming increasingly integrated through linked production centres, commodity chains, and information networks that are reshaping the global market economy. Second, these developments are based on technological developments in transportation and communications that accelerate the flows of commodities, people, capital, and information in time and space. Third, this is accompanied by an ideological rationale based on a triumphant neo-liberalism that sees globalization universally increasing economic wealth within the market system.

This is not a discourse that the authors of this book engage to any great extent and, yet, implicit in their analysis of the changes that are occurring in the Massif is the realization that improved communications and transport are freeing up space to move, interact, and trade, allowing the people of the Massif to become more mobile. For example, in Vietnam, the use of motorbikes has been pivotal in breaking down the barriers of isolation and an inadequate transportation structure. These have facilitated the extension of social networks of ethnic groups even beyond national boundaries.

Within the urban context of Southeast Asia, globalization has become a more influential paradigm. As many writers have shown, the globalization trends accelerate urbanization (particularly the growth of the multi-functional port cities), as well as internal changes in urban space that have encouraged the universal outward spread of urban activity into surrounding areas. This has led to the breaking down of the boundaries between rural and urban and has precipitated the need to imagine new ways of thinking about rural and urban relationships in space in a similar way to the extensions of ethnic networks through national boundaries in the Massif.

Modernization and "Developmentalism"

Now the third hegemonic paradigm. All the trends listed in the previous section have been driven by a state-led push for modernization throughout Southeast Asia (Myanmar offers a peculiar kind of exception to this statement) in which, even in the hybrid socialist states, there is an increasing determination to seek techno-economic policies that are basic to this form of developmentalism. In this model of urbanization, technological change is seen as the catalytic element for modernism and economic growth. Recent research into the urbanization process has begun to question this model, particularly as it relates to the challenges posed by climate change, increases in energy prices, and the American-led recessions (McGee 2008).

Reinventing Research Paradigms, Vernacularizing Modernity (Grounded Knowledge)

A second theme relates to the need to reinvent research paradigms so that processes of change are seen from the perspectives of ethnically and culturally diverse groups of people actively negotiating these processes at the grassroots level. This approach is central to *Moving Mountains*. For instance, in the Conclusion, Michaud makes a sophisticated argument as to why the prevailing paradigms of modernism (summarized in the discussion of the first theme) set up a hegemonic view on the part of lowland majorities that portrays the locally embedded traditions stemming from ethnicity and culture as backward. These traditions have to be "normalized" through education, technological change, and, in some cases such as Laos, through dislocation and establishing new settlements. Developmentalists, often working for international agencies, tend to see ethnic minorities as people whose condition is one of poverty that is measured in terms of material and supposedly objective facts, such as agricultural yields, transport costs, and so on. The contributors to this book start off from a very different position. They see the upland ethnic groups as actively engaging these processes with awareness and subtlety. To quote Michaud from his Conclusion, "Authors in this book have relied predominantly on qualitative factors: beliefs and spirituality, customary wisdom (indigenous knowledge), social organizations, oral history, fears, desires, and more. Across the board, their studies have benefited from long and recurring fieldwork periods, intense participant observation, life stories, loosely structured and repeated interviews, and perhaps most importantly, a marked empathy for their subjects, for their fate, and for their right to participate fully in deciding their own future."

This same process is observable in urban areas. As urbanization has increased in Southeast Asia, the poor – squatters, street hawkers, *becak* drivers – have been portrayed as "people who get in the way." In the view of the policy makers, they illegally occupy land, they cause congestion in the streets, and they block development. However, grounded research that relies on both quantitative and qualitative data has constantly emphasized the contribution that the poor make to cities in which they reside and their efforts that show how vigorous and adept they are at making livelihoods and at what I have previously called "making out" in the urban setting (McGee 1976). Grounded research in the urban areas of Southeast Asia constantly reminds us that, like the upland ethnic minorities, the urban poor deserve the right to participate more fully within the urban areas.

Reassessing the Relationship of People and the State (Underground Knowledge)

The final theme I wish to approach relates to the relationship between the state, the market, and people. In my rather simple view of it, this relationship is governed by the power and access to resources of different economically and socially positioned groups, which in my admittedly Marxist-influenced youth we used to call classes. The exploration of this relationship has been a constant theme of Southeast Asian research – for example, the work of Yeoh (1996) and Kusno (2000). One important thread of this research is the resistance of people who are marginalized in terms of access to the power of the state and participation in the market. Throughout most of rapidly urbanizing Southeast Asia (again with the exception of Myanmar), this relationship often involves liaison between the state and the major participants in the market, to which the growing middle classes are given complete access, while sizable proportions of the low-income communities and poor are given only marginal access. The study of resistance in the urban context of Southeast Asia is, in the highly factionalized urban society, complex and indicates that overt resistance (for example, student demonstrations at the end of the Suharto era) has led to changes in political power. But resistance in the economic arena has been much less successful. In the political economy of hybrid socialism in which the upland ethnic communities live, where the centralized one-party states exert considerable power, this nexus between state, the market, and people is far more nuanced. Although Laos, China, and Vietnam are opening up spaces for the market economy as part of a modernist vision, there is only a limited discussion of open resistance presented in this book. However, there is ample evidence of covert resistance. These actions represent a degree of defiance that remains most of the time under the radar, and, to again quote Michaud from his Conclusion to this book, "it is the particular contours of customary social relations, local culture, and agency that decide the balance between the two." In a way, this is not surprising given the general geographical and linguistic fragmentation of the upland ethnic minorities, the lack of real civil society, and their history of violent repression.

Critically Evaluating Homogenizing Paradigms

Finally, I would like to return to the anecdote I told earlier. All my assumptions about the ethnic minority village close to Dalat had been conceived out of an understanding of the world of upland ethnic minorities in Southeast Asia that had been formulated from the "colonial geographies" of Pierre Gourou and K.J. Pelzer, along with an uncritical acceptance of the minorities ideology that was a part of Asian socialism. These were, of course, part of a genre of homogenizing understandings that my work on urbanization in Southeast Asia had increasingly come to question (McGee 2002). The great strength of this book is that, in addition to being a major contribution to the study of upland ethnic communities in hybrid socialist societies, it creates space to reconceptualize our understandings of the processes of social, political, and economic change among the people of the urban worlds of Southeast Asia and other parts of the world. But this also involves us in critically evaluating the homogenizing paradigms that currently often guide our assumptions about the processes of social, political, and economic change; the ways we acquire this knowledge; and how we listen to the voices of the people in local settings. This is a task about which the majority of the authors in this volume seem to be quite hopeful and is already well advanced. But as the Mien saying that introduces this foreword suggests, this is no easy task.

References

Kusno, A. 2000. *Beyond the Postcolonial: Architecture, Urban Space and Political Cultures in Indonesia.* London: Routledge.

McGee, T.G. 1976. Hawkers and hookers: Making out in the Third World city – Some Southeast Asian examples. *Manpower and Unemployment Research,* April: 3-16.

–. 2002. Reconstructing *The Southeast Asian City* in an era of volatile globalization. In *Critical Reflections on Cities in Southeast Asia,* ed. Tim Bunnell, Lisa B.W. Drummond, and K.C. Ho, 31-53. Singapore: Times Academic Press.
–. 2007. Many knowledge(s) of Southeast Asia: Rethinking Southeast Asia in real time. *Asian Pacific Viewpoint* 48(2): 270-80.
–. 2008. Managing the rural-urban transition in East Asia in the 21st century. *Sustainability Science* 3(1): 155-67.
Scott, J.C. 1985. *Weapons of the Weak: Everyday Forms of Peasant Resistance.* New Haven, CT: Yale University Press.
–. 1990. *Domination and the Arts of Resistance: Hidden Transcripts.* New Haven, CT: Yale University Press.
Yeoh, B. 1996. *Contesting Space: Power Relations and the Urban Built Environment in Colonial Singapore.* Kuala Lumpur: Oxford University Press.

Acknowledgments

This book is the result of four years of work and talks. Discussions were often held via the Internet – at times, some authors could meet in person – and most congregated for a four-day workshop in Québec City, Canada, in October 2007. Financial support for that workshop was provided by the Social Sciences and Humanities Research Council of Canada (Aid to Research Workshops and Conferences).

On that occasion and in conjunction with the bi-annual conference of the Canadian Council for Southeast Asian Studies, also held in Québec City, four panels were set up. In addition to the book's contributors, the following people contributed to these panels: Isabelle Henrion-Dourcy and Marise Lachapelle (Laval), Yves Goudineau and Christophe Caudron (EFEO, Paris), and Ménaïque Légaré-Dionne (Montréal). The editors thank them warmly for their valuable contributions.

Terry McGee, of the University of British Columbia, immediately agreed to write a Foreword to the collection, for which we are most grateful. Our author and colleague Sarah Turner generously contributed much of her time to significantly enhancing the whole manuscript. Laura Schoenberger also helped with careful editing.

The editors would also like to express their gratitude to Emily Andrew and Megan Brand from UBC Press for their excellent collaboration, as well as UBC Press's anonymous readers for making enlightening and stimulating suggestions.

Moving Mountains

1
Rethinking the Relationships between Livelihoods and Ethnicity in Highland China, Vietnam, and Laos
Tim Forsyth and Jean Michaud

In the far south of China and the neighbouring lands of Southeast Asia there is a mountainous zone that stretches some thousand kilometres from the South China Sea to the Himalayas. This land is not snow-capped nor entirely rocky but instead features a mixture of forest, rain-fed agriculture, and rice terraces that sometimes extend to the very top of steep slopes in deep valleys that criss-cross the region. More than 200 million people distributed over eight countries live in this zone, of which about half belong to ethnic minorities living chiefly in scattered hamlets, villages, and market towns in a staggering array of cultural diversity.[1] This vast region, which we call the Southeast Asian Massif (Michaud 2000b), is now increasingly opening up to investment, regional planning, and development interventions, often as countries change from socialism to more liberal markets and political systems. Yet, despite its size and importance, there has been little in-depth research about how people make a living or about the interconnections of cultural diversity, political and economic change, and livelihoods in these highlands.

This book presents a number of rich analyses of livelihoods and cultural diversity in selected parts of this region. More specifically, the authors of the chapters here investigate the relationships between livelihoods and ethnicity in the high borderlands of socialist China, Vietnam, and Laos, which together represent more than two-thirds of the Massif's surface and an even greater proportion of its population. The aim of the book is to present locally grounded analyses of how ethnic minorities there fashion livelihoods and to question how ethnicity affects, and is influenced by, economic and political changes in relation to these livelihoods. We believe this discussion provides much-needed local information about this complex region. It also demonstrates the role of cultural and ethnic networks as an under-acknowledged influence in the livelihood strategies of so-called "poor people." This approach is crucial for better informing discussions on poverty alleviation and livelihoods in general; perhaps even more so for the countries of China,

Vietnam, and Laos, which have now opened up to marketization and political reform after years of centrally planned economies under state socialism.

Together, the authors in this book make three key arguments. First, we suggest that the ways local populations on the margins of centralized states in the Southeast Asian Massif make a living and maintain their identities are shaped both by external forces – such as the state and the market – and by their own agency. Indeed, marginal highland groups demonstrate particular, locally rooted, and culturally informed agency that, in our opinion, is often overlooked in generalized approaches to livelihoods within development practice.

Second, we believe that understanding highland livelihoods in the Southeast Asian Massif as a whole requires a more nuanced appreciation of transnationalism than considering highland people simply in terms of "national minorities." Many upland groups engage in cross-border trade, or have current or historical social networks across state borders. Some existing analyses of upland marginal groups in Asia fail to notice this transnationalism. *Civilizing the Margins: Southeast Asian Government Policies for the Development of Minorities*, edited by Christopher Duncan (2004), is an important work that summarizes problems and challenges for minority peoples in almost all the countries officially located in Southeast Asia. While having many merits, it overlooks not only cross-border issues within Southeast Asia but also the situation in the adjacent uplands of China, Bangladesh, and India. The overall picture thus produced is country-focused, fitting chiefly the needs of modern political analyses determined by state boundaries – *national* policies addressing *national* minorities. Moving on from such an approach, we demonstrate in this book that there is a compelling logic in choosing to study highland groups in the Massif transnationally and, in particular here, those of southwest China along with those adjacent in Vietnam and Laos, where borderlands opened only recently to outside scholarly inquiry, with little research of this kind having yet been published (see Lim Joo Jock 1984; Evans, Hutton, and Kuah 2000).

Third, we choose to adopt a more complex stance toward assumptions made about this region being a single and, in some ways, coherent social space. Willem van Schendel (2002, 647) proposed to call the wider mountainous region from the coast of Vietnam to Tibet – and even to Afghanistan, as he suggested later – "Zomia," and claimed it was unexamined because it "lacked strong centers of state formation, was politically ambiguous, and did not command sufficient scholarly clout." Along those same lines, political scientist James C. Scott (2009), in his thought provoking book *The Art of Not Being Governed: An Anarchist History of Upland Southeast Asia*, picks up the baton and labels Zomia – which he confines, however, to the eastern section of van Schendel's original Zomia, thus equating Zomia with the same region on which this book focuses – as "the last great enclosure."[2] For Scott, this is where a wide variety of populations have historically taken refuge from the surrounding "civilizations" in order to pursue an age-old or, in some cases, a renewed interest in the remarkable project of living in a stateless society (or at least in a space where the state does not control people significantly).[3] Although we look at such considerations, made from a distance sympathetically, we argue for a more refined reflection from the ground up and a more dynamic understanding of the relationships between (marginal) local subjects, (global) market forces, and (national) states.

In other words, the authors of this book use locally grounded studies to reveal the unexpected ways in which people on the margins do not just get onboard and accept (socialist) modernity, but, rather, use their agency to maintain direction over their lives and livelihoods despite current and far-reaching changes to economic conditions and political authority.

The Southeast Asian Massif
We will expand more on the claims outlined previously and their rationales shortly, but first, it is helpful to more precisely locate the subjects of this book. The Southeast Asian Massif, as we define it, brings together the highlands of all the countries sharing a large chunk of the southeastern portion of the Asian land mass. These lie roughly east of the lower Brahmaputra River, in India and Bangladesh, and south of the Yangtze River in China, all the way to the Isthmus of Kra in Thailand at its southernmost extension (see Figure 1.1; Michaud 2006). As of 2008, as we mentioned, about 100 million of the Massif's inhabitants belong to ethnicities that are distinct from the lowland majorities who form the cultural core in each of these eight countries, that is the Han (China), Kinh (Vietnam), Burman (Burma/Myanmar), Bengali (Bangladesh and northeastern India), Thai (Thailand), Lao (Laos), and Khmer (Cambodia) majorities. Over the course of centuries, these dominant lowland ethnic groups have – more or less firmly – ruled the highlands and their populations, albeit often with important disagreements. As such, one of the themes we address in this book is how these relationships have affected ethnicity and livelihood strategies.

We have selected three socialist states for analysis: the People's Republic of China, the Socialist Republic of Vietnam, and the Lao People's Democratic Republic. These are countries where, because of their participation in the world's Communist "brotherhood" (Evans and Rowley 1984), a fused ideology has guided state dealings with "minority nationalities" (Michaud 2009, 30). Academic research on these populations by non-Communist academics was virtually impossible for several decades, roughly from 1945 to 1990. It is therefore useful and timely that the authors included in this book have been able to perform lengthy field-based investigations in these socialist

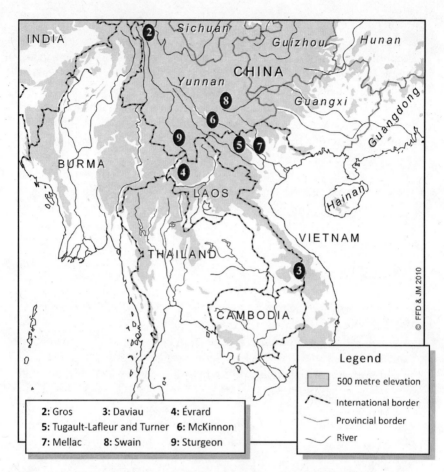

Figure 1.1 The Southeast Asian Massif and the eight case study chapters

settings and that they have developed intimate knowledge of the lived experiences of ethnic minorities in these highlands, and of what making a livelihood on the margins of a Communist state involves.

Some may argue that nowadays, what are often called the post-socialist regimes of China, Vietnam, and Laos have little in common beyond the worn-out veneer of previously being highly centralized revolutionary regimes, which have gradually departed from Marxist orthodoxy and have now opened up to the liberal market economy – China in 1978, Vietnam and Laos in 1986.[4] Certainly, all three countries are liberalizing their economic activities. But at the same time, these three regimes share a unique ideology that directs the relationships of the state with minority groups dwelling within their national borders. In China, Nicholas Tapp (2001) has shown that the Soviet model, based on Josef Stalin's considerations (1913) of the "nation," and the policies they eventually entailed, served in the 1930s as a template for strategies of alliance building between the Communist Party of China and minority groups whose support was essential to ensure victory over Republican forces. In Vietnam, the strategy that linked the Viet Minh's political project with highland minorities closely followed the Chinese model, in this and many other aspects of the revolutionary struggle (McAlister 1967; Michaud 2000b). Furthermore, Yves Goudineau (2000) showed that the USSR-China-Vietnam ideological stance on minorities triggered a similar response in Laos.

Indeed, the parallels in approaches to ethnic minorities in China, Vietnam, and Laos raise several important questions for ethnicity, livelihoods, and state-society relationships. Many authors have acknowledged that the various national Communist revolutions in these locales could not have been successful without strategic wartime alliances with minority groups on the margins. For example, it is well known now that in China, the Yi of Yunnan sheltered and protected the fleeing Communist troops during the Long March of the 1930s (Mueggler 2001; Harrell 2002). In Vietnam, the Tày of Bac Thái province hosted and fed Viet Minh leaders in hiding from French colonial troops for years, while the Thái in northwestern Vietnam were instrumental in the decisive victory at Dien Bien Phu in 1954 (Michaud 2000a, 352-53).[5] In Laos, with the majority of its national territory located in mountainous areas, the Communist triumph was possible only with the support of scores of highland allies (Goudineau 2000; Pholsena 2007). In all three countries, revolutionary leaders had to provide assurances of political autonomy to highland peoples, and included this in early drafts of national constitutions. This way, many ethnic minorities decided to ally with the Communist forces in hope of some political reward (McAlister 1967; MacKerras 2003).

Yet, once Communist victories were achieved, the new socialist states cunningly backtracked in unison. They argued that wartime pledges could not be carried out effectively without endangering the socialist project and the very existence of the new socialist nations. Early commitments to grant political autonomy were toned down, diluted, or sometimes plainly forgotten. In clear contradiction to all the promises made, these socialist states instead took the stance that highland margins and their populations could not be given real self-government. On the contrary, minorities had to readily accept being ever more firmly attached to the central state and to the socialist project of establishing a unified citizenship seeking uniform and predefined goals. Ironically, an important tool to achieve this forced marriage involved a decoy strategy of setting up showcase, largely powerless "autonomous territories" where sizable numbers of minority occupants were dwelling – one of Stalin's original precepts. In China's southwestern upland border zone, this practice became policy for the first time shortly after the Communist victory of 1949, while in the Democratic Republic of Vietnam (North Vietnam), these came into existence in 1955, right after independence.

The modern practice of organizational segregation of mountainous areas in the Southeast Asian Massif can be traced back to British Burma, which set up administrative enclaves in the nineteenth century for numerically important ethnic groups, such as the Shan, Chin, and Kachin. Not long after, the French in Indochina took the same route with the Military Territories policy implemented in 1891 (Condominas 1978; Michaud 2000a, 344). As elsewhere throughout the colonial world, these constituted rather crude attempts at dividing local societies to rule them more efficiently, in this case, by encouraging an upland-lowland fracture rooted in ancient cultural distinctions. For the colonial powers, to ally with upland minority leaders served the purpose of thwarting nationalist sentiments and weakening resistance among the lowland majorities. It is not surprising that, in time, victorious socialist regimes in the region pragmatically accepted this heritage and used it to their own ends, blending it with original Soviet ideology.

Today, highlanders in the socialist portion of the Southeast Asian Massif are still facing governments that in large part lack dependable information about their history, cultural distinctiveness, and aspirations for the present and the future. More importantly, it seems these governments, taken by their fast-paced neo-liberal national growth agendas, often lack even the interest to learn more about ethnic minorities. Instead, they vigorously implement nationwide policies of cultural integration and economic standardization. Education, for instance, in principle a tool for emancipation, is geared instead toward Sinization, Lao-ization, and Vietnamization (Goudineau 2000; Potter 2007).[6]

For the most part, the region's state programs are attuned to growth and progress. The dominant rhetoric, after decades of applied social evolutionism inherited from strict Marxist ideology, has now moved increasingly toward the language of economic growth and development. Development agencies from the affluent world are joining governments to apply the technology of the international development industry to ethnic minority health, education, and agricultural practices; in the process, traditional practices end up being labelled as obsolete or even harmful, especially to the environment. Although the general indicators of health and education undeniably show an upgrading among highland populations, these initiatives also play directly into the national governments' strategies of integrating minorities into the central national economy and identity. In the process, cultural distinction is paid only subsidiary attention, with an array of other issues being judged incomparably more urgent.

China clearly has a strong central policy of controlling and integrating *shaoshu minzu*, minority nationalities, in its southwestern borderlands (Unger

1997; Baranovitch 2001; MacKerras 2001, Michaud 2009).[7] This region is politically sensitive because it touches several international borders. It is also rich in natural resources important to the national economy, it provides a substantial portion of the country's diet through intensive agriculture, and it is a land of migration for many lowland citizens (Blum 2002; Wilkerson 2003). From the state's viewpoint, migration of lowland Han people to the margins of China might be motivated by a desire to eventually outnumber locals and take final political, economic, and cultural control over these margins (Harrell 2001; MacKerras 2003). Indeed, China's Go West campaign is an ambitious state-sponsored series of investments and land use plans that aim to bring development to provinces that would not usually attract the same level of industrialization as the seaboard. Started in 2000, the campaign aims to steer state investment, outside expertise, foreign loans, and private capital into western provinces of China, especially Yunnan, the province that occupies much of China's portion of the Southeast Asian Massif. Some of these activities include turning existing towns and cities into regional centres of economic development, such as the provincial capital Kunming. Yet, there has also been resettlement of villages in order to change the distribution of population in affected areas, and the reforestation of previously agricultural land by plantation forestry. Some commentators fear that the non-Han populations living in southwest China will find their societies, languages, and cultures threatened by these activities and the in-migration of lowland Han (Plafker 2001). Picking up on this program, four chapters in this book consider various aspects of the Go West campaign (Gros, McKinnon, Swain, and Sturgeon). They illustrate that, in remote locations of southwest China, resistance to such programs exists, while taking covert, restrained forms.

In Vietnam, the state has officially made its peace with its *các dân tộc thiểu số*, the minority nationalities, through their legal enshrinement in official polity since the late 1970s (McElwee 2004). But the Vietnamese government still considers dangerous political resistance to be simmering in the Central Highlands and elsewhere. The government has denounced political support for minorities coming from mainly US-based organizations, often made up of Vietnamese who fled the country in the 1970s and whom the government branded reactionary (Anonymous 2002; Salemink 2003). Christian missionary activism is a bone of contention, chiefly in the south, but increasingly in the northern highlands too. As a countermeasure, education is seen as a tool for the state to preserve carefully selected and benign features of local highland cultures (Nong Quoc Chan 1978) while showing the public eye the face of a benevolent state preserving minority cultures (McElwee 2004).

In Laos, the government has adopted a vigorous relocation program in order to move some minority ethnicities *(sonphao)* from upland areas to the lowlands and to force scores of highland villagers into larger groupings (see

Daviau, Évrard, this volume). This approach allows highlanders to be placed directly under the Lao state's gaze – a form of national panopticon as it were. Also, a deeply rooted mistrust between the socialist state and old royalist factions among certain highland groups has ensured that armed struggles endured long after the revolution was officially over in 1975. The Xaysomboun Special Region in northern Laos, an area sealed off from outside observers, was enforced from 1994 to 2006 to isolate pockets of minority resistance to the Laotian forces. Clearly, however, with nearly half its population belonging to one or another of many non-Lao ethnicities, Laos cannot afford to wage an all-out confrontation on its minorities, and a degree of negotiation has to prevail (Goudineau 2003; Ovesen 2004; Soukamneuth 2006).

The Implications of Ethnicity
In this culturally complex, mountainous transnational setting, authors in this book reflect on the relationships between ethnicity and livelihood practices on the frontiers of the state (see Brown 1994; Donnan and Wilson 1994; Lamont and Molnar 2002). But what do we mean by "ethnicity"? And why is this important in state-society relations and livelihood strategies?

Within the expansive field of identity studies, ethnicity generally refers to kinship, group solidarity, common culture, and shared strategy (see Barth 1969, 1999; Glazer and Moynihan 1975; Cohen 1978; Gordon 1978; Yinger 1985; Nash 1989; Thompson 1989; Banks 1996; Hutchinson and Smith 1996; Eriksen 2002; Cornell and Hartmann 2007). With the possible exception of increasingly industrialized urban settings where anonymity can sometimes prevail over most other components of individual and group identity (Fong and Shibuya 2005), blood ties and regionalism have always played, and still do play, a crucial role in defining individuals as part of groups, and groups as distinct from each other (Rata and Openshaw 2006).

But it would be a mistake to presume that ethnicity thus implies an essential, fixed, or unchanging form of identity rooted only in biology and location (Melucci, Keane, and Mier 1989).[8] For many years during the European colonial era and then during Communist regimes in the twentieth century, defining an ethnic group was above all an act of classification and control. Administrators saw indigenous cultures as fixed entities – "tribes" (Sahlins 1968) – with permanent characteristics in the likes of skin colour and facial features, and circumstantial evidence such as location and dress, as determining exactly who was or was not Karen, Masai, or Maori (see Sollors 1996).

The social sciences have since come a long way. Ethnicity today is believed to refer to personal and collective decisions, circumstantial strategies, and various other influences that sustain a discrete and negotiable form of collective identity (Jenkins 1997). Indeed, this was a tenet of the influential *Political Systems of Highland Burma* by Edmund Leach (1954), which found that the ethnic group called the Kachin was actually far more differentiated than initially thought, and communal identities were more contingent on short-term strategies and needs than outsiders predicted. As later summarized by Eriksen (2005, 353), ethnicity came to be seen as comprising aspects of both symbolic meaning and instrumental utility. These forces may be defined as desires to fit in (such as via belonging or compliance) and strategies to opt out (via distinction, resistance, or defiance), which together compose an astoundingly complex and highly localized set of factors forming the agency of a particular group (Sollors 1989). Indeed, agency is a vital notion in this book; it is the instrument by which local responses to external pressures for change are conceived and put in practice (Holland et al. 2001). It is the highly localized element defying the routine elaboration and application of overarching models of development and integration of local societies into nations, the market, and the global world.

The ethnic factor is everywhere. Around the world, internal hostility toward ethnically distinct groups within national borders surfaces with a stubborn regularity in Burma, the Sudan, Iraq, India, China, Indonesia, and Brazil to name just a few zones where ethnic tensions flare (see Eller 1999). The so-called developed world is not immune either, as the recent incidence of ethnic war and ethnic cleansing experienced in Eastern Europe demonstrate (Cigar 1995). Furthermore, policies of singling out and excluding specific ethnic identities are still rampant in the United States, Canada, Mexico, Australia, Germany, Switzerland, and France (Dean and Levi 2003). Ethnic factors can be invoked to support both affirmative action and the harshest political projects (Ceuppens and Geschiere 2005). But the ethnic factor, in all its fluidity, is also a powerful tool for understanding human behaviour in context, including, for our purpose here, how certain peoples in given locations negotiate their livelihoods (Lamont and Molnar 2002). In fact, it is so powerful that we contend that neglecting ethnicity and its local cultural determinants will ensure the long-term failure of effective good governance and development programs. Many contemporary approaches to livelihoods and development, we contend, do not pay sufficient attention to this challenge.

Recent debates on ethnicity have been lively. Essentialists (see Fuchs 2005), primordialists (Geertz 1963; Eller and Coughman 1993), and sociobiologists (van den Berghe 1987) have long insisted on blood ties and locality as the key elements of ethnicity over other possible dimensions. This position is fragile: Is one's brother really automatically one's best ally or trading partner? Are different ethnic groups necessarily prohibited by custom to marry across ethnic boundaries? Clearly, interracial, inter-ethnic, or cross-class cooperation occurs and is not routinely doomed, even if social customs exist to ascribe limits to it. At the other end of the spectrum, instrumentalists insist that, nowadays, ethnicity is not rooted in essence. They argue that ethnicity is in fact nothing but a short-term, instrumental construction that is used by specific actors to achieve specific ends. This drastically opposite position is equally fragile: Can a Hindu really move across castes freely and without hindrance (Reddy 2005)? Will the Sicilian mafia, the Japanese Yakuza, and the Chinese Triads smoothly admit members from any racial background? Indeed, could the American voters elect a black president without ever raising the issue of race? And finally, in parallel, Marxist analyses have argued against ethnicity being related to any of the above. Friedman's classic work (1979) challenged Leach's emphasis on local explanations for ethnic identity and instead claimed that ethnicity and indeed culture are themselves produced through market forces and modes of production (see also O'Connor 1995; the new introduction to Friedman in 1998; Robinne and Sadan 2007).

Efforts at bridging the gap between such extremes have led to a middle ground based on propositions such as those supported by transactionalist and ethnosymbolist arguments (Poutignat and Streiff-Fenart 1995; Hutchinson and Smith 1996). The majority of proponents of such conciliatory positions see ethnicity as partly biological (visible in marriage preference, inheritance patterns, preferred trading association, clustering in times of adversity, and so on), and partly subjective and political (visible, for instance, in strategic grouping and modern urban lifestyles that allow diverse, competing identities encouraged by volatile technologies, challenges, and living circumstances) (Sanders 2002; Dean and Levi 2003; Fong and Shibuya 2005). The balance between these sets of characteristics can vary hugely across time and space but, overall, all are believed to play a role (Fuchs 2005; Ceuppens and Geschiere 2005; Cornell and Hartmann 2007).

Clearly, we should be careful in transferring concepts developed in settings such as modern industrial societies or post-industrial cities to locations such as the Southeast Asian Massif. For our purpose in this book then, ethnicity refers to blood ties, cultural variety, local agency, and the political agendas of highland peoples dealing with opportunities and constraints. Ethnicity helps people reproduce an identity they believe in. This is especially important when a group has to maintain itself in the face of fast-changing circumstances such as those related to globalization and, as in our case studies here, when attempting to create viable livelihoods while negotiating particular standardization constraints created by socialist regimes. In turn, this means paying attention to both the growing role of national and global trade flows in these regions, as well as local explanations of distinctiveness. This is an approach that is shared by all the authors in this book.

The Dilemmas of Livelihoods and Development

Let us also explain what we mean by "livelihoods," and how these may connect with ethnicity in the Southeast Asian Massif. But, to begin, how can livelihood studies help us understand socio-economic change and "development" in this region?

At the most basic level, livelihoods are the means by which people make a living, such as through agriculture, trade, and waged employment. A common image of highland livelihoods in the Southeast Asian Massif focuses on scattered villages following customary ways, with the occasional road or access to electricity, and with inhabitants engaged in a combination of subsistence agriculture (that is, farmers' land used for food production), cash cropping, gathering of forest products, and subsidiary trade. This image includes the cultivation of upland dry (non-irrigated) rice, frequently on steep slopes, and the growing of vegetables and maize, the latter mainly as feed for pigs or as an ingredient for alcohol making. Furthermore, a common form of agriculture in the past was "pioneer" shifting cultivation (Conklin 1963), in which migratory groups, such as Miao-Yao speakers, would use land and forests exhaustively before relocating villages every ten to twenty years.[9]

Yet, these classic images of livelihood practices in the Massif are questionable. Subsistence agriculture and shifting cultivation certainly exist in this region, but many highland peoples in northern Vietnam and southwest China, for instance, have been sedentarized (that is to say, settled on a semipermanent or permanent basis) for centuries, especially those using irrigated rice terraces under local feudal chiefdoms. Added to this, other villages are becoming sedentarized either through choice or because they have been forced to resettle to lowland sites by state campaigns (see both Daviau and Évrard, this volume). Consequently, challenges to such allegedly classical images of highland livelihoods in the Massif have appeared, in part, because academics and development agents have come to realize that many researchers had been influenced by their experiences with the so-called "hill tribe" minorities in northern Thailand. For many years, researchers from the First World found themselves confined to Thailand because it was next to impossible to gain access to China, Vietnam, and Laos, and their findings bear that signature. With approximately one percent of the total highland ethnic minority population of the Massif, the Thailand heritage has been given an importance that today appears disproportionate. For several reasons relating to politics (the advent of socialism), demography, and history (including colonialism), research findings arising from this relatively constricted research hotbed are not often easily transferable to China, Vietnam, and Laos. Contributing to bridging this gap, scholarship based in these three countries is at last flourishing, helping to correct this discrepancy, and conveying a more attuned picture of the highland realities there.

Upland agriculture has often been cited as a reason to encourage resettlement or sedentarization. Highland practices such as shifting cultivation have been blamed for various environmental problems, including lowland flooding and upland erosion. Undoubtedly, much classic shifting cultivation occurred on land that was previously forested, and farmers burnt forest and other vegetation in order to plant crops and add nutrients to the soil. But ecological geographers and anthropologists have argued that shifting cultivation, in locales with low population density, and without interference from the state or rival communities, is sustainable for upland societies (Conklin 1963; Boulbet 1975). More recently, hydrological researchers have shown that the links between upland agriculture and these environmental problems are likely to be exaggerated because fluctuations in soil, rain, and water flows are complex and not always linked to agriculture, and because many upland farmers adjust practices to many of the risks they face (De Koninck 1999; Bonell and Bruijnzeel 2004; Bruijnzeel 2004; Forsyth and Walker 2008). These findings have been claimed for traditional forms of shifting cultivation, as well as for cultivation under higher population densities or with newer commercialized crops. This work does not suggest that upland agriculture has no environmental implications but questions the certainty with which environmental degradation has been cited by states and other actors to justify resettlement or reforestation.

It is now also widely acknowledged that subsistence agriculture has been supplemented for years through trading or bartering products, or by paid labour. Labour has been an income source from the post-feudal era (that is, roughly from the mid-nineteenth century) until the collectivization of the economies in China, Vietnam, and Laos in the mid-twentieth century. During that period, trade in agricultural products such as opium and home-brewed alcohol was complemented by trading livestock, timber, and a mind-boggling variety of non-timber forest products, including live and dead animals, or parts of animals. Waged agricultural labour also grew markedly after the end of the collectivized era (from the 1950s to the 1980s). In addition, non-agricultural incomes in larger settlements in the Massif grew considerably following numerous state-led industrial projects as part of overarching modernization plans. Indeed, Rigg (2005) notes that one should not only focus on assessing sources of agricultural income from the land around villages, but also acknowledge the growing importance of paid employment and remittances from off-farm labour.

Moreover, it is important to assess to what degree long-term customary land tenure systems have continued to operate in these uplands, or have been reformed or challenged by new systems imposed by successive national regimes over the last century. As China, Vietnam, and Laos undergo economic and political liberalization, opportunities for highland peoples are changing, local decision making has taken on new urgencies, and new property rights and forms of agriculture are merging with ancient ones. Moreover, as land use rights (but not land ownership) are now transferable and marketable, there is increased competition for land (see Mellac, this volume).

These insights into how highland people gain livelihoods are vital for understanding social and economic change in the Massif today. Yet, "livelihoods" mean more than the activities people use to make a living. Understanding livelihoods also requires looking at the less obvious social resources, organizations, local politics, and ethnic and social networks and decision making that underpin economic activities and can effectively reduce or increase social vulnerability to economic and political change.

The language of the development theorist Amartya Sen is particularly useful in understanding the wider basis of livelihoods (Sen 1984, 1987). Sen suggests that livelihoods are a means of achieving *capabilities,* or the range of a person's life options, and are not only a means of achieving an economic income. Similarly, livelihoods reflect the availability of *assets,* or those valued items that also enhance an individual's ability to achieve life goals and lifestyles. Such assets might include a combination of physical, natural, and social properties such as infrastructure, land, and social networks along with human talents and skills, and financial resources that provide access to certain livelihoods. Accordingly, a livelihoods approach focuses not only on activities but also on access to these and on how changing social contexts might change the underlying means by which people can seek suitable livelihoods on a long-term and rewarding basis (Ribot and Peluso 2003). Ethnicity, or the social and cultural networks that maintain local identity, is clearly an important variable for understanding sources of capabilities and assets, as well as access to them.

Recent discussions, regarding long-term and rewarding livelihoods, within anthropology, human geography, and development studies have used the concept of sustainable livelihoods to refer to how one might make a living that can continue despite upsets or threats to income. Chambers and Conway (1992, 1) define a sustainable livelihood as one that "can cope with and recover from stress and shocks, maintain and enhance its capabilities and assets and provide sustainable livelihood opportunities for the next generation." Sensibly, this framework focuses on addressing the vulnerability and poverty of affected peoples as they themselves see these (Chambers and Conway 1992; Scoones 1998; Ribot and Peluso, 2003), and requires "an examination of critical elements such as a livelihood's impact on resources and its relationship to poverty reduction, security, equity, well-being, and capability" (Turner 2007, 403).

To identify livelihood strategies, many sustainable livelihoods approaches recognize five kinds of capital, or forms of assets available to an individual or to a household, village, or region. These capitals are human capital (educational and practical skills, health); natural capital (resources such as land and forests); physical capital (infrastructure such as roads); financial capital (savings, credit); and social capital (networks and relationships of trust) (Bebbington 1999). These assets, in turn, are deemed to allow vulnerable people to increase livelihood options through three broad strategies: first, agricultural intensification (such as increasing the number of crops per year, including the use of fertilizers, mechanization, or access to more productive land); second, incomes diversification (including access to non-agriculture income in addition to agriculture); and third, creative uses of migration as a means of securing incomes (for example, involving one household member working for cash elsewhere, or an individual travelling to a city to engage in non-agricultural activities on a cyclical, seasonal basis). These capitals have been used by development agencies such as the United Nations Development Programme and the United Kingdom's Department for International Development as the basis of livelihood analyses and aid programs.

Critics, however, propose that seeing diverse communities through the lens of these capitals is to adopt a cookie-cutter style of analysis, a mechanical model that assumes these factors will create success, regardless of context, and overlooks the assumptions employed when using them. According to Hinshelwood (2003, 254, 243) these capitals are "merely a confused diagram and a wordy manual." Others have suggested that using words such as "capitals" in uncritical, easily transferred ways may reduce the ability for local people to assert their own values in framing development policy (Arce 2003, 204). Indeed, some social analysts have suggested that using the word "capitals" to describe social networks and culture reflects a market-driven outlook; unsurprisingly, the capitals approach was developed largely in countries with liberal economies.

Accordingly, critics have argued that any focus on the five capitals should be matched by an awareness of what these capitals mean in different cultural contexts. Similarly, there is a need to understand how specific cultural and/or political factors govern access to different assets (Ribot and Peluso 2003; Forsyth 2007; Scoones 2009). Assets are not accessible to all citizens equally, including in socialist regimes. Consequently, some observers have argued that we need to incorporate more rigorous forms of bottom-up, rights-based analyses into livelihood studies. Such approaches would consider how ethnic minorities or poor people assert their needs and make decisions, rather than, in the case of development programs, achieving top-down "sham participation" by the poor in pre-set development goals (Baumann 2000, 34; Carney 2003).

To that end, in this book, we question how far ethnicity, encompassing cultural identity and linkages, should be considered an agent of access, or indeed as an asset itself when wishing to better understand ethnic minority livelihoods in the socialist portion of the Southeast Asian Massif. If one takes on board the five capitals approach, discussed above, then it is the concept of social capital that is assumed, most commonly, to include social associations and networks, ties, and linkages. Some analysts, however, have argued that actors such as the World Bank have used the concept of social capital in ways that overlook various deeper and indeed, more negative forms of power and control (Portes and Landolt 2000; Woolcock and Narayan 2000; Harriss 2002; Radcliffe 2004). Other critics have suggested that this approach avoids deeper understandings of social connectivity – one example being Bourdieu's earlier formulation (1972) of social capital – along with that other form of capital bypassed by more recent livelihood analysts, namely, cultural capital. Under Pierre Bourdieu's formulation (1972), cultural capital focuses on shared meanings within societies and cultures, which – knowingly or unknowingly – may be used both positively to include more people in decision making or negatively to reinforce existing political power.

In sum, cultural factors, or the presence of shared values and understandings, are a crucial source of support and creativity within livelihood strategies. Yet, many critics, including the authors, feel that current approaches to the analysis of livelihoods do not take culture and ethnicity sufficiently into account (Ellis 2000; de Haan and Zoomers 2005). As noted earlier, the aim of this book is therefore to question how and to what extent ethnicity impacts the fashioning of local livelihoods and how it interacts with other oft-forgotten variables such as political relations and social change.

Rethinking the Relationships between Livelihoods and Ethnicity

What, then, needs to be done to better understand the relationships between ethnicity and livelihoods, and how can we illustrate this in the highlands of the Southeast Asian Massif?

As we stated at the start of this chapter, this book is based on three key arguments. First, local people's ability to forge livelihoods is a product of both external changes, such as political and economic changes, as well as of their own agency, always influenced by ethnic identity and culture. Second, ethnicity is best understood on a transnational basis relating to the existence of cultural and trading links across borders rather than within the restrictive and artificial (at least culturally speaking) context of single countries. And third, we need to view the Massif area in more complex and dynamic terms that go beyond categorizing ethnic minorities as just statecontrolled or stateless, or considering all local people as sharing the same political, cultural, and economic characteristics.

We propose a few central routes to advancing these new understandings of the Massif. First, we suggest that studying and understanding ethnicity and culture assists in helping highland peoples achieve effective livelihood strategies. By stating this, we propose that there is a need to indicate how, and in which ways, culture can be assessed and better understood. This has been a recurrent concern for social anthropology in particular, which has advocated research methods adapted to local circumstances and involving long-term observation (Bernard 2005), rather than rapid rural appraisal or the largely quantitative strategies that are used by governments or development agencies and tend to focus on current activities rather than on livelihoods as embedded in longer term decision-making processes and taking into account the nuances of ethnicity.[10] All the chapters in this book offer telling examples of ways to approach local cultures that can lead to more refined understandings of how the inclusion of ethnicity, along with its associated trading and migration links, in the development equation can offer more diverse strategies for enhancing livelihoods while simultaneously retaining – or attempting to retain – a core identity (see Jonsson 2005). In the words of Sarah Turner (2003, 198): "Culture is never static but is constantly being recreated and negotiated by conscious actors. Accordingly, a framework designed to examine [local economic agents] must incorporate the cultural context as a dynamic dimension of human agency."

Another avenue is to realize how livelihood strategies influence ethnicity. Clearly, it is argued throughout this book that ethnicity bears a significant influence on the local definition and achievement of livelihoods. The substantivist argument (see Stanfield 1986) suggesting that the economy is embedded in cultures and that it cannot be studied advantageously outside its particular local context is convincing in the Southeast Asian Massif but also in the lowlands around it. Turning this proposition around is also true, or more exactly, a retroaction is to be expected: changes in livelihood options will affect ethnic identity through local responses to important political or economic changes, including the indigenization of state reforms or increasingly pervasive markets (Sahlins 1999; Engel Merry 2006).

One example of how identities may change comes from James Scott's classic work *Weapons of the Weak*, written after a substantial period of field research on socio-economic change in a Malaysian rural community following mechanization and the introduction of new cropping practices. Scott argues that the withdrawal of customary, kinship-based, and village-based social welfare practices following these changes undermined the livelihoods of poorer villagers and altered the nature of social identities. These alterations occurred because of what he calls the "euphemization of property relations" (Scott 1985, 305) into practices that today's researchers might call social and cultural capital, such as providing access to food, loans, and social networks between richer and poorer peasants. Yet, in keeping with both the positive and negative aspects of cultural capital, Scott argues that these changes did not simply result in a "victim class" but also created a new class of peasants-turned-capitalists that shattered the old village hegemony. These new capitalists changed identities by disregarding custom in favour of new commercialism. In other words, going back to Sahlins' typology (1968), these changes tipped the balance of reciprocity in the village of Sedaka in favour of rampant negative reciprocity, in which social linkages became obsolete and the pursuit of personal profit grew dominant. This kind of research by Scott underscores the value of long-term field investigation, familiarity with a local group, and the resulting deeper insights into how cultural and economic changes interconnect.

A third avenue is to operationalize these lessons for livelihood practices and, especially, understand the role of local agency. As we argue above, the agency of local communities is not merely the willingness and ability to accept and comply with new market opportunities, land reforms, and socio-economic circumstances under globalization and liberalization. Rather, as Sherry Ortner (2006) and Saba Mahmood (2004) argue, it is more fertile to see agency as a locally and culturally informed type of self-maintenance, even resistance, that allows minorities to uphold identities and customary practices that may counteract the external forces of change, even if these have an apparently overwhelming weight.

To some extent, the recent economic-liberalization changes in China, Vietnam, and Laos are still so new that we are only beginning to understand how peasants might respond to the resultant globalization processes and cultural change (Burawoy and Verdery 1999; Sturgeon and Sikor 2004). One cultural analyst, Arjun Appadurai is relatively optimistic. He argues: "Those social orders and groupings that were apparently passive victims of large forces of control and domination were nevertheless capable of subtle forms of resistance and 'exit' ... that seemed to be not primordialist in any way" (Appadurai 1996, 145). In other words, even if many do succumb to degrees of subordination and compliance, a fair number of simple farmers can succeed in avoiding domination in restrained, yet successful ways (Kerkvliet 2005, 2009).

How might peasants assert their culture and identity while also complying with new political and economic orders that can at times take the shape of hegemonies? Several authors in this book suggest that new livelihood strategies are, for the subjects in the Massif, experiments in finding solutions to basic needs, while at the same time asserting identity in accordance with their economic potential *and* the moral dimensions of local cultures. In the terms of James C. Scott (1990) again, the public projects of state reform and marketization coexist with local hidden transcripts, which provide marginal people space to confer among themselves and seek ways to maintain and assert who they want to be, and even profit economically, without feeling prey to the reforms. Within these forms of resistance lie the combinations of ethnicity and resourcefulness that offer significant assets for livelihood strategies.

How the Chapters Tackle These Themes

This book is a vast and rather ambitious project. When recruiting contributors, transnational research experience, as well as an intimate knowledge of the realities on the ground for the local groups each proposed to write about, were two qualities we sought. In terms of disciplinary background, we were eager to build a degree of diversity within the social sciences in order to disembed case studies from potentially restrictive intellectual disciplinary boundaries, often tied to partisan discourses that do not always stand the test of time well. We contend that transdisciplinary considerations enrich our understanding of a complex object such as the Southeast Asian Massif and its populations.

Thus, contributors to this book are evenly spread among the fields of social anthropology, development studies, and human geography. They have in common broad field experience in one or several highland areas in the Southeast Asian Massif – particularly the socialist segment of it – combined with critical publications on the highland minority groups in the region. In addition, beyond these disciplines and the six countries the authors originate from, half belong to French-speaking academia and thus bring an intellectual tradition and a series of insights on the region that many among the English-speaking audience are not always entirely familiar with. This combination of disciplines, experience, and intellectual background brings a unique depth to this collection.

The case studies have been arranged according to the degree to which the livelihoods of the groups under investigation are integrated into the market economy, ranging from those most remote from the market to those most dynamically involved in it. Each chapter is based on a given ethnic group's profile and signature agency, not in relation to a specific national situation, which would run against the transnational objective we favour. The resulting picture shows, among other details, that integration in the market is intimately linked to the degree of political and economic formalization each group achieved before the Communist takeovers in the three countries under consideration. The initial chapters are based on lineage groups (for whom social organization was or is based primarily on kinship), such as the Drung, Tarieng, Khmu, and Hmong. These groups show the least degree of market integration and sometimes also the weakest forms of agency in dealing with outside influences. Geographical isolation, which has sheltered some of these groups from the unmediated reach of state administration (Scott 2009), could be part of the explanation as to why this situation exists. The book then moves to ethnic groups that were functionally integrated into a feudal system before colonization or Communist victories, either as a dominant group or as commoners, and which seem to have adopted market practices more rapidly. Does this mean that their agency is also weak and they simply give in to modernizing pressures? Not necessarily so, as the cases of the Hani, Tày/Thái, Yi, and Dai seem to suggest. Does that mean that the more integrated in the market they are, the more hazy their ethnic identity becomes? Nothing is less sure. Ethnicity, let us recall, is fluid and prone to strategizing.

Turning now to each chapter, the following four chapters, Chapters 2 to 5, focus on lineage groups. In Chapter 2, geographically as much as culturally, the Drung, a small *shaoshu minzu* of Yunnan province, stand uncommonly remote from the political centres of China's southwest. In this chapter, "Economic Marginalization and Social Identity among the Drung People of Northwest Yunnan," Stéphane Gros, a social anthropologist, discusses ethnic identity and political as well as economic change through time in this distant northwestern corner of the province. The Drung have long been pushed to the extreme of dependency and exploitation by more powerful neighbours. It was only at the end of the imperial era in the early 1950s, when the revolutionary administration finally reached them, that they experienced a welcome relief from chronic domination. By retracing the Drung people's history of relationships with their powerful neighbours and their inclusion into the People's Republic of China, Gros shows how they experienced successive forms of dependency that eventually impacted their sense of identity. The Drung embody the notion of the isolated and subjugated "tribe" in the highlands of the Southeast Asian Massif, a politically weak society falling prey to predation and, later, struggling to "get a grip" on socialist modernity. New economic opportunities such as tourism, Gros assesses, appear to be just another way for the Drung to remain marginalized.

Only slightly less isolated but more numerous than the Drung, the Tarieng dwell on the border between southern Laos and central Vietnam. Also a lineage society, the Tarieng have been active through history, in a dominant role to some groups in their vicinity when the opportunity to trade slaves presented itself, while just as often falling victim to the lowland powers surrounding them. Times have changed since the 1950s, though, with the Vietnam War and the sudden geostrategic value of their customary territory, located on the Ho Chi Minh Trail. Since 1975, socialism has also had its impacts. As such, in Chapter 3, "Integration of a Lineage Society on the Laos-Vietnam Border," Steeve Daviau, a social anthropologist, looks at Tarieng identity by analyzing the recent changes in their lives stemming from their adaptation to state-led resettlement programs. The Tarieng, like many other highland minorities in Laos, face overwhelming external vectors of change. Forced resettlement and compulsory clustering of small villages are efficient mechanisms of surveillance and control of such non-Lao, animist minorities and speed up their integration into the Lao nation. These mechanisms leave Tarieng farmers with few options, one being to start to move, looking for unskilled, low-paid wage work in the mid- and lowlands. However, despite a totalitarian political climate, the Tarieng population is not altogether passive. The Tarieng undertake elaborate and diverse strategies, reactions, and forms of resistance at the local level in an attempt to maintain some autonomy. Nevertheless, their case exemplifies some of the ways in which a strong state can put minority groups under economic, social, cultural, and political integrationist pressures and use its strategic power to break down ancient social fabric.

Also in Laos, this time in the north of the country, close to Burma and China, the case of the Khmu appears somewhat more encouraging. Here, Olivier Évrard, a development anthropologist, has researched the historical emergence of identities and new livelihoods among Laos' largest minority group, with half a million people. He especially considers, in Chapter 4, "Oral Histories of Livelihoods and Migration under Socialism and Post-socialism among the Khmu of Northern Laos," the role of migration as part of households' livelihood strategies and points to the fact that livelihoods are not just located on one's own farming land or trading premises but also exist through travel and by connecting into helpful commercial networks. Évrard also provides a useful example of a biographical method for investigating how specific individuals express their agency in seeking specific livelihoods.

In spite of being classified as one of the most primitive and poor minority nationalities in Vietnam, the Hmong farmers and traders in Lào Cai province, discussed in Claire Tugault-Lafleur and Sarah Turner's Chapter 5, "Of Rice and Spice: Hmong Livelihoods and Diversification in the Northern Vietnam Uplands," show a high degree of cultural adaptability in negotiating modernity while jealously protecting a core identity. Tugault-Lafleur and Turner, two human geographers, focus on how Hmong have engaged with cardamom production and trade within broader complex livelihood strategies. They take an actor-oriented approach to livelihoods as they root, focusing on local ethnic relations and culturally rooted decision-making processes. After an examination of Hmong livelihood coping tactics during the socialist and post-socialist periods more generally, the authors focus on current-day Hmong livelihood portfolios while unravelling the adoption of strategies of income diversification that allow Hmong households to adapt to local-level political and economic transformations. These transformations have included the creation of a national park in the district and consequent restrictions on forest use, a ban on opium production and timber felling, as well as new market integration opportunities.

In the next four chapters, sedentarized groups long embedded in feudal systems take the front stage. With 1.5 million people, the Hani in southern Yunnan are one of the more numerous *shaoshu minzu* of China; their representatives, under the ethnonym Akha, can be found across the borders in several adjacent countries in the Massif. Two chapters in this book focus on the Hani (Chapters 6 and 9). Chapter 6, "Hani Agency and Ways of Seeing Environmental Change on the China-Vietnam Border," is written by John McKinnon, a development geographer long acquainted with highland Thailand and who then studied Hani communities of Yunnan in the course of a New Zealand development aid, participatory research project. McKinnon focuses on the adoption of state directives, and later, cash crops, in Hani villages near the Vietnam border and the environmental outcomes of these, as well as how Hani identity appeared to be subjugated by state directives. McKinnon describes how Hani communities received and then attempted to "indigenize" the development options put to them. He further shows how their ethnic identity was able to reappear when their communities were brought together to face the environmental consequences of recent livelihood decisions. McKinnon criticizes years of outside intervention by the state and development agencies that have not sufficiently appreciated local values and customs. As an alternative, he illustrates how local Hani leaders have been able to assert their identity and some autonomy through traditional land use conservation measures. Whether the Hani will now be able to circumvent the far-reaching implications of the Go West national program of modernization in the highlands remains to be seen.

Chapter 7, "Land Reform and Changing Identities in Two Tai-Speaking Districts in Northern Vietnam," explores the links between land reform and identities in communities of northern Vietnam belonging to the Thái and Tày minority nationalities. Marie Mellac, a human geographer, considers how recent changes to land allocation and related laws have allowed local groups to negotiate, with uneven success, access to land and the relationship that these changes have with the adoption of non-agricultural income and hence livelihood diversification. Land tenure stands at the core of territorialization processes and takes an active part in the social organization of these formerly feudal groups. As such, large-scale land reforms carried out by (post-) socialist Vietnam over the last twenty years have interfered with customary social rights within each community and have altered the political and economic balance between neighbouring groups, also affecting the farmers' relationships with political institutions at every level. Mellac surmises that these reforms may lead to the homogenization of local society with mainstream Vietnamese culture through the erosion of ethnic identities.

Yunnan tourism in the early twenty-first century relies heavily on merchandizing ethnic diversity as a local renewable resource. Studying the case of the Yi, social anthropologist Margaret Swain analyzes, in Chapter 8, "Commoditized Ethnicity for Tourism Development in Yunnan," the recent tourism boom in Yunnan and how such change influences Yi identity and livelihoods. Using the examples of groups in two tourist sites – the Sani in Stone Forest (Shilin) and the Bai in Dali – Swain looks at issues of equality in terms of gender, ethnicity, and class, and the promise of cosmopolitan discourse to shape opportunities for selling one's own (or someone else's) ethnic identity. Building on a growing body of research on the tourist industry in the region, she argues that tourism offers great diversity for non-agricultural incomes among minorities. Yet, as has been observed in many other similar situations, the downside is the tendency, rampant throughout China, to commoditize ethnicity as an attraction; an ethnicity, that is, that has been reduced to benign exotic characteristics and devoid of any political potency. She suggests, in these cases, that while staged identities are presented to visitors, more meaningful changes still occur within groups but remain less visible and more difficult to assess.

Finally, the case of communities among the Dai (Tai Lue) and Hani (Akha) groups in Xishuangbanna in the far south of Yunnan, near Laos, appear like a success story. Development geographer Janet Sturgeon, in Chapter 9, "Rubber Transformations: Post-Socialist Livelihoods and Identities for Akha and Tai Lue Farmers in Xishuangbanna, China," observes the influence and impact of state-led programs for rubber plantations in Yunnan on local livelihoods and identities among these two *shaoshu minzu*. Sturgeon argues that the new trend of taking up rubber plantation production represents an extension of neo-liberal governance to this region following the entry of China to the World Trade Organization. It turns out, she explains, that Hani rubber farmers emerge as savvy entrepreneurs renegotiating land use and entering markets in this globalizing moment, though not without unsettling the identities of both themselves and state farm workers. As state rubber farms slide toward bankruptcy, Akha rubber farmers, Sturgeon argues, are getting rich. It is suggested that the evolution of new governance offers opportunities but also presents new dilemmas for highlanders, as the state requires them to take more responsibility for providing social services such as education and health care. Nationalism appears as a means of asserting identity and livelihoods in the face of changes imposed by the Chinese state.

Finally, in the Conclusion to the book, "Lesson for the future," Jean Michaud draws from these case studies the lesson that, to fruitfully rethink the relationships between ethnicity and livelihoods and to assess how well highland minorities in China, Vietnam, and Laos are faring in these turbulent times, agents of development would gain much from learning to pay closer attention to local factors such as culture and agency. Michaud proposes that deadlines and tangible results should not be the only guiding lines along which projects are designed and implemented. If more importance could be placed instead on factoring in local historical and cultural ways of sharing and understanding the relationships between livelihood strategies, agency, local politics and resistance, then the programs put in place by state development actors, overseas development practitioners and academics, and nongovernmental organizations would stand a better chance of yielding long-term dividends for ethnic minorities in the Southeast Asian Massif.

Notes

1. The notions of ethnic minority and national minorities are being used cautiously here as a historical construct that is a consequence of the installation of the modern nation-states in the region (Michaud 2006).
2. On Zomia, see the thematic issue of the *Journal of Global History* (Michaud 2010).
3. For a global presentation of the Zomia debate, see Michaud 2010.
4. It should be noted here that in this book some authors speak to the current situation in these locales as "socialist" while others use the term "post-socialist." This is personal choice, but in all cases, authors are cognizant of the recent liberalization of these economies, including their opening up to outside market integration forces, while politically these states retain certain socialist principles of rule and a firm hand over political organization as well as specific "takes" on ethnic minorities, discussed here.
5. The Thái and the Tày in Vietnam are not to be confused with the Thai of Thailand. All belong to the "Tai" language sub-family, which refers to any speaker of the Tai branch of the larger Tai-Kadai language family, which includes all speakers of one form or another of that vast cluster of languages found in Guangxi, Guizhou, Yunnan, Burma, Assam, Vietnam, Laos, or indeed Thailand, where most of them dwell (Michaud 2006).
6. Recent history suggests that it is only in southwestern China and northeastern Burma, where some minority groups such as the Zhuang, Yi, Hani, Shan, or Dai reach several million people, that forms of resistance to cultural assimilation can sometimes arise. For most of the other groups, resistance must be subtle, sometimes covert, often hidden (see Scott 1990, 2009).
7. Based on Michaud (2009).
8. Essentialism implies ascribing an eternal and discrete sense of identity to peoples, rather than seeing how ethnic identities coexist with other social and cultural factors.
9. The name "swidden" has been given to fields that are cleared and cultivated in these ways.
10. We do also acknowledge that for many, time *is* of the essence, especially where the state might not look particularly favourably on long-term research by outsiders. A summary of faster yet effective ways to use anthropological methods can be found in publications such as Handwerker (2002).

References

Anonymous. 2002. Vietnam: Indigenous Minority Groups in the Central Highlands. UNHCR Centre for Documentation and Research, Writenet Paper no. 05/2001, 2002.

Appadurai, A. 1996. *Modernity at Large: Cultural Dimensions of Globalization*. Minneapolis: University of Minnesota Press.

Arce, A. 2003. Value contestations in development interventions: Community development and sustainable livelihoods approaches. *Community Development Journal* 38(3): 199-212.

Banks, M. 1996. *Ethnicity: Anthropological Constructions*. London: Routledge.

Baranovitch, N. 2001. Between alterity and identity: New voices of minority people in China. *Modern China* 27(3): 359-401.

Barth, F., ed. 1969. *Ethnic Groups and Boundaries*. Bergen/London: Universitet Forlaget/ George Allen and Unwin.

–. 1999. Boundaries and connections. In *Signifying Identities: Anthropological Perspectives on Boundaries and Contested Values*, ed. A. Cohen, 17-36. New York: Routledge.

Baumann, P. 2000. *Sustainable Livelihoods and Political Capital: Arguments and Evidence from Decentralization and Natural Resource Management in India*. London, Overseas Development Institute Working Paper 136.

Bebbington, A. 1999. Capitals and capabilities: A framework for analyzing peasant viability, rural livelihoods and poverty. *World Development* 27(12): 2021-44.

Bernard, H.R. 2005. *Research Methods in Anthropology: Qualitative and Quantitative Approaches*. Lanham, MD: Altamira Press.

Blum, S.D. 2002. Margins and centers: A decade of publishing on China's ethnic minorities. *Journal of Asian Studies* 61(4): 1287-1310.

Bonell, M., and L.A. Bruijnzeel. 2004. *Forests, Water, and People in the Humid Tropics: Past, Present, and Future Hydrological Research for Integrated Land and Water Management*. New York: Cambridge University Press.

Boulbet, J. 1975. *Paysans de la forêt*. Vol. 55. Paris: Publications de l'EFEO.

Bourdieu, P. 1972. *Esquisse d'une théorie de la pratique: Précédé de trois études d'ethnologie kabyle*. Paris: Librairie Droz.

Brown, D. 1994. *The State and Ethnic Politics in Southeast Asia*. London: Routledge.

Bruijnzeel, L.A. 2004. Hydrological functions of tropical forests: Not seeing the soil for the trees? *Agriculture, Ecosystems and Environment* 104(1): 185-228.

Burawoy, M., and K. Verdery. 1999. Introduction. In *Uncertain Transition: Ethnographies of Change in the Postsocialist World*, ed. M. Burawoy and K. Verdery, 1-17. Lanham, MD: Rowman and Littlefield.

Carney, D. 2003. *Sustainable Livelihoods Approaches: Progress and Possibilities for Change*. London: UK Department for International Development.

Ceuppens, B., and P. Geschiere. 2005. Autochthony: Local or global? New modes in the struggle over citizenship and belonging in Africa and Europe. *Annual Review of Anthropology* 34: 385-407.

Chambers, R., and G. Conway. 1992. *Sustainable Rural Livelihoods: Practical Concepts for the 21st Century*. IDS Discussion Paper 296. Brighton, UK: Institute of Development Studies.

Cigar, N.L. 1995. *Genocide in Bosnia: The Policy of "Ethnic Cleansing."* Texas: A&M University Press.

Cohen, R. 1978. Ethnicity: Problem and focus in anthropology. *Annual Review of Anthropology* 7: 379-403.

Condominas, G. 1978. L'Asie du sud-est. In *Ethnologie régionale II: Asie, Amérique, Mascareignes*, ed. J. Poirier, 283-375. Paris: Encyclopédie de la Pléiade.

Conklin, H.C. 1963. *The Study of Shifting Cultivation*. London: Routledge and Kegan Paul.

Cornell, S.E., and D. Hartmann. 2007. *Ethnicity and Race: Making Identities in a Changing World*. 2nd ed. Thousand Oaks, CA: Pine Forge Press.

de Haan, L., and A. Zoomers. 2005. Exploring the frontier of livelihoods research. *Development and Change* 36(1): 27-47.

De Koninck, R. 1999. *Deforestation in Vietnam*. Ottawa: International Development Research Centre.

Dean, B., and J.M. Levi, eds. 2003. *At the Risk of Being Heard: Identity, Indigenous Rights, and Postcolonial States*. Ann Arbor: University of Michigan Press.

Donnan, H., and T.M. Wilson, eds. 1994. *Border Approaches: Anthropological Perspectives on Frontiers*. Lanham, MD: University Press of America.

Duncan, C.R., ed. 2004. *Civilizing the Margins: Southeast Asian Government Policies for the Development of Minorities*. Ithaca, NY: Cornell University Press.

Eller, J. 1999. *From Culture to Ethnicity to Conflict: An Anthropological Perspective on Ethnic Conflict*. Ann Arbor: University of Michigan Press.

Eller, J., and R. Coughnan. 1993. The poverty of primordialism: The demystification of ethnic attachments. *Ethnic and Racial Studies* 16(2): 183-203.

Ellis, F. 2000. *Rural Livelihoods and Diversity in Developing Countries*. Oxford: Oxford University Press.

Engel Merry, S. 2006. Transnational human rights and local activism: Mapping the middle. *American Anthropologist* 108(1): 38-51.

Eriksen, T.H. 2002. *Ethnicity and Nationalism: Anthropological Perspectives*. 2nd ed. London: Pluto Press.

–. 2005. Economies of Ethnicity. In *A Handbook of Economic Anthropology*, ed. J.G. Carrier, 353-69. Cheltenham, UK: Edward Elgar.

Evans, G., C. Hutton, and Kuah Khun Eng, eds. 2000. *Where China Meets South-East Asia: Social and Cultural Change in the Border Regions*. Singapore/Canberra: Institute of Southeast Asian Studies/Allen and Unwin.

Evans, G., and K. Rowley. 1984. *Red Brotherhood at War: Indochina since the Fall of Saigon*. Sydney: Pluto Press Australia.

Fong, E., and Kumiko Shibuya. 2005. Multiethnic cities in North America. *Annual Review of Sociology* 31: 285-304.

Forsyth, T. 2007. Sustainable livelihood approaches and soil erosion risks: Who is to judge? *International Journal of Social Economics* 34(1/2): 88-102.

Forsyth, T., and A. Walker. 2008. *Forest Guardians, Forest Destroyers: The Politics of Environmental Knowledge in Northern Thailand*. Seattle and London: University of Washington Press.

Friedman, J. 1979. *System, Structure and Contradiction: The Evolution of "Asiatic" Social Formations*. Copenhagen: National Museum of Copenhagen.

Fuchs, S. 2005. *Against Essentialism: A Theory of Culture and Society*. Cambridge, MA: Harvard University Press.

Geertz, C. 1963. The integrative revolution. In *The Quest for Modernity in Asia and Africa: Old Societies and New States*, ed. C. Geertz, 108-13. New York: Free Press.

Glazer, N., and D.P. Moynihan, eds. 1975. *Ethnicity, Theory and Experience*. Cambridge, MA: Harvard University Press.

Gordon, M. 1978. *Human Nature, Class and Ethnicity*. London: Oxford University Press.

Goudineau, Y. 2000. Ethnicité et déterritorialisation dans la péninsule indochinoise: Considérations à partir du Laos. *Autrepart* 14: 17-31.

–, ed. 2003. *Laos and Ethnic Minority Culture: Promoting Heritage*. Paris: UNESCO.

Handwerker, W.P. 2002. *Quick Ethnography: A Guide to Rapid Multi-Method Research*. Lanham, MD: Altamira Press.

Harrell, S. 2001. The anthropology of reform and the reform of anthropology: Anthropological narratives of recovery and progress in China. *Annual Review of Anthropology* 30: 139-61.

Harriss, J. 2002. *Depoliticizing Development: The World Bank and Social Capital*. London: Anthem.

Hinshelwood, E. 2003. Making friends with the sustainable livelihoods framework. *Community Development Journal* 38(3): 243-54.

Holland, D., W. Lachicotte Jr., D. Skinner, and C. Cain. 2001. *Identity and Agency in Cultural Worlds*. Cambridge, MA: Harvard University Press.

Hutchinson, J., and A.D. Smith. 1996. Introduction. In *Ethnicity*, ed. J. Hutchinson and A.D. Smith, 3-16. Oxford: Oxford University Press.

Jenkins, R. 1997. *Rethinking Ethnicity: Arguments and Explorations*. London: Sage.

Jonsson, H. 2005. *Mien Modernities*. Ithaca, NY: Cornell University Press.

Kerkvliet, B.J.T. 2005. *The Power of Everyday Politics: How Vietnamese Peasants Transformed National Policy*. Ithaca, NY: Cornell University Press.

–. 2009. Everyday politics in peasant societies (and ours). *Journal of Peasant Studies* 36(1): 227-43.

Lamont, M., and V. Molnar. 2002. The study of boundaries in the social sciences. *Annual Review of Sociology* 28: 167-95.

Leach, E. 1954. *Political Systems of Highland Burma: A Study of Kachin Social Structure*. Cambridge, MA: Harvard University Press.

Lim, Joo Jock. 1984. *Territorial Power Domains, Southeast Asia, and China: The Geo-Strategy of an Overarching Massif*. Singapore: Institute of Southeast Asian Studies.

MacKerras, C. 2001. China's minority cultures at the turn of the century: Issues of modernization and globalization. *Archiv Orientali* 69(3): 447-64.

–. 2003. Ethnic minorities in China. In *Ethnicity in Asia*, ed. C. MacKerras, 16-47. London: RoutledgeCurzon.

Mahmood, S. 2004. *Politics of Piety*. Princeton, NJ: Princeton University Press.

McAlister Jr., J.T. 1967. Mountain minorities and the Vietminh: A key to the Indochina War. In *Southeast Asian Tribes, Minorities and Nations*, ed. P. Kunstadter, 47-83. Princeton, NJ: Princeton University Press.

McElwee, P. 2004. Becoming socialist or becoming Kinh? Government policies for ethnic minorities in the Socialist Republic of Vietnam. In *Civilizing the Margins: Southeast Asian Government Policies for the Development of Minorities*, ed. C.R. Duncan, 182-213. Ithaca, NY: Cornell University Press.

Melucci, A., J. Keane, and P. Mier, eds. 1989. *Nomads of the Present: Social Movements and Individual Needs in Contemporary Society.* London: Hutchinson Radius.

Michaud, J., ed. 2000a. The Montagnards in northern Vietnam from 1802 to 1975: A historical overview from exogenous sources. *Ethnohistory* 47(2): 333-68.

–. 2000b. *Turbulent Times and Enduring Peoples: The Mountain Minorities of the South-East Asian Massif.* London: Curzon Press.

–. 2006. *Historical Dictionary of the Peoples of the Southeast Asian Massif.* Lanham, MD: Scarecrow Press. (Reprinted in 2009 with the title *The A to Z of the Peoples of the Southeast Asian Massif.*)

–. 2009. Handling mountain minorities in China, Vietnam, and Laos: From history to current issues. *Asian Ethnicity* 10(1): 25-49.

–. 2010. Editorial: Zomia and Beyond. *Journal of Global History* 5(2): 187-214.

Mueggler, E. 2001. *The Age of Wild Ghosts: Memory, Violence, and Place in Southwest China.* Berkeley: University of California Press.

Nash, M. 1989. *The Cauldron of Ethnicity in the Modern World.* Chicago: University of Chicago Press.

Nong, Quoc Chan. 1978. Selective preservation of ethnic minorities' cultural tradition. *Vietnamese Studies* 52: 57-63.

O'Connor, R. 1995. Agricultural change and ethnic succession in Southeast Asian states: A case for regional anthropology. *Journal of Asian Studies* 54(4): 968-96.

Ortner, S.B. 2006. *Anthropology and Social Theory: Culture, Power, and the Acting Subject.* Durham, NC: Duke University Press.

Ovesen, J. 2004. All Lao? Minorities in the Lao People's Democratic Republic. In *Civilizing the Margins: Southeast Asian Government Policies for the Development of Minorities,* ed. C.R. Duncan, 214-40. Ithaca, NY: Cornell University Press.

Pholsena, V. 2007. *Post-War Laos: The Politics of Culture, History and Identity.* 2nd ed. Singapore: Institute of Southeast Asian Studies.

Plafker, T. 2001. China's "Go West" drive seeks to funnel aid to poor region. *International Herald Tribune,* 8 May 2001. http://www.iht.com.

Portes, A., and P. Landolt. 2000. Social capital: Promise and pitfalls of its role in development. *Journal of Latin American Studies* 32: 529-47.

Potter, P.B. 2007. Theoretical and conceptual perspectives on the periphery in contemporary China. In *The Chinese State at the Borders,* ed. D. Lary, 94-119. Vancouver: UBC Press.

Poutignat, P., and J. Streiff-Fenart. 1995. *Théories de l'Ethnicité.* Paris: Presses Universitaires de France.

Radcliffe, S. 2004. Geography of development: Development, civil society and inequality – Social capital is (almost) dead? *Progress in Human Geography* 28(4): 517-27.

Rata, E., and R. Openshaw, eds. 2006. *Public Policy and Ethnicity: The Politics of Ethnic Boundary Making.* Basingstoke: Palgrave Macmillan.

Reddy, D.S. 2005. The ethnicity of caste. *Anthropological Quarterly* 78(3): 543-84.

Ribot, J., and N. Peluso. 2003. "A Theory of Access." *Rural Sociology* 68(2): 153-81.

Rigg, J. 2005. *Living with Transition in Laos.* London: RoutledgeCurzon.

Robinne, F., and M. Sadan. 2007. *Social Dynamics in the Highlands of Southeast Asia: Reconsidering Political Systems of Highland Burma by E.R. Leach.* Leiden: Brill.

Sahlins, M. 1968. *Tribesmen.* Englewood Cliffs, NJ: Prentice Hall.

–. 1999. What is anthropological enlightenment? Some lessons of the twentieth century. *Annual Review of Anthropology* 28: i-xxiii.

Salemink, O. 2003. *The Ethnography of Vietnam's Central Highlanders.* Honolulu: University of Hawai'i Press.

Sanders, J.M. 2002. Ethnic boundaries and identity in plural societies. *Annual Review of Sociology* 28: 327-57.

Scoones, I. 1998. *Sustainable Rural Livelihoods: A Framework for Analysis.* IDS Working Paper 72. Brighton, UK: Institute of Development Studies.

–. 2009. Livelihoods perspectives and rural development. *Journal of Peasant Studies* 36(1): 171-96.

Scott, J.C. 1985. *Weapons of the Weak: Everyday Forms of Peasant Resistance*. New Haven, CT: Yale University Press.
—. 1990. *Domination and the Arts of Resistance: Hidden Transcripts*. New Haven, CT: Yale University Press.
—. 2009. *The Art of Not Being Governed: An Anarchist History of Upland Southeast Asia*. New Haven, CT: Yale University Press.
Sen, A. 1984. Rights and capabilities. In *Resources, Values and Development*, ed. A. Sen, 307-24. Oxford: Basil Blackwell.
—. 1987. *The Standard of Living*. Cambridge, Cambridge University Press.
Sollors, W., ed. 1989. *The Invention of Ethnicity*. New York: Oxford University Press.
—, ed. 1996. *Theories of Ethnicity: A Classical Reader*. New York: New York University Press.
Soukamneuth, B. 2006. The political economy of transition in Laos: From peripheral socialism to the margins of global capital. PhD diss., Cornell University.
Stalin, J. 1913. Marxism and the National Question. *Prosveshcheniye* 3-5 (March-May 1913). Transcribed by Carl Kavanagh.
Stanfield, J.R. 1986. *The Economic Thought of Karl Polanyi: Lives and Livelihood*. London: Macmillan.
Sturgeon, J., and T. Sikor. 2004. Introduction: Postsocialist property in Asia and Europe – Variations on "fuzziness." *Conservation and Society* 2(1): 1-17.
Tapp, N. 2001. *The Hmong of China: Context, Agency, and the Imaginary*. Leiden: Brill Academic.
Tapp, N., J. Michaud, C. Culas, and G. Yia Lee, eds. 2004. *Hmong/Miao in Asia*. Chiang Mai: Silkworm Books.
Thompson, R.H. 1989. *Theories of Ethnicity: A Critical Appraisal*. New York: Greenwood Press.
Turner, S. 2003. *Indonesia's Small Entrepreneurs: Trading on the Margins*. London: RoutledgeCurzon.
—. 2007. Trading old textiles: The selective diversification of highland livelihoods in northern Vietnam. *Human Organization* 66(4): 389-404.
Unger, J. 1997. Not quite Han: The ethnic minorities of China's southwest. *Bulletin of Concerned Asian Scholars* 29(3): 67-76.
van den Berghe, P.L. 1987. *The Ethnic Phenomenon*. New York: Praeger.
van Schendel, W. 2002. Geographies of knowing, geographies of ignorance: Southeast Asia from the fringes. *Environment and Planning D: Society and Space* 20(6): 647-68.
Wilkerson, J. 2003. Disquiet on the southwestern front: Studies of the minorities of Southwest China. *Pacific Affairs* 76(1): 79-91.
Woolcock, M., and D. Narayan. 2000. Social capital: Implications for development theory, research, and policy. *The World Bank Research Observer* 15 (2): 225-49.
Yinger, J.M. 1985. Ethnicity. *Annual Review of Sociology* 11: 151-80.

2
Economic Marginalization and Social Identity among the Drung People of Northwest Yunnan

Stéphane Gros

Recent Chinese government policies to enhance the livelihoods of the Drung, a small minority nationality of northwestern Yunnan, China, are – paradoxically – far more destructive than any previous hardships the Drung have endured. An examination of their history and their relationships with other social groups and the state demonstrates how the Drung have incurred successive forms of dependency and marginalization that have impacted on their past and current ethnicity.[1]

The Drung numbered just 7,400 people in China's 2000 census, with most living in Yunnan province's northwestern corner, known as Gongshan Autonomous County (see Figures 2.1 and 2.2). This land is shaped by high, steep mountains and three great rivers, the Nujiang (Salween), the Lancangjiang (Mekong), and the Jinshajiang (Golden Sand). It is in this area that the administrative boundaries of the Tibetan Autonomous Region, the provinces of Yunnan and Sichuan, and Burma meet. Gongshan Autonomous County is chiefly the home of Tibetans but also of several Tibeto-Burman-speaking groups such as the Naxi, Lisu, Nung, and Drung, among others.[2] The closest town to the Drung Valley is Gongshan, which is approximately 850 kilometres from Kunming. The Drung Valley, where most of the Drung population live, is also where they form the majority of the population, approximately 95 percent.

Not surprisingly for this remote location, the Drung (or Dulong in Chinese official parlance) are known for being poor and isolated. The first dirt road to the Drung area was completed only in 1999, putting an end to the use of horse caravans for the transportation of goods and supplies. The road has been central to, and the starting point of, various exogenous development plans aimed at improving the livelihoods of the "poor."[3] In my opinion, however, this road neither changed the economic circumstances of the valley nor fundamentally alleviated poverty.

After a ban on logging in 1998, tourism became one of the main pillar industries for Yunnan province. Moreover, northwestern Yunnan has become

Figure 2.1 Nujiang Lisu Nationality Autonomous Prefecture and Gongshan Dulong and Nu Nationalities Autonomous County (Yunnan Province).

a major tourist destination for both domestic and international tourists since the early 1990s because of the marketing of local minority cultures and the region's rugged valleys and hills. The old town of Lijiang, the cultural centre of the Naxi people, became a UNESCO World Heritage site in 1997, attracting increasing numbers of visitors. Further north, the Tibetan town of Zhongdian has been officially renamed Shangri-La to better highlight its cultural and environmental qualities (McKhann 2001; Hillman 2003). Since the early 2000s, a collaborative venture between the Yunnan provincial government and the environmental organization The Nature Conservancy, called the Great Rivers Project, aims at transforming northwest Yunnan into a huge eco-tourism zone (Litzinger 2004). Increasingly, more remote parts of this region are also affected by international initiatives aimed at preserving nature and culture, accompanied by a series of state policies to support these discourses. For the Drung, however, these developments are yet another form of marginalization.

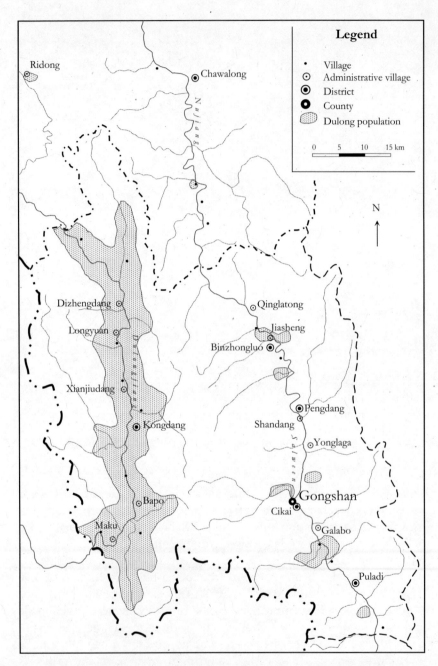

Figure 2.2 Distribution of the Dulong population in Gongshan County (northwestern Yunnan).

Current state-led assistance to the Drung is the latest of various interventions that began during the period of social transformation following the Liberation (*jiefang* or Communist victory) in 1949. Older Drung people often remember the transition to socialism fondly and tell stories about how the Communist Party helped the Drung in this period. This perception is likely linked to the fact that before the Communist victory, the Drung paid heavy tributes and taxes to Tibetan chiefs and the Chinese Empire, under whom they lived in abject submission. But significantly, the stories told by elders contrast with how younger Drung people today describe the help coming from Kunming and Beijing. This chapter considers the shifts between these three periods and assesses the Drung's responses and livelihoods in the context of political and economic marginalization. In particular, I discuss the exchange system between the Drung and their neighbours, and what changing political circumstances mean for negotiating forms of dependence.

The Drung and Enforced Servitude

Historically, the northwestern borders of Yunnan province lay at the junction of several competing political centres. Long a theatre of unceasing conflicts, this remote area was coveted by Tibetans, Naxi, and Chinese. In the middle of this zone lived three Tibeto-Burman-speaking peoples, the Drung, Nung, and Lisu, who were expected to obey the requests of these dominant groups or pay dearly for their resistance. The Drung stood at the lower end of the political and cultural hierarchy.

For centuries, the Chinese state governed the fringes of its empire through the indigenous chiefs system *(tusi zhidu)*, which gave a degree of autonomy to local leaders in return for their loyalty to the empire. During the Qing dynasty (1644-1911), this system changed to direct administration by mandarins (state-appointed officials), yet China still had only nominal authority in this area. Until the first half of the twentieth century, this patch of remote land was like an open zone, where only local chieftains retained real authority. These chieftains included the indigenous leaders (or *tusi*) of the Naxi (known then as the Moso), and the independent Tibetan chiefs of Tsarong (a region of southeast Tibet) (see Figure 2.3).

For a long time, the Drung were "eaten" – their own expression – by their more powerful neighbours. The Drung's past, still vibrant in oral memory, is a history of deprivation and excessive demands, fear, and extreme forms of dependence and marginalization. It is a history that is little known. Their inability to pay taxes sometimes led them into domestic work. These facts are not reported in detail in historical documents (which were invariably written by outsiders), but some Drung women, men, and children were indeed at times exchanged for oxen or taken away to become slaves in an alien land. Some were victims of raids by their immediate neighbours, mainly

32 Stéphane Gros

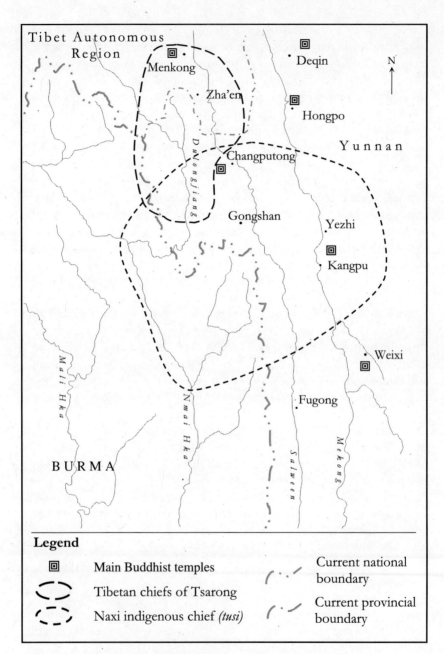

Figure 2.3 Main political spheres in northwestern Yunnan (*c.* 1900).

the Lisu. Recurring motifs in oral histories concerning that period are of living in fear of such raids and abductions of women and children.

The Drung's political dependency arose from trading with and accepting loans from commercial agents and the intermediaries of local rulers. These traders were willing to lend to Drung people, and the inability of some borrowers to pay led to debt, economic dependence, and eventually political servitude. The Tibetan chiefs who levied taxes on the Drung were themselves rich merchants holding a trade monopoly in southeast Tibet on the border with Yunnan. Similarly, the Naxi, who had been the main ruling elite in this area when the Qing dynasty extended the indigenous chiefs system *(tusi zhidu)*, had firmly established themselves early on in some villages of the upper Salween valley. Some Naxi traders, operating as agents of the native chiefs *(tusi)*, travelled each year to the Irrawaddy Valley to buy gold and medicinal plants. Loans to Drung with interest were common practice, not only among the Naxi *tusi* and their agents but also among various Buddhist temples and the Tibetan chiefs, who were the main actors for commercial transactions, especially for salt, tools, iron utensils, and wool clothing. It was a great source of income and a means through which many Drung (or impoverished Nung and Tibetan themselves) became indebted.

The practice of providing credit was particularly developed at the expense of weaker groups, such as the Drung and their neighbours the Nung, who were often obliged to accept the terms of the transaction. When the creditors eventually came to claim their due, many were not able to pay back their loans. The Tibetan chiefs from Tsarong (referred to by the Drung as *lenbu*) collected taxes, undertook trade, and carried out local administrative duties. Public administration was, therefore, mixed with private profiteering and sometimes abuse. In other words, the chief and the creditor were often one and the same.

Today, many observers would call this system of debt dependency a form of slavery (see the discussion in Testart 2001). But it seems that the "victims" adopted a more nuanced understanding. Clearly, debt played an important role in the domination of the Drung, but the relationship between creditors and debtors has to be considered in terms of exchange and reciprocity.

Exchange and the Nature of Slavery

The Drung today refer to the past relationship with the Tibetans chiefs and their agents as *bang-nam*. The term implies a friendship between two individuals, in particular, a sincere relationship made manifest by frequent exchanges, gifts, and counter-gifts. It is best translated as "companions of exchange." Among other things, the *bang-nam* relationship was the framework for transactions involving oxen exchanged for people who would ultimately become "slaves."

In the Southeast Asian Massif, many regions were prone to frequent raiding by neighbours. In consequence, Communist Chinese observers described the phenomenon among the Drung as a direct result of Tibetan feudal domination (Dulongzu Jianshi Bianxiezu 1986; Gros 2001). The ideological positioning of these critical sources presented the Tibetans as tyrants, while the Drung were forced into poverty and slavery. By far the main form of exchange during this period was the enslavement of marginalized individuals through trade, and with the tacit agreement of the slave-releasing community. In fact, if the Tibetans owned Drung slaves, they had often acquired them through exchanges for oxen, an important ritual good for the Drung.

Drung slaves were typically orphans, individuals who did not manage to start a family, the poor who could not pay taxes or tribute, or thieves and even sorcerers. These categories of people were regarded as not having a valid social existence and so were rejected by Drung society. Drung trade intermediaries, or *shu-tap*, played an essential part in the transfer *(shu dv-bon)* of the slaves *(ladu)*. These intermediaries were generally "companions of exchange" *(bang-nam)* of the Tibetans of Tsarong. The former took people to the latter and carried out the exchange.

What was it like to be a slave? Numerous testimonies from the region (Rockhill 1881, 285; Bacot 1912, 273; Goré 1992, 106) indicate that the living conditions of enslaved individuals were not extremely difficult. However, the most important aspect of slavery was considered to be the sense of exclusion. As Testart (2001, 24) writes, "The slave is a man without an identity." The (legal) status of the slave is marked by the total exclusion from his or her society of origin. It is often said by the Drung that the people who were traded for oxen were – in this patrilineal society – children without recognized fathers. Fundamentally, in Drung society, exclusion referred to kinship.

By contrast, the Tibetans in Tsarong identified inclusion through the community of shared language, culture, and religious identity. Slaves therefore usually originated from non-Buddhist groups, considered to be ethnically different (Lazcano Nebreda 1998, 229-31). Thus, for the Tibetans, the origin of potential slaves was important: people could be pawned for debt, but enslavement resulted only from the change in status of the pawned person, which became more likely over time (Testart 2001, ch. 3). Consequently, slavery among the Tibetans coexisted with other types of service labour that did not include a deep sense of exclusion. Accordingly, when an individual was pawned for debt, the bond with the community of origin was preserved and hence there was the possibility of returning to the community at a later time. This opportunity also existed for abducted or voluntarily enslaved people.

Goods and people, and people as goods, therefore, circulated in this region. Indeed, local oral histories and written documents show the movement of oxen and slaves as completely entangled. Moreover, several spheres of influence in terms of religion and political power were in place, resulting in multiple, and sometimes competing, systems of authority. The Drung were thus in the middle of various overlapping spheres of influence, which involved them in multiple ties of allegiance.

The Drung's very existence was linked to these vast, overlapping systems. To be Drung is a structural relationship vis-à-vis others. In particular, ethnicity is and has been constituted by a wider set of social and spatial relationships. The Drung define themselves and their surrounding social and political environments by these lenses of hierarchy and asymmetrical power relations. Within this situation, slaves were excluded from kinship ties and were placed at the lowest position within asymmetrical relationships. But this extreme form of dependency also offered benefits to Drung society. The Drung were not only the victims of economic and political domination that led to extreme dependence. They also participated in upholding this hierarchical exchange system as it played an important role in creating their sense of locality and identity. In this sense, Drung society, while at the margins of its powerful neighbours, was itself fully defined by the same asymmetrical principles as its neighbours.

These hierarchical and unequal relationships influenced people's perceptions of their identity and their sense of group belonging. Yet, when the Drung were integrated into the newly founded People's Republic of China, these unequal yet balanced relationships ended. From a slave-releasing society exploited in a "backward" feudal system, the Drung were upgraded to the status of a nationality *(minzu)* and, in relation to the Han majority nationality, a minority nationality *(shaoshu minzu)*.[4] This change established the Drung, in principle, as part of the People with rights equal to those of everyone else in the People's Republic. But it also created important challenges for the identity of the Drung and how they related to their neighbours.

The Impacts of the Communists
After the Communist victory in China in 1949, the Drung were affected in various ways. One important change was in the official classification of their group and the rights afforded to them as a result of this classification. As Forsyth and Michaud discuss in Chapter 1, systems of classification were derived from an agenda of rationalization and control. This is especially true for peoples such as the Drung who lived in politically contested areas, as around the Sino-Burmese border.

Up to the mid-1950s, the Chinese used the term "Qiuzi" to designate the present-day Drung and some of their immediate neighbours in upper Burma. (Indeed, a few Western sources also used this term, written as "Kiutzu" or "Kioutsé.")[5] The British, having settled in Burma since the end of the nineteenth century, employed a different ethnonym: Nung. The name Nung was originally a Jinghpaw (Kachin) term used to indicate two groups: the Daru

(Daru Nung) and Rawang (Rawang Nung). The British, however, used the category of Nung to encompass whole populations along the Sino-Burmese border, including the Qiuzi and, on occasion, the Luzi (Nu) as well (Gros 2004). Anthropologists call these terms exonyms because they refer to names given to an ethnic group by people who do not belong to that group.

Both the Nung category of the British and the Qiuzi category of the Chinese overlapped in the context of the highly politicized Sino-Burmese border, a frontier region contested by both parties. These larger political powers imposed systems of classification on similar people in order to make their own processes of border demarcation clearer. In turn, the connection between border demarcation and ethnic classification played a part in how the Communists defined ethnic groups or *minzu* (nationality). During the 1950s, the exonym "Qiuzi" remained in use and had been considered as a possible official name. In 1962, the Chinese and Burmese governments agreed on the location of the Sino-Burmese frontier, and the name Dulong was chosen to refer to this group (Gros 2004). Consequently, the ethnic boundary of the Dulong category finally coincided with the political boundary between the two neighbouring countries.

The crystallization of the Chinese categories of Qiuzi and Dulong therefore depended on complex and changing political factors. Inventing new labels and redrawing the ethnographic map also had impacts on how people understood these labels; how they used them in social, historical, and political discourses; and how they related to them as internal or external identifiers. In other words, ethnic categories were reimagined within the new political context. This cognitive aspect is important, and it situates the workings of ethnicity within what Harrell (2001) has called the "triangle of discourses," that of ethnohistory, *minzu* categories, and local identities.

The advent of the New China under Communism brought immense changes and economic improvements to the valley. But many of these socialist-then-modernist policies also brought new forms of dependency that reinforced marginalization. One example of this is the state distribution of economic subsidies, which played a relatively important role in assisting Drung livelihoods but which also introduced new problems of dependency.

The case of one old man – whom we will call Duri – illustrates these problems. Duri was a widower and had mourned his wife for almost a year when I visited in 2003. Because of his age, he was unable to remain economically independent and had stayed at the house of his younger brother. As Duri was one of the poorest people in the village, the local government allocated him a subsidy of fifty kilograms of rice per year. But the rice had not yet arrived. One evening he complained to his nephew, who was a newly appointed leader at the village level. "And my rice, where is it?" he asked, "I heard nice words, but in fact it was a lie!" That evening, Duri drank too much and spoke more strongly. "They lied to me! Even the family lies to me!" At first, some people tried to make him understand that he had indeed been allocated the subsidy but that he would have to collect the rice and carry it back to the village. This task, however, would take three days, and Duri could not be the one to carry it on his back. Nothing helped, and in the end, Duri put his head under his covers, grumbling.

Yet, only a few days later, during a discussion with close relatives around the fire, Duri started to express how much better life was since the Liberation. This apparent contradiction is explained later in the chapter. About the improvements, Duri said:

> People are happy since President Mao ... President Mao, he's good, look ... Previously, we, the people, we suffered, we were oppressed, we had to gather the items [for the tribute], at the time of the Guomindang it was like that. Previously, the chiefs were not good, they did not rule correctly ... Since the [Communist] Party, since President Mao, we, the people, we have clothing. Previously, we had nothing, nothing to wear; it is true, we slept here, on the sides of the fireplace ... When the tribute had to be gathered, there was no pot to use anymore, no [iron] tripod left [for the hearth]. Now, since President Mao's rule, one can set the tripod.[6] It has been forty, fifty years that all is very well, since the party, President Mao arrived in the Drung country. For those who suffered, it improved, one has something to eat and drink, no need to chew more roots of *mang*, *jit*, and *peuri*.[7]

Duri's statement summarizes an important shift in the relationships between local people and their rulers during the twentieth century. According to Duri, before the Liberation, the chiefs "did not know how to rule"; but today, they know how to give. This is a familiar experience for the Drung. Older members of Drung society are always prompt to evoke the suffering of the times before Communism, when villagers had to pay tributes to old chiefs, which frequently left villagers in a state of extreme poverty. Back then, the lords and chiefs took a lot but did not give much in return. The relationship has now been reversed. Today, the chiefs are the ones who give, and the term "chiefs" often links local governors, the party, and President Mao, whose timeless figure still haunts the present. For Duri, as for others, the state *(guojia)* and the Communist Party *(gongchandang)* are personified and merged with the immutable figure of President Mao in an entity that is one and the same, and that is made real by the distribution of goods.

Duri's statement about the suffering and oppression caused by the chiefs of the "old society" *(jiu shehui)* could possibly be compared with the practice of "speeches of bitterness" *(suku)* of the revolutionary period, which allowed people to express grievances in public. In turn, this encouraged people to view society and interpret their history according to the logic of class struggle.

Peasants were told to recount, in a narrative form, their experience of poverty, domination, and exploitation by the dominant class, learning how to formulate the past injustice in the light of their recent "Liberation" (see also Makley 2005). These accounts effectively served to obliterate the past and enhance the socialist revolution by encouraging citizens to express their pain from previous exploitation and seek redemption through punishing the culprits. The deprivation that characterized the previous oppression would be resolved by a new era of equal distribution of wealth.

Moreover, Duri's speech resonates with a more general narrative of lack, or poverty, among the Drung. In the past, the Drung adopted a myth relating to injustice that is often recalled to underline or justify the poverty and the ignorance of the Drung themselves. The myth referred to an omnipotent celestial divinity who distributed wealth and knowledge among all people. At this time, certain characteristics of environment, aptitudes, and living conditions were also distributed. But the Drung did not receive much:[8]

> At the time of our ancestors, at the time of the flood when humankind developed, just when the flood started, when the men were to be, here is how it was ... Among the men, the one Drung, the story tells, almost fell asleep.
>
> Dozing, he asked for grass seeds and vegetables. He held his basket open, but the bottom was pierced. "I'm staying awake, give the grass seeds," were his words. "I'm staying awake." The grass seeds were given in sufficient quantity, but the basket was never full; it's what the story tells. Then, not being able to fill in his basket, he looked toward earth, and down there the seeds had already become green, the grass had grown, all green. For this reason, here on earth there is grass. And one says for this reason that he was not very smart.
>
> Thus, the Drung ended up not knowing how to sing, not knowing all kinds of things. How has that happened? The Chinese, they write books, the Tshawalong, they have the Tibetan script to write and some write on stones.[9] The Drung do not have writing.
>
> He held his basket open, and holding his basket, all fell by the hole; by the hole of the basket, the songs had fallen. After all had fallen, here we knew nothing; it's for this reason. We know nothing, [whereas] the others write, have a writing system. Carry it in your heart, he [the dozing one] said, and it is by heart that the stories are told ... And if they were not thus transmitted, there would be no stories.

Since these primordial times, the social positions were defined. The dozing Drung, "not very smart," who seems to be the only one to blame, obtained almost nothing of what was distributed among men. This unequal distribution of the goods and knowledge helps explain the historical and current reality in which the Drung find their place as the most deprived group.[10]

The political hierarchical order, past and present, is also rationalized by a further story that describes how the Drung, from time immemorial, have been under the domination of the "people of the East" *(shar vtsang)*. Following the Flood *(ngang kizin zin)*, a new order succeeded in recreating humankind. From an original pair of siblings forced to commit incest, nine couples were formed and dispatched across the nine valleys making up the terrestrial abode. This territorial distribution then went according to the hierarchy among the couples (who became different ethnicities) and the establishment of fixed political relations between them. A shooting contest was then held to determine which couple should hold authority on all other topics: the couple who hit the target most with their arrows would become the chief *(pon)*, and all others would be the people *(prase)* who pay the chief tribute *(kri)*. The oldest couple won and were sent toward the east. This direction is consequently associated with the place, generally identified as China, where the dominators of the Drung have always lived (be it the empire or the Naxi chiefs, or at times even the Tibetan, regardless of whether they are actually to the north). The mythical tournament thus justified the giving of tributes between elder and juniors and, following that, between the communities of the descendants of the nine primordial couples.

For the Drung, the hierarchical order appears natural and instituted since ancient times. But contrary to this mythical logic of inescapable and fixed hierarchy, the statements of Duri and others make it possible to identify contemporary causes of poverty that do not refer to oppressors from the old society, or, more specifically, the former Tibetan chiefs.

As we have seen, before the founding of the People's Republic of China, the Drung were under the concomitant rule of distinct authorities. Each placed them in a different hierarchical relation. The Tibetan chiefs could make their rule heavier by direct control and by imposing an annual tax, whereas the imperial state delegated control of their subjects to intermediaries such as the local Naxi chiefs. Retrospectively, the Drung tend to minimize their oppression by "the people of the east" (the empire and its intermediaries) compared to that of the Tibetans. As an old Drung man put it during a conversation about their past political situation:

When the people of the east received the tribute, it was not very important. In the same way, people of the east did not oppress the population. Just like now: all the things that we use are things that were provided by the Communist Party. The other countries did not give anything, but the Communist Party of China gave a lot. The other countries did not even give a piece of fabric. It all came from China.

The coming of the Communists is thus considered by many Drung as the beginning of a new type of political relation, one that is clearly opposite to the relations based on giving tribute that connected them to the Tibetan chiefs. Even if, at the time of Tibetan domination, the Drung were not as deprived as some of them say, the Liberation after 1949 allowed them to present the Chinese state as a benefactor because it provided economic assistance. This situation explains Duri's incomprehension: logically, his rice should have arrived, and for him, it was inevitably the local cadres, his nephew among them, who caused this delay. But Duri's reaction also refers to a more general dissatisfaction with the fact that the state today plays its role of benefactor less efficiently. It is no longer like under Mao's rule. The idealization of this earlier period could be viewed as a strategic discourse produced in a specific context and aimed at addressing current concerns. To some extent, it is a way to give oneself the means to justify more requests. It also tells the extent to which, even if strategically, the Drung are now expecting support from the state and, finally, how much they now depend on it.

Recent state policy must then have satisfied people like Duri: the state, once again, took charge of the Drung's future. After a decision to implement a policy of "returning the fields to the forest" *(tuigeng huanlin)* on a large scale, the Drung were asked in late 2003 to stop planting crops and to instead receive a monthly subsidy in rice. To understand this new situation fully, we must first review successive reforms and the politics of aid to the Drung.

Analyzing State Reforms
As discussed above, the official identification after 1949 of a "Dulong nationality" symbolized a radical change. The choice of the name, a Chinese transcription of their vernacular, was in itself recognition in the full sense of the term. The rejection of old derogatory terms (such as "Qiuzi" or "Tchòp'a") meant that the state wanted the Drung to appreciate that their historic unequal relationship was over. The Dulong could consequently have representatives within the Gongshan Dulong and Nu Nationalities Autonomous County created in 1956, and the first appointed head of the county was Dulong.

In official publications, various figures emphasize the government assistance allotted to the Drung. At the time of the integration of the valley into the People's Republic of China, from 1951 to 1952, the government gave two hoes to each "labor force," as well as thirty-six oxen (Zhang 2000, 37). Clothing was also distributed, each adult receiving trousers and a jacket. In October 1952, 2,164 new pieces of clothing were distributed. In 1953, after several allowances for the poorest households (275 items), 1,569 additional working suits were distributed (100), for an estimated total population in the Dulong valley of twenty-five hundred people. These initial gifts, among other distributed goods, remained alive and well in the memory of elders. They forged the idea that the Communist Party has prestige.

Since the 1950s, many forms of assistance have reached this remote township. The current policy continues that put in place at Liberation. At the end of October 1998, Ling Hu'an, then secretary of the Party Committee for the province of Yunnan, visited the Dulong valley by foot. The visit created a sensation because it was the first time that such an important leader showed, with his own sweat, that he was interested in, and supported, the Drung. The prestige of the party was reaffirmed, especially as Ling Hu'an decided to launch a three-year plan to improve agricultural production by granting additional access to seed crops (maize and potatoes), introducing new standards for houses, increasing the local stock of cattle, rebuilding schools, and installing small hydroelectric power stations and satellite antennas for receiving three national television channels in the main villages of the valley. In the 1990s, the average cereal production in the Drung locality was approximately 170 kilograms per capita, and the average income was 217 yuan per year. Under the development program launched by Ling Hu'an, the production would, within three years, reach the national standard of 300 kilograms per capita, and the average standard of living would rise to an annual income of 800 yuan per family. Together, these steps would constitute dramatic improvements to local livelihoods.

Until recently, the Dulong valley was accessible only by walking for three days on a mountain path. A state-owned caravan – the last one in China – was in charge of transporting the cereals (up to four hundred tons annually) and other products (drugs, articles sold in the state shops, and so on), for a total of approximately nine hundred tons per year (65 percent by mule caravan, 35 percent by porters). The maintenance of the mule track and the caravans cost an average of 600,000 yuan per year (roughly US$90,000). If the costs of buying and maintaining mules are added, the total can be estimated at 2 million yuan per year. The paradox is that because of this cost, the price of food in the Dulong valley was higher than elsewhere. On 1 July 1995, construction of a motor road officially began in order to connect the valley of the Salween (Nujiang) to that of the Drung (Dulongjiang), to the west. The road, which runs ninety-six kilometres across a mountain range, was finished in autumn 1999; the total investment can be estimated as 98 million yuan, or approximately more than one million yuan per kilometre.[11] There was one death during construction. Because of the steep slopes and high levels of rain- and snow-fall, the new road remains impassable for more than half the year. It is an astounding level of investment for this small valley and its twenty-five hundred inhabitants.

To understand how the Drung perceive the state and what they expect from it, it is important to consider some of the key aspects of political power in this society. As discussed above, the Drung often regard the state, or the party, as the provider of goods. This relation contrasts with previous political relations based on the payment of taxes. But despite this opposition, there are still similarities between the current state and past regimes based on the concepts of prestige and circulation of goods.

As we saw, the Drung were formerly in a complex position of allegiance toward several authorities to which they paid tribute: indigenous Naxi chiefs acting as intermediaries of the Chinese Empire, and the Tibetan chiefs of Tsarong. The political domination relied heavily on the establishment of a creditor-debtor relationship, which was at the root of dependence, expressed through the payment of tributes. From the Drung's point of view, those in a position of power demonstrated their status by distributing goods. And very significantly, this demonstration of generosity in the past often involved the most prestigious goods (often obtained in exchange for a slave) – oxen.

The oxen were used among the Drung mainly for sacrifice *(dvruq-wa)*, which ensured the prestige *(koksang)* of those who organized the rituals. The meat was divided, and this distribution was part of the flow of exchange and reciprocity within the social network. The logic of the sacrifice and the distribution of meat relates to what Stevenson ([1943] 1970) had called "the economy of prestige" when describing the Feasts of Merits of the Chin people of Burma. This sheds another light on the meaning of the exchange of slaves for oxen. But it also offers the chance to look at the political relationship differently and assess the implications for local livelihoods in more culturally contextualized ways.

The Drung considered the Tibetan chiefs the "masters of the place" *(mvli aqkang)* and paid them an annual tax. This relationship was established in a particular way. According to one Drung story, the Tibetans of Tsarong arrived in the Drung Valley with nine oxen and established their authority by distributing meat: all those who had received a share were from then on to pay taxes to them. The distribution of meat thus was a key element in the establishment and acknowledgment of the Tibetan chiefs' domination. In this context, taxation appears as a gift in return for an initial distribution of meat, which legitimates the political structure (Gros 2007). Interestingly, the Drung refer to these oxen sacrifices as *dvruq-wa*, literally meaning "to make the group."

Even if oxen sacrifices are now prohibited by the modernist socialist state, it seems reasonable to assume that these historic associations concerning the distribution of goods are always present in the local representation of power. In particular, the Drung assume that claims to power must be validated by generosity. From this perspective, the various forms of aid coming from the state are an integral part of its legitimacy. Without these distributions, the state would lose its legitimacy.

From Dependence to Development, and Back Again

So, how have these state reforms and perceptions of political hierarchy influenced local livelihoods in the Drung region? Over the last two decades in the Drung country, significant inequalities progressively developed among villagers, not only because of the economic liberalization launched in the 1980s but also because of the increasing influence of family networks, which favoured some households above others. Dissatisfaction also grew during the construction of hydroelectric power stations, which villagers were obliged to take part in by working "voluntarily" *(yiwugong)*. The same voluntary labour was required for transporting sand and stones during the rebuilding of local schools. And, between 2000 and 2005, each household had to provide two family members for a full month of voluntary work on the construction of the road in the valley.

According to the development plan, state aid in the form of seeds, manure, and plastic film for agriculture had to be paid for at the rate of one yuan per kilogram as a partial contribution toward the cost of these items' transportation from Gongshan. All these products had to be transported by the villagers themselves, often involving several days of walking. Many Drung villagers did not consider this required level of participation to be fair, and some complained.

Just like Duri, who was still expecting his bag of rice, some believed that the new form of assistance provided by the state "is not giving; to give is to bring at your door." In the same way, the free distributions of worn-out clothes in the schools are often considered degrading. For some, the comparison is obvious: in the time of Mao, they received new clothes. For many Drung, accepting worn-out clothes would imply that they are moving backward toward the old status of poverty and inferiority. Many younger Drung would prefer to have an entitlement to the same benefits and standards that they now see on television. It would seem that the Drung have begun to reject their old way of acting as assistants and are showing signs of wanting parity with other social groups, including majority Han Chinese.

Yet, there is also strong resentment of outsiders, as well as of the local leaders, over the exploitation of local resources. For instance, at the beginning of the 1990s, there was a boom in the exploitation of camphor oil. In the north of the valley, many Drung had abandoned fields to pursue camphor production. But the money they earned was quickly spent, and the largest profits were carried out by non-Drung traders who collected the oil. This economic activity is now prohibited because the Dulong valley has been incorporated into a nature reserve. The government enforces environmental protection, and hunting is prohibited as well. Many Drung feel that these steps have deprived inhabitants not only of a source of food but also of incomes related to the sale of by-products.

The local leaders, themselves Drung, are thus often accused of leaving the best share to "foreigners" and of being negligent in assuring the best assistance to the Drung population. Locally, the main role conferred upon mediators (village head, party secretary) is to obtain as much as possible for the villagers. If they obtain overall benefits for the community, they are considered legitimate leaders. When local government representatives make their yearly visit to the more remote villages in the valley, they are often expected to give donations from their own pockets. The leaders must play a part in this redistributive chain of which the party is the source. Their presumed elite status increases their social distance from the villagers, who often see them as the ones who "eat and drink with excess" *(dachi dahe)*, at the expense of the community.

Since the early 2000s, the largest development project affecting the Dulong valley is the vast national undertaking known as the Great Western Development *(Xibu da kaifa)*.[12] One important objective of this project is to convert mountain fields into a plantation forest *(tuigeng huanlin)*, which, in turn, will require the resettlement of people and agricultural fields. Indeed, the province of Yunnan has been allocated 1.4 billion yuan to deal with displaced populations. Starting in the fall of 2003, in the north of the Dulong valley, the inhabitants of some isolated hamlets were resettled further south. As a whole, the Drung are now banned from practising agriculture on mountain slopes; yet, 85 percent of the arable land in the valley is on slopes greater than thirty-five degrees. They preserve the right to cultivate only wet rice (planted only in a few villages in the central part of the valley), with some permanent land around houses allocated for small-scale agriculture. According to official statistics, before 2003, the total cultivated surface in the valley amounted to 14,804 *mu* (1 *mu* is 0.0667 hectare), and the conversion of the fields to forest absorbs 14,000 *mu*. This plan would therefore leave only some 800 *mu* for agriculture, among some 860 households.

How can a population that lives off agriculture, hunting, and collecting natural resources subsist if it loses the right to cultivate the land or to take advantage of the natural resources? How can such a drastic curtailing of the customary means of livelihoods be achieved without a serious threat to social reproduction? The project's answer to these questions has been to provide a supply of food to the villagers, which effectively means that villagers live on rice the government provides. Originally, each household was to receive grain subsidies on the basis of the land area converted. In practice, the local government decided to allocate the subsidy on a per capita basis, with all inhabitants receiving 180 kilograms of rice per year (see Wilkes and Shen 2007). In addition, the state paid twenty yuan for each *mu* converted and planted with varieties of trees supplied by the Forestry Office.

At the time of research in 2003, villagers had immense confidence that these subsidies would reach them. People assumed the state would play its part. Of course, evidence presented in this chapter suggests that this largesse may not be forthcoming. Moreover, some Drung were ambivalent about these changes. They realized that this project would make them totally reliant on assistance, and also that it probably meant the gradual loss of some of their cultural practices and heritage. The prestige of the party, which survives today through the policy of assistance to the Drung, also denies them their agency and anything but the right to be poor.

Evidence from the project's initial stages suggests that it has indeed created a high degree of dependency on the government. It has also reduced agricultural activities, including the transmission of agricultural knowledge to younger generations. For the 860 households on the land in 2005, the total remaining cultivated surface was only 2,998 *mu* (199 hectares), or 0.051 hectares per capita (Li Jinming 2008, 81). Some younger Drung do not know how to adopt the farming practices of earlier generations. According to a short survey conducted in 2005, the implementation of the field conversion policy (to controlled land use and forest) has further eroded agro-biodiversity (Xiao Jianwen 2005). Since its implementation, many crops and varieties that used to be grown in the swidden fields have declined, and the land has been planted with forest monoculture. Among the forty-nine crop varieties identified, five had apparently disappeared in 2005, and seventeen were kept by only a very few households. Only eight varieties were still regularly planted on the small remaining cultivated areas.

The conversion policy has also restricted grazing pasture such that livestock herding is becoming difficult, further weakening livelihoods. Many Drung no longer work, depending on grain and relief from the government instead. A few households have kept seeds suitable for swiddens, but since these are no longer allowed to be cultivated and some are for crops unsuited to non-swidden fields, it is unlikely that such crops can be kept for much longer.

Conclusion

The discourse about Drung identity, as well as the Drung's discourse about themselves, is fuelled by a standardized vocabulary derived from political imperatives. Indeed, the villagers generally evoke their situation in terms of an absence, or lack, of what is rightfully theirs. Because they have belonged to a socialist state that has explicitly promoted "development" for at least fifty years, it is not surprising to hear them speak about themselves in ways that reflect outsiders' views of them as being poor, needy, and lacking the skills needed to develop on their own. These stereotypes also reflect the imperatives of the new Chinese modernity developed in the twentieth century that emphasizes the "concerted construction of the 'people' in terms of lack, unready for political sovereignty, but ... disciplined and rendered docile for the employ of global capital" (Anagnost 1997, 78).

The question of poverty and its associated categorizations plays an important role in the relationship the Drung maintain with the outside world today. In sociological terms, according to Simmel ([1908] 1998), poverty does not come initially, followed by assistance. Rather, being identified as people who should receive assistance is what makes a people "poor." The poverty of the Drung and other groups are officially and objectively defined according to national standards of basic needs. And this system is justified in part by the state's exclusive right to determine needs and, consequently, provide assistance according to its own criteria. Thus, the state, by monopolizing the legitimacy required to define the collective needs, can be a provider. But as the Drung are now realizing, the assistance from the state comes with a price tag.

The categorization in terms of needing and lacking resonates with the Drung's own discourse on their sense of not having had their fair share. But if the Drung make use of official vocabulary and external stereotypes imposed on them, it is also an indirect way to justify particular living conditions and require more than what is already being received.

Today more than ever, the socialist state is adopting the role of the giver in this region. At first, the Drung praised the initial period of Communist rule and gave the impression that they would be happy to live in complete dependence on the state. This impression was the result of the historic association of political authority with generosity or redistribution, and the Drung's history of having lived through a long succession of forms of dependency with groups that were better off or more powerful than they. With the victory of Communism in 1949, the historic pattern of domination was ruptured, and the old tributary system of allegiance ended. From then on, the Drung became the only ones to receive, without having to give in return.

Since 1949, state aid assigns each person a place in society based on a hierarchy of social categories. But if what it aims at, from the official point of view, is economic and social development, it leads in reality to the formation of a new dependence through welfare. The action of the state has effectively destroyed the customary system of reciprocity by replacing it with a system of institutional responsibility. The state, with its gifts that do not imply any reciprocity or debt, symbolically takes from the Drung a part of themselves. There is no choice left to the Drung but to accept this gift without returning anything, which makes them even poorer.

The state's redistributive policy has aimed to address a certain perception of social problems and needs and has contributed to forms of social categorization, according to ethnic or other terms. Interventions targeting parts of the population considered to be particularly needy reinforce established categories. For the Drung, the present period is characterized by a new form of dependency in which all reciprocity disappears. Formerly, the Drung's preferred form of political relations, although asymmetrical, implied exchange and the circulation of goods. Now the policy-driven assistance is only one way. The Drung's rhetoric likes to emphasize their indigence or ethnic distinctiveness as a means to appeal to Communist social categorization in order to obtain more state-provided resources. Their official recognition as a nationality represents an asset. Their status of nationality has reinforced their identity and allows them to present their ethnic characteristics as set in stone. The Drung's response to the classification established by the state is a kind of contractual acceptance of improved integration and better access to wealth. But, ironically, the progressive increase of their dependency on the state has led to the progressive disappearance of their means of subsistence.

The Drung's inclusion in a hierarchical political system is a story of successive forms of dependency. State policies have aimed at empowering the Drung by granting them political status and providing them with the technological means of improving their living conditions. But, in turn, state policies have contributed to a higher degree of dependence on the state, which has total control of defining the rationale for development. New government initiatives to include the Drung in livelihoods projects or nature conservation, as witnessed by the Great Western Development project, ultimately produce no opportunities for the Drung other than for marginalization.

Notes
1 This chapter is based on fieldwork among the Drung between 1998 and 2005 for a total of eighteen months, funded largely by a Franco-Chinese Bilateral Grant (1997-98), a Lavoisier grant from the French Ministry of Foreign Affairs (1999), the France Foundation (1999), and the Louis Dumont Fund for Social Anthropology (2003).
2 For recent studies in English on Naxi (and Moso), see, for example, Oppitz and Hsu (1998) and Mathieu (2003). For the Lisu people of the upper Salween valley, see the detailed Introduction in Dessaint and Ngwâma (1994). "Nu" and "Dulong" are respectively the standardized form and official name in Chinese of these two groups. The Drung are part of a broader linguistic group that also includes the Nung and Rawang of Burma. See Gros (2004) for an analysis of the relationships between these groups.
3 See Michaud (2009) for a recent discussion of Communist China's policies for the economic and cultural development of its minority nationalities *(shaoshu minzu)*. See Harrell (1995) for an historical overview of the center-periphery relationship in the Chinese context.
4 Thoraval (1990) is a good discussion on the use of the most-debated *minzu* concept in China.
5 The Chinese name Qiuzi is itself most probably derived from the Lisu name Tchòp'a.
6 Iron pots and tripods, and metal items in general, are key elements of wealth for a Drung household.
7 These are the roots of wild plants that were one of the important elements of the Drung's diet.
8 Known locally as "Story of the Dozing One," the following transcription is a version recorded in the winter of 2001. The story was told by an old man in a familial setting, after his adult son inquired about it.

9   Tshawalong here refers to the Tibetans.
10 Myths portraying ancestors as foolish, or that aim at affirming one's inferiority vis-à-vis more powerful or erudite neighbours, are found among many minorities of southwest China and Southeast Asia. For example, Proschan (2001, 1025) refers to this tendency in the myth of origin of the Khmu people of northern Laos. This also resonates in other ways with the rhetoric of lack or indolence in identity claims of difference; see Yeh (2007) for the case of the Tibetans.
11 These figures were given to me in 2000, and since then I have not been able to find reliable official figures detailing the costs of construction.
12 About the Go West initiative and the Great Western Development in China, see also Swain and Sturgeon (both this volume), Lai (2002), and Goodman (2004).

References

Anagnost, A.S. 1997. *National Past-Times: Narratives, Representation, and Power in Modern China*. Durham, NC: Duke University Press.

Bacot, J. 1912. *Le Tibet révolté: Vers Népémako, la terre promise des Tibétains, suivi des Impressions d'un Tibétain en France* [Tibet in revolt: Toward Nepemako, promised land of the Tibetans, followed by Impressions of a Tibetan in France]. Paris: Hachette.

Dessaint, W., and A. Ngwâma. 1994. *Au sud des nuages: Mythes et contes recueillis oralement chez les montagnards lissou (tibéto-birmans)* [South of the clouds: Myths and tales collected orally among the Lisu Montagnards (Tibeto-Burmese)]. Paris: Gallimard.

Dulongzu Jianshi Bianxiezu, ed., 1986. *Dulongzu jianshi* [Concise history of the Dulong]. Kunming: Yunnan minzu chubanshe.

Goodman, D.S.G. 2004. The campaign to "open up the West": National provincial-level and local perspectives. *China Quarterly* 178: 317-34.

Goré, F. [1939] 1992. *30 ans aux portes du Tibet interdit* [Thirty years at the gates of forbidden Tibet]. 2nde éd. Paris: Éditions Kimé.

Gros, S. 2001. Du politique au pittoresque en Chine: À propos des Dulong, nationalité minoritaire du Yunnan [From politics to picturesque in China: About the Dulong, a minority nationality of Yunnan]. *Ateliers* 24: 28-68.

–. 2004. The politics of names: The identification of the Dulong (Drung) of northwest Yunnan. *China Information* 18(2): 275-302.

–. 2005. Le nouveau partage du monde: Pauvreté et dépendance dans les marges du Yunnan (Chine) [A new partition of the world: Poverty and dependence on Yunnan's margins, China]. *Moussons* 8: 61-88.

–. 2007. The missing share: The ritual language of sharing as a "total social fact" in the eastern Himalayas. In *Social Dynamics in the Highlands of Southeast Asia: Reconsidering Political Systems of Highland Burma by E.R. Leach*, ed. F. Robinne and M. Sadan, 257-82. Leiden: Brill.

Harrell, S. 1995. Introduction: Civilizing projects and reaction to them. In *Cultural Encounters on China's Ethnic Frontiers*, ed. S. Harrell, 3-36. Seattle: University of Washington Press.

–. 2001. *Ways of Being Ethnic in Southwest China*. Seattle: University of Washington Press.

Hillman, B. 2003. Paradise under construction: Minorities, myths and modernity in northwest Yunnan. *Asian Ethnicity* 4(2): 175-88.

Lai, H.H. 2002. China's western development program: Its rationale, implementation, and prospect. *Modern China* 28(4): 432-66.

Lazcano Nebreda, S. 1998. La cuestion de la servidumbre en el sudeste de Tibet y regiones colindantes del Himalaya Oriental hasta la ocupacion China de 1950 [The question of slavery in Southeastern Tibet and surrounding regions of the Eastern Himalayas to the Chinese occupation of 1950]. *Boletin de la Asociacion Española de Orientalistas* 34: 221-37.

Li Jinming. 2008. Shengtai baohu, minzu shengji kechixu fazhan wenti yanjiu: Yi Dulongjiang diqu Dulongzu wei li [On the problem of environmental protection, subsistence, and sustainable development: The example of the Dulong people of the Dulong Valley area]. *Yunnan Shehui Kexue* [Social Sciences in Yunnan] 3: 81-85.

Litzinger, R. 2004. The mobilization of "nature": Perspectives from north-west Yunnan. *China Quarterly* 178: 488-504.
Makley, C. 2005. "Speaking bitterness": Autobiography, history, and mnemonic politics on the Sino-Tibetan frontier. *Comparative Studies in Society and History* 47(1): 40-78.
Mathieu, C. 2003. *History and Anthropological Study of the Ancient Kingdoms of the Sino-Tibetan Borderland – Naxi and Mosuo*. Mellen Studies in Anthropology, 11. Lewiston, NY: Edwin Mellen Press.
McKhann, C.F. 2001. Tourisme de masse et identité sur les marches sino-tibétaines: Réflexions d'un observateur [Mass tourism and identity on the Sino-Tibetan Marches]. *Anthropologie et Sociétés* 25(2): 35-54.
Michaud, J. 2009. Handling mountain minorities in China, Vietnam, and Laos: From history to current concerns. *Asian Ethnicity* 10(1): 25-49.
Oppitz, M., and E. Hsu, eds. 1998. *Naxi and Moso Ethnography: Kin, Rites, Pictographs*. Zurich: Völkerkundemuseum.
Proschan, F. 2001. Peoples of the gourd: Imagined ethnicities in highland Southeast Asia. *Journal of Asian Studies* 60(4): 999-1032.
Rockhill, W.W. 1881. *The Land of the Lamas: Notes of a Journey through China, Mongolia and Tibet*. New York: Century Company.
Simmel, G. [1908] 1998. *Les Pauvres* [The Poor]. Paris: PUF.
Stevenson, H.N. [1943] 1970. *The Economics of the Central Chin Tribes*. Bombay: The Times of India Press.
Testart, A. 2001. *L'esclave, la dette et le pouvoir: Etudes de sociologie comparative* [Slaves, debt and power: Studies in comparative sociology]. Paris: Éditions Errance.
Thoraval, J. 1990. Le concept chinois de nation est-il "obscur"? À propos du débat sur la notion de *minzu* dans les années 1980 [Is the Chinese concept of nation "obscure"? About the debate on *minzu* in the 1980s]. *Bulletin de sinologie* 65: 24-41.
Wilkes, A., and Shen Shicai. 2007. Is biocultural heritage a right? A tale of conflicting conservation, development, and biocultural priorities in Dulongjiang, China. *Policy Matters* 15: 76-83.
Xiao Jianwen. 2005. *Dulongjiang tuigeng huanlin dui nongye shengwu duoyangxing de yingxiang: Chubu diaocha jieguo* [Preliminary survey of the impact of sloped land conversion on agro-biodiversity in Dulongjiang township]. Report 24. Kunming: Center for Biodiversity and Indigenous Knowledge.
Yeh, E.T. 2007. Tropes of indolence and the cultural politics of development in Lhasa, Tibet. *Annals of the Association of American Geographers* 93(3): 593-612.
Zhang, Q. 2000. *Dulongzu wenhua shi* [A Cultural history of the Dulong]. Kunming: Yunnan minzu chubanshe.

3
Integration of a Lineage Society on the Laos-Vietnam Border
Steeve Daviau

The Tarieng minority on the Laos-Vietnam border has asserted diverse forms of agency and resistance to authoritarian political regimes, achieving forms of livelihoods coherent with their cultural traditions despite the pervasive influence of state policies, development projects, and foreign investment schemes.[1] The Tarieng are a Mon-Khmer minority group of about fifty thousand people, indigenous to the land now straddling the Laos-Vietnam border located in the highlands of the Xay Phou Louang or Annam Range (see Figure 3.1). Equally distributed across this border in Sekong and Attapeu provinces in Laos and Quảng Nam and Kon Tum provinces in Vietnam, the Tarieng are a lineage society primarily involved in subsistence farming, animal husbandry, forest food gathering, fishing, hunting, and bartering. Through time and thanks to its relative isolation, this small highland society has managed to preserve a relatively high level of cultural and political autonomy. During colonial times, the French administration never fully pacified this group and, accordingly, had labelled it a *"tribu insoumise."* In the late 1940s, the area then sheltered a Viet Minh base, playing a key role in the First and Second Indochina Wars and was crossed by segments of the Ho Chi Minh Trail that facilitated communist troop movement and supplies to South Vietnam. Today, the Tarieng remain geographically isolated from mainstream Lao and Vietnamese societies; for example, during the rainy season, it takes several days to walk from any provincial capital to reach their dwelling sites.

The Disciplinary Regime of the Lao State
Focusing on the Tarieng now living in Laos, the Lao socialist state exercises multiple forms of control over the country's politics, ideology, livelihoods, and social life at every level, creating the situation I analyze in this section, based chiefly on my own observations and fieldwork experiences during the twelve years I spent researching and living in Laos. This analysis uncovers

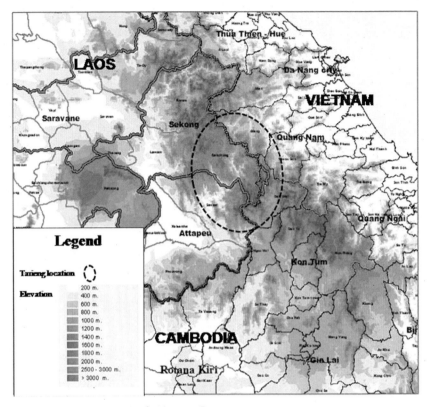

Figure 3.1 Tarieng area in the Annam Range.

the state's agenda of indiscriminate hegemonic control over the entire Laotian population including ethnic minorities such as the Tarieng.

The modern Lao state, in the Foucauldian sense, is a hegemonic apparatus whose raison d'être is control and administration of the population or the "government of conducts" (Foucault, 1975). While considering the relationship between the Lao state and the Tarieng, it is useful to employ the Foucauldian notions of governmentality and the panopticon to describe the Lao totalitarian regime and disciplinary technologies. It is my contention that the political practices of the Lao state are a form of panopticon, or a mechanism of surveillance and conditioning of individuals' identities, behaviour, and livelihoods under the guidelines of state socialism.

In Laos, after the socialist revolution was over in 1975, the new regime rapidly curtailed individual freedoms and traditional values for the whole population. In addition, highland minority populations – nearly half the population of the country – were metaphorically confined to a "lower grade" of the new social order and "drowned" in the darkness of ignorance and incompetence.² The new state sponsored nationalism by promoting national unity and creating the identity of New Socialist Man for all to emulate (Doré 1982; Zasloff and Unger 1991).

The new regime focused on "the three revolutions": the revolution of the relations of production, the scientific and technical revolution, and the social and ideological revolution. The objective of the latter, in particular, was to create New Socialist Man by eradicating neo-colonial and imperialistic influences through actions such as banning newspapers and publications in foreign languages, prohibiting foreign cars, and sometimes even excluding foreigners (Evans 1998). From 1976 onwards, the government arrested representatives of so-called social "plagues" (drug addicts, prostitutes, political opponents to the regime, and the like), who were sent to re-education camps – dubbed "seminars" – where political indoctrination, vigorous discipline, along with torture and execution, were commonplace (Zasloff and Unger 1991). Redemption was only possible through self-criticism; once released, individuals had to demonstrate their political awakening by voluntarily assisting with the political re-education of the wider population (Doré 1982, 107; Évrard, this volume).

Under the socialist regime, social mobility was possible only in terms of *phone ngan,* positive achievement, which could be attained in three ways. First, through revolutionary vigilance or *sati pativat,* which was achievable through a zealous militancy proving individual worth via dedication by exposing the enemy (a situation that usually tempted militants to anticipate reality in order to gain results), while anyone could report on their superiors'. misbehaviour and inform on anyone else's illegitimate acts. The second way was through agricultural production, the results of which were compiled every six months (number of animals vaccinated, hectares cleared, and so on). The third way was through political consciousness or the devotion to political ideals regarding international socialist solidarity *(samakhi).* In reality, this meant a willingness to favour the Lao People's Revolutionary Party's implementation of "the three revolutions" and promotion of New Socialist Man (Chou Norindr 1982) – just as in socialist Vietnam next door.

The pre-colonial and pre-socialist feudal regimes in Laos allowed local leaders a high level of autonomy, generally as a recompense for paying tribute to an overlord or a powerful neighbour (also see Gros, this volume). The socialist regime, however, could no longer tolerate such autonomy and exerted its authority inside each village (see Figure 3.2). The state became the companion of every individual through systematic control and domination in the name of collective mastery undertaken through the Lao People's Revolutionary Party (Doré 1982).

Verdery (1991, 430) underlines that in socialist situations, the control of communication through language is vital in transforming individual as

Figure 3.2 Original Tarieng village setting. *Photo by author*

much as collective consciousness. Language is thus instrumentalized by the regime to serve as a means of ideological advancement. In their effort to shape consciousness and social life, socialist leaders impose a certain form of discourse. The semantic structure of this discourse is static, and one can observe an extreme codification that is censured, ideologized, and laden with taboos. Consequently, the non-authorized use of official language constitutes an offence.

Accordingly, in socialist Laos, New Socialist Man was formed through the elaboration of a new national language, a task performed in 1967 by Phoumi Vongvichit.[3] In one way, the pro-Vietnam regime tried to promote the new socialist Lao language by dissociating it from its closest relative, the Thai language spoken in neighbouring Thailand (Enfield 1999). At the same time, all explicit references to the pre-socialist monarchist regime (for example, literary styles and hierarchies in terms of address and politeness) were purged. From then on, the Lao language was deemed accessible, functional, and suitable to New Socialist Man.

These changes in official language impacted the political control of Lao society. In socialist, as much as in "post-socialist" Laos now, one cannot easily dissociate the party *(pak)* from the state *(lat)*. Those two terms have become fundamentally indistinguishable: people now refer to political power as *pak-lat*. According to this model, the party rules, the government manages, the mass organizations implement national policies, and the military upholds the party line. The political structure is divided between the *say tang* (vertical line) of the party and the *say kouang* (horizontal structure) represented by the government or mass organizations. This all becomes encapsulated in the modern Lao maxim *"Pak si nam, lat nam pha, pasason pen chao"*: "The party shows the path, the government leads, and the people are in charge."

Despite increased access to alternative channels of information in urban centres, notably through the Internet, in rural Laos, the party controls political power and all sources of information. Villagers are not made aware of their rights, and state-monitored information is spread through compulsory meetings, state-controlled mass media, and the omnipresent public loudspeakers.[4] These guarded communication channels represent the only public information available nationally and are transmitted only in the Lao language, regardless of the ethnicity of the targeted audiences. For example, the official slogans promoted during the Seventh Party Congress held in 2001 focused on poverty alleviation *(lout-phone kouam touk niak)* and referred to the "tranquillity" of the regime *(haksa kouam sangob)*. Since 2001, it became clear that these notions, diffused through all available means, have encouraged passive social responses in line with state goals. The subsequent Five-Year Plan, presented at the Eighth Party Congress in 2006, explicitly maintained these priorities (Khamtay Siphandone 2006). This approach was made possible due to mass organizations that are present at every echelon: national, provincial, district, and village. These take five shapes: the Lao Women's Union (LWU), Lao Youth Union (LYU), the village chief *(naiban)*, the militia *(khornglon)*, and the Lao Front for National Construction *(neo hom)*.

The disciplinary system is further reinforced by strong territorial control at the village level. A short description suffices to reveal the intricacies of these surveillance and disciplinary systems. Each district throughout the country harbours a military base *(kong tap)* where troops maintain surveillance of the local population while also guarding national borders, infrastructure, and strategic areas. In addition, police forces stress their presence on occasions when the regime's security may be threatened – a constant obsession for the regime – such as on Lao National Day, during government party plenums, or during occasional meetings of the Association of Southeast Asian Nations in the capital.

Administratively speaking, the country's population is divided into territorial sections called *noy*, each with its head *(houana noy)*, who controls surveillance and informs the public about compulsory activities, curfews, and various other disciplinary rules. Monthly meetings *(pasoum)* are held in community houses, village offices, or Buddhist temples and require attendance from each household; absentees must explain themselves. Each household must maintain a residence booklet *(samanokoua)* in which household members are registered, their personal data and pictures displayed, and their movements and travels meticulously recorded for future inspection. Each member must obtain formal authorization from the village head or the president of a mass organization prior to migrating (even if temporarily) to a new settlement. Villagers wishing to change location must present a relocation permit on reaching their new place of residence. This tracking system allows the state to monitor labour movements and helps in planning the unavoidable monthly unpaid public works, based on the amount of labour available in each household.

Even home architecture is strictly set. The government requires that proper houses have wooden floors, wood boards on the walls, squared stilts, and corrugated iron roofing. These features are required regardless of the ethnicity of the proprietors and dwelling site; together they replicate the standard ethnic Lao house. Consequently, round timber stilts, bamboo walls, and thatched roofs, well adapted to the local climate and available free from forest materials, are discouraged because they are linked to pre-socialist misery and primitivism. In the state strategy for poverty eradication by 2020, these traditional highland characteristics define the poorest households and pinpoint those residents who must replace their transient dwellings with more permanent ones. In the worst cases, longhouses, frequent among Mon-Khmer groups in the south of the country, are dismantled and inhabitants divided into nuclear families, each living under a single roof.

On the spiritual side, all "superstitious" rituals involving animal sacrifice, such as those customarily performed by animist highland groups, are prohibited by law for being counterproductive. By extension, and defying logic, all art and cultural forms that differ from the dominant Lao model, such as dance, weaving, traditional songs, and musical instruments, are discouraged, while the Lao majority's traditional dance *(lamvong)* is imposed on ethnic minorities via the Youth Union's artistic education. Women are required to wear the Lao skirt *(sin)* if they work at or enter locations of power such as government offices at the national, provincial, and district levels, as well as in temples and during official ceremonies.

All these forms of control, from the most subtle to the most crude, became dominant after the 1975 revolution and were implemented relentlessly throughout the 1980s. But after the opening up of China and Vietnam to the market economy and the collapse of leading socialist regimes in the Eastern bloc in 1989, and the Soviet Union in 1991, Laos saw the flow of goods from friendly Communist regimes dry up. The country had to turn to international financial institutions for help and, like its two neighbours, Vietnam and China, opened its economy to regional and world markets under what is known in Laos as the New Economic Mechanisms (NEM). Starting in 1986, concurrently with Đổi Mới (economic and political renovation) in Vietnam, the reforms enacted under the NEM laid the basis for a transition toward a market economy, and the national agenda reflected the adoption of policies dictated by international financial institutions. These economic reforms and political changes rehabilitated the role of the market in the economy, renovated the public enterprise sector, promoted the private sector, and improved macroeconomic financial management (Rigg 2005).

This liberalization, however, did not translate in Laos into political softening (Stuart-Fox 1991, 1997). The monopoly of the party was actually reinforced in the hands of Lao generals and veteran militants with politically conservative stances, and the political aspects of socialism were further legitimized, using Buddhist symbolism dear to the heart of all Lao.[5] The first version of the NEM package coincided with the Third Party Congress in 1982 (Thayer 1983), which became the first opportunity for the government to state its intention to stabilize shifting cultivation as a development priority, or even prevent it through resettlement and sedentarization (see also Évrard, this volume, and Figure 3.3). From then on, state discourse and policy measures were designed to meet international objectives for environment protection and development, and highland peoples suddenly found themselves at the heart of this global strategy.

From 1985 onwards, international organizations started to support the Lao policy of forest protection. The Tropical Forestry Action Plan of 1990 re-emphasized the importance of stabilizing slash-and-burn cultivation, a priority of the Lao government since the Fourth Party Congress of 1986. This was a turning point in government policy toward the highlands and their inhabitants (Goudineau 1997). Much as elsewhere in Southeast Asia, the government set up the first serious plan concerning the creation of national biodiversity conservation areas (NBCA) and forest conservation. People whose livelihoods were intimately linked to the forest were categorized as environmentally destructive, institutionalizing a practice now common in Southeast Asian countries: casting the blame for deforestation on forest dwellers.

In this context, shifting cultivators, the vast majority of whom were non-Lao ethnic minorities, became castigated in state discourse as deviant and were depicted to the rest of the country as backward *(lalang)* and superstitious. They were publicly rendered an obstacle to development and the common good.[6] Having become the main culprits responsible for national deforestation, non-Lao ethnic minorities were relocated outside forested areas by the state, which sought to "Laoize" them by the same token.

Figure 3.3 Resettled Tarieng village. *Photo by author*

Resettlement of highland dwellers is presented today by the Lao government as a strategy for social and economic development in the global agenda of modernization. But it is also an efficient mechanism of surveillance and control of non-Lao, animist minorities, a form of panopticon as theorized by Michel Foucault (1975, 235). A panopticon refers to a system of control by which individuals internalize surveillance patterns out of fear that their actions will be seen and punished. These actions helped bring the shifting cultivators closer to the Lao Lum model (lowland Lao), the national standard. Their fate was decided by the ideals of a (post-)socialist regime, along with the neo-liberal dogma supported by multilateral institutions promoting, for forest encroachers, a one-way transition from subsistence economy to global capitalism.[7]

The Tarieng: Transnational Dwellers in the Annam Range
So how exactly do these national trends impact remote highland areas and populations of southern Laos, along with their livelihoods? To address this question, I propose that we first meet the subjects, the Tarieng. As mentioned

briefly in the introduction, the Tarieng number about fifty thousand and are equally distributed across the Laos-Vietnam border in the Annam Range. They live in Sekong and Attapeu provinces in Laos and in the Phước Sơn and Đắk Glei districts in Quảng Nam and Kon Tum provinces in Vietnam. This kinship-based society has an animist spirituality, and descent is traced through the female side – that is, they are matrilineal – and reflected in the customary sharing of power. They chiefly practise rotational shifting cultivation and are primarily involved in subsistence farming, animal husbandry, forest food gathering, fishing, and hunting. What cannot be obtained through these means is obtained through barter.[8] Undoubtedly, the Tarieng nicely fit the general characterization of a horticultural society as defined by Johnson (1989).

The remoteness of their villages, combined with rare economic contact with surrounding Lao settlements further down slope, have encouraged the Tarieng to make economic, cultural, and political exchanges with dwellers in Vietnam instead. This has caused a constant cross-border exchange of wealth, resources, people, livestock, and cultural models.

On the Laos side, the one I focus on in this chapter, the bulk of the Tarieng population lives in the Dakcheung and Sanxay districts (with a combined population of about 39,000 people), at altitudes between 500 and 2,000 metres. The climate is monsoonal, with a dry season that lasts about three months and yearly rainfall ranging between 2,500 and 3,000 millimetres. Until 2009, the uplands in both districts were accessible only via segments of the wartime Ho Chi Minh Trail. Access remains difficult during the rainy season, with frequent landslides, deep muddy areas, and the absence of bridges across most waterways. Access is not possible at all during three months of the year, even though a new road has linked Attapeu to Kon Tum since the early 2000s.

In both districts, the Tarieng are the most numerically important ethnic group with eighty-one villages, followed by the Yeh (twenty-one villages), the Alak (thirteen villages), the Dakang (twelve villages), and the Triu (nine villages). All are indigenous to the area. The first three groups belong to the Bahnaric ethnolinguistic family while the other two are Katuic; both categories are part of the Mon Khmer linguistic group within the larger Austronesian language family. Historically, communities were monoethnic. The mixed villages that exist today are the result of government resettlement, consolidation policies, and migration, as is the case in the district capitals.

Today, the resettlement of Tarieng shifting cultivators takes place under the legal framework called Khumban Phathana (Village Development Clusters, or VDCs; see Figure 3.4). The VDCs are implemented in accordance with party instruction 09/CPPB, linked to the party's Seventh Congress. This policy is directly associated with rural development and Prime Minister Decree 01, 2001, which summarizes the village consolidation plan. This sets

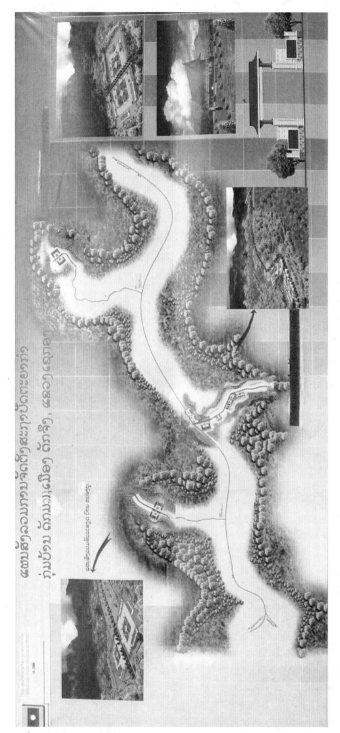

Figure 3.4 Village development cluster, Xieng Louang, Dakcheung district. *Photo by author*

minimum population standards for lowland villages (one thousand households), mid-slope villages (five hundred households), and upland villages (two hundred households) (Government of Laos 2003). The resolution also planned to establish VDCs by gathering five to seven villages together to ensure national security *(haksa kouam sagnob)* and socio-economic development (Government of Laos, Committee for Planning and Cooperation 2002). Notably, this policy is directly supported by the United Nations Development Programme in the framework of the National Growth and Poverty Alleviation Strategy (NGPES).

The Village Development Clusters policy is, in fact, the third generation of sedentarization projects, the first ones being initiated at the beginning of the 1990s when resettlement was openly declared a government strategy targeting 25 percent of the national population. In the 1996-2000 Rural Development Program, resettlement took place in the framework of the controversial focal sites. I argue in this chapter that the Village Development Clusters are the latest technology of power to be implemented by the socialist state to finalize the sedentarization process and the control of ethnic minority space.

In Sekong province, provincial authorities have already set up six VDCs directly managed by the provincial authorities: two in Lamam district, two in Thateng district, one in Dakcheung district, and one in Kalum district, totalling thirty-five villages, 2,345 households, and 16,487 people. In Dakcheung district, there are fourteen VDCs managed by three levels of government administration: the Dak Mouan VDC is directly managed by Vientiane, the Xieng Louang VDC is managed by the provincial authorities, and the twelve other VDCs are directly managed by the district. The entire district population, totalling eighty-eight villages or 18,603 people, has been brought under this new technology of power.

On the ground, however, VDC implementation does not yet proceed according to plan due to contradictions in the administrative structure. This means that the subdistrict unit still acts as the territorial and administrative operational framework in Dakcheung. As a new structure, VDCs have not yet rooted themselves in Dakcheung, whereas they are becoming operational in two areas: Xieng Louang (ten villages) and Dak Mouan (four villages). In both cases, state representatives are stationed in the two main villages and are charged with resolving conflicts, lecturing villagers on the Party line, and getting villagers increasingly involved in development activities.

In official documents, conversations, and interviews with government officials, it is interesting to note, Khumban Phathana is also called *choutsoum phathana,* meaning "focal sites." The focal sites approach, a key strategy of the 1996-2000 Rural Development Program, proved highly controversial because it involved large resettlement schemes that carried adverse consequences, now well documented, which culminated in 1997 in a donor ban on resettlement (see Évrard, this volume; also see Goudineau 1997, 2000; Daviau 2001, 2003a, 2003b, 2005; Alton and Houmphanh 2004; Évrard and Goudineau 2004). This does not mean, however, that the scheme has been totally abandoned. During field work in June 2007, I observed that the implementation of the VDC strategy in Dakcheung district acted as a screen to large-scale resettlement schemes similar to the old focal sites strategy. The official discourse has changed, but the Lao government carries on, at least in some places, with the forced resettlement of upland shifting cultivators.

In Dakcheung district, the VDC strategy is based on moving more than half the district population. Fifty-four villages (77 percent of villages) are slated for resettlement, totalling 10,046 people (54 percent of the total population of 18,603). In the case of Xieng Louang's VDC, four villages out of ten are earmarked to be resettled, totalling 774 people. And in Dak Mouan VDC, three villages out of four, totalling 326 people, are to be resettled.

Most of the time, Village Development Clusters are located in areas suitable for paddy cultivation and market-oriented production and away from foreign investment projects; yet, this is not always the case. Dak Mouan VDC lies within the Sekaman 3 hydropower project site, the largest Vietnamese investment made in Laos to date. Similarly, the Xieng Louang VDC is located near a Chinese bauxite mining and aluminum-processing factory project. Both Vietnam and China are neighbours with which Laos has strong political and economic connections. The two VDCs are guarded by military personnel to prevent any contestations from emerging at the grassroots level and, in both cases, teams of government agents and Vietnamese workers take charge of infrastructure building and impose new market-oriented production activities on villagers.

Non-governmental organizations are actively directed by the state toward such VDCs in order to help provide basic services and training coherent with the wider scheme. Their actions, even if based on praiseworthy ideals, thus directly endorse the national policy, and these NGOs are used in government development rhetoric to convince communities of the merits of resettling. I argue that the VDC framework is the latest technology of power in upland Laos: a control and sedentarization mechanism targeting Tarieng shifting cultivators and turning them into an unskilled transient workforce needed in the national transition to a market economy.

Dak Mouan VDC: Bilateral Khumban Phathana on the Laos-Vietnam Border

The VDC groups in Dak Mouan consist of four Tarieng communities that previously lived in Dak Taok Noy, Dak Mouan, Dak Mat, and Nong Bu. The head of Dak Taok Noy village, when I interviewed him in 2004, explained that the community initially refused resettlement because members felt that the proposed new site, located along the road to Vietnam, was inadequate.

Villagers would have refused resettlement, he said, even if the new site were closer to their paddy fields because it would have moved them away from pasture land for cattle and buffalo, which is essential in the community livelihood system (see Figures 3.5 and 3.6). Furthermore, the village already had a clean water system, whereas there was less clean water in the government-proposed resettlement site.

The fate of the community, however, was decided on by a bilateral development project linked to the Sekaman 3 hydropower development. The Dak Mouan VDC, managed directly at the national level, was supported 40 percent by the Vietnamese government and 60 percent by the Lao government. Thirty-three Lao civil servants were based in the village to implement the development plan until December 2009. An additional fifty Vietnamese workers were based in the village to construct a health field station, schools, and a few other infrastructure projects. The human resources from the outside who were injected into this single VDC totalled nearly 80 people, while the overall population of the VDC is only 550 people.

Development opportunities offered to the Tarieng villagers, revolving around new livelihood schemes, were designed from above. A Vietnamese company has already signed a contract with the government for a cassava cash crop program, but villagers – not involved in the approval process or the signing of the agreement – will be the ones planting the cassava. The crop will then be shipped to a processing unit that is scheduled to be built only after the completion of the Sekaman 3 hydropower project.

Other cash crops in this area – where villagers otherwise focus on subsistence agriculture – were introduced in the mid-2000s. The impacts of these new crops on culturally significant spaces such as sacred forests, sacred ground, and cemeteries, remain highly questionable. Outside technical staff members have noted that many villagers do not understand the concept of development and remain "too attached" to their own cultural beliefs and the "natural way" of doing things. Concurrently, during interviews, villagers have not been at all enthusiastic about these changes. The heavy reliance on outsiders to undertake such development activities has, ironically, increased the villagers' burdens because they have to participate in activities such as clearing land for cassava and coffee plantations and undergo training. Villagers felt overstretched and lacked time for their usual subsistence tasks. This situation delayed the development plans because, despite the outside contingent of civil servants, villagers' labour is still needed to implement such development activities. Some activities, such as paddy cultivation, are completely new to many villagers, who only practised rain-fed dry-rice cultivation before. Consequently, a lack of experience both in managing water for terraces and in ploughing the land leads to tremendous difficulties in implementing the transition from shifting cultivation to sedentary farming livelihoods.

Figure 3.5 Free-roaming buffaloes typical of Tarieng husbandry. *Photo by author*

Figure 3.6 Customary buffalo sacrifice ritual among the Tarieng. *Photo by author*

Figure 3.7 Educational board by German Agro Action promoting good agricultural practice on the right of the river and condemning "inefficient" ones on the left. Photo by author

The Xieng Louang VDC: Bauxite Mine and Aluminium Factory

Xieng Louang, the second VDC discussed in this chapter, is linked to a new aluminum factory funded by a Chinese company in partnership with the Lao Aluminium Industry Company. When completed, the project will cover twenty-five square kilometres and be licensed to operate for twenty-seven years, at a total investment value of US$329 million. The company aims to export overseas starting in 2010.

In this VDC, there are about twenty-five hundred people living in ten villages. Initially, four villages did not agree to the factory because they were not offered compensation for the loss in land use. But, as the head of the Energy and Mines Office in Sekong province later explained, the company, the government, and the four Tarieng village heads sat together and eventually came to an agreement in a meeting in Vientiane. "We were happy when the village heads understood the point of this matter" said the provincial head (Khonesavanh Latsaphao 2007). The Lao Aluminium Industry Company agreed to compensate the four communities by providing new land, houses, schools, electricity, health centres, roads, and sanitation.

This example illustrates the types of negotiations that occur around development projects in the area and the forms of village participation they involve. Village heads are invited to the capital to be informed of and to agree to such projects on behalf of their communities – with whom no other consultation is being held. This was probably the first time these four men had travelled to the capital, and one can imagine the unease of these shifting cultivators sitting in the air conditioned Energy and Mines Office with Vientiane officials and foreign investors putting pressure on them. An agreement was duly hammered out, but there were no discussions regarding how the new land would be distributed, how those it previously belonged to would be dealt with, and the possible community reactions to the agreement as a whole.

From Resignation to Resistance: Individual and Collective Forms of Agency within Tarieng Livelihoods

From 1975 onward, the Lao Revolutionary Party institutionalized its position using iconography and revolutionary frescos adorned with the hammer, sickle, bayonet, and flag. It did not allow protests, castigating them as counter-revolutionary. The country is, in true Marxian parlance, under the "dictatorship of the proletariat" according to which the people hold the reins of power via its "avant-garde," the Communist Party; no form of dissent is allowed to be shown to the national project. This situation is reflected in the national Lao language where, ironically, *pathivat* (revolutionary) is in contrast with *pathouang* (rebel).

But despite the blocked political climate and the might of the repressive arm of the state, minority ethnic groups employ multiple strategies, consciously or not, to react to or resist state policies, development projects, and foreign investment schemes that infringe on their livelihood goals. The presence of the Lao state's panopticon limits the extent to which local people can protest, but individuals, households, lineages, communities, and even local party representatives are not simply passive subjects of the state. They adopt diverse strategies that James C. Scott (1985) has called "everyday forms of peasant resistance." These "weapons of the weak" involve covert disagreement and tactics meant to pursue a local agenda while raising as little suspicion from the state as possible. In official statements to the authorities, forms of such everyday resistance used by the Tarieng may include, for instance, the underestimation of land surface, lies about the quantity and quality of yields and about the number and health of buffaloes, the underestimation of income, illegal border crossings, the selling of protected animal species, and many other tactics put into play with the aim, among other things, of dodging taxation.

Some of these tactics also involve civil servants of local extraction. According to Prime Ministerial Decentralization Decree 01, 2001, the province is the strategic unit, the district is the planning unit, and the village is the implementation unit (Government of Laos 2001). But scholars are skeptical about the extent to which the decree actually achieves decentralization. Chagnon and Van Gansberghe (2003, 9) argue that "there is not much evidence that Decentralization has broadened decision-making authority beyond the ranks of the Party-appointed political elite of each level. Especially at the district and village levels, the cores of administration leaders remain largely the same, largely due to the Party's control over elections and to the limited number of qualified persons."

In Dakcheung district, local ethnic representatives do fill a number of the political and technical positions in various departments, including agriculture, health, and education; ethnic Lao tend not to be very present in these positions because, generally, they do not wish to stay very long in this isolated region. Locally recruited civil servants are thus familiar with the names and locations of villages and if they wish, they can communicate with the population by means other than official channels. Their ordeal is to remain both loyal to the party while helping to lead their people out of poverty and toward a better life. In this latter respect, they are open to development alternatives proposed by local and international NGOs, and there is room for dialogue at the local level. The agency of these Tarieng civil servants lies between publicly embracing state ideology and privately showing local belonging. Or in Scott's terms (1990), they must perform a balancing act between convincingly waving the public transcripts expected by the state and supporting, even nurturing, the hidden transcripts behind the scenes at the local scale.

The state is aware that there may be a deficiency in the determination and political willingness of civil servants of Tarieng origin to implement national directives uncritically. The Tarieng civil servants at the district level are directly linked to the provincial administration, which is mostly composed of ethnic Tarieng from Dakcheung. Good students of the revolution, the Tarieng provided key resources for resisting the French colonials during the First Indochina War. Dakcheung district had also sheltered Viet Minh representatives and the Lao Revolutionary Forces base during the Second Indochina War, and was an important strategic zone for the liberation of southern Vietnam. One would think that with these credentials, Tarieng state agents could be trusted. But the provincial authorities have worked to maintain control over them by establishing a new head of the Planning Office in Dakcheung district, in order to ensure that ethnic Tarieng party members remain committed to the party. The director of this office is an ethnic Lao from neighbouring Saravane province, who is expected to be less hesitant in implementing resettlement plans.

Community Reactions and Adaptations to Government Plans

Local communities do indeed react to government plans that significantly alter their livelihoods and daily life. They use what power they have to attempt to adjust these vectors of change to their local reality, and acts of resistance from communities are common.

For highland villages targeted by government resettlement plans, an internal consultation process is initiated first. Representatives from mass organizations (head of the village, head of the elders, Lao Women's Union's representatives, and so on) position themselves in favour of or against the plan, and diverse strategies are played out. The final decision is rarely unanimous. For instance, generational differences of opinion exist within each community. Elders are usually little inclined to leave their customary environment while younger people are usually more receptive to resettlement plans and their promises. Frequently, elders eventually accept the resettlement in order to allow younger generations to have better opportunities in the "new era," one in which the elders' traditional knowledge is depreciated, contested, and made largely irrelevant.

Resettlement also allows some people to instate new forms of social organization that break away from traditional forms of authority. The class of new youth leaders often stems from those with a military background. They have been drafted and have served in the Lao National Army, and they have been trained to be receptive and uncritical of the party ideology. When re-entering civilian life in their villages, they automatically command a salary, the best land in the resettlement sites, a model house for other villagers to emulate, and can speak with a louder voice in village meetings. They have been formally educated and can read and write, and thus have all the necessary qualities for becoming local representatives of the state by bypassing the customary channels for access to power positions in their communities. One result of this process is the deterioration of vernacular customary institutions and community leadership.

But a possible compensation for this deterioration is that modern forms of administrative leadership might allow the community to be better heard and to ask for safeguards regarding the relevance of the resettlement sites, the services provided, and the support given for resettling. This is the case of Tang Brong village, the most important Tarieng community in terms of population (867 people), and well known for its social cohesion and strong traditional leaders. In 2006, this community commissioned the village president of the Lao Front for National Construction to send a letter to the district governor explaining that the community wanted to remain in situ and would not agree to the proposed resettlement plan. In this case, astutely, party-supported mass organizations were used to channel this message of defiance. The strategy seems to have worked: four years later, Tang Brong remains in its original location and successfully opposes top-down resettlement plans. By contrast, in the case of very small hamlets of the Yeh ethnicity such as Dak Ying, Dak Jrang Ngai, and Vangli, with twenty-nine, thirty, and fifty-four people respectively, this kind of negotiation is not conceivable. By the early 2000s, these villages were resettled without further ado to more accessible zones and merged with other communities to satisfy official definitions of the minimum size of communities (Government of Laos 2001).

Communities can also react to resettlement plans by adopting new forms of mobility beyond the state's gaze. If a village does indeed become resettled, the final picture may often be far from the model planned by the authorities. Facing government pressure to resettle, communities can elaborate answers such as compromise, fragmentation, or plain refusal. In this way, the final place of resettlement is often some distance from that initially pinpointed, but the government does not usually punish the deviant villagers since it considers it has at least succeeded in making people move from their original location.

Spontaneous verification can also occur. In Dakdin khumban phathana, the six communities included in the district resettlement plan – Dak Noy, Dak Euy, Dak Din, Kounxay, Dak Sieng, and Dak Sa – sent their own scouts to assess a proposed resettlement site. These scouts reported that the site had insufficient clean water and was unsuitable for a gravity-fed water distribution system needed for local livelihoods. Consequently, the villages refused the proposed site and are still in their original locations.

Villagers are usually well aware of the regulations that legally define the shape of an acceptable rural community that may become permanent. Accordingly, one of the strategies communities implement to remain in situ is to try to meet state criteria defining the right of existence for a village. To be allowed to remain in its current upland location and avoid resettlement, a community must fulfill five conditions: a minimum population of thirty to fifty households; access to a school; access to clean water; access to a road or river; and access to permanent farming land such as rice terraces (Government of Laos 2001). To meet the first condition, a community can choose to welcome new migrants or help previously resettled people return if they have experienced difficulties gaining a livelihood in the lowlands. Some communities manage to seal their territorial borders to avoid an uncontrolled exodus of their population. Others try to avoid depopulating by heavily fining households that plan to leave the community, an approach I observed in Done En village, in Nalae district, Louang Namtha province (Daviau 2003b). Regarding the other four conditions, some may decide to develop road access to avoid being resettled. Communities also alter their livelihoods, developing permanent agriculture such as paddy rice on suitable plots within their community. Some communities are also investing in building schools and recruiting teachers.

But some communities appear to decide, for better or for worse, that the best strategy is to comply and follow the plan to move to the site selected by the authorities. Such apparent conformity to state policy can at times be analyzed as a strategy to become eligible for benefits, but it also often simply reflects the difficult situation of many upland communities. In Xieng Louang Khumban Phathana, Dak Chak village was not initially included in the resettlement scheme, and village leaders, afraid to be left behind without any more development initiatives, volunteered to be included in the resettlement. This does not necessarily forecast a happy ending. The Tarieng village of Chavan was resettled on 17 January 2002 at nine o'clock in the morning – a deadline remembered well by villagers. Twenty-eight households (140 people) moved together, while four households left instead for another upland village. The house structures left behind were swiftly dismantled and the wood stolen by villagers from another community that had remained in the uplands. The twenty-eight households then had to squat for two months in abandoned district administrative facilities while building their new houses from scratch – at a time when they would normally have undertaken swidden cultivation. Initially, relocated villagers were not overly worried by this turn of events as they had been promised one paddy field, a *mai ketsana* (eaglewood tree) nursery, rice, and a few other things on resettling. However, in reality, all they received was twenty kilograms of salt per household. In 2005, three years after having been resettled, the new Chavan village still did not have land, not even an administrative existence as the village space is set on former military land, while the promised paddy fields are stuck in an ownership imbroglio. Facing difficult odds for the first year, Chavan villagers farmed on the land of other resettlers with the latter's permission. Villagers declare that the harvest was poor because the District Agriculture and Forestry Office had given them rice seeds unsuitable for this new type of land. Moreover, buffalo herds belonging to a neighbouring village destroyed the swiddens that were maintained as a safeguard. Villagers asked district authorities for assistance, to no avail. During interviews conducted with village elders, my Tarieng hosts waited until the state representatives accompanying me were asleep to drag me out of my mosquito net, sit me around the jar of khanien alcohol, and speak without inhibition about their frustration and sufferings. They mentioned the possibility of returning to their former upland village since, as they put it, "there are more people there now, we can see the road, and there is merchandise available."

The Effect of Resettlement on Tarieng Livelihoods

Resettlement impacts upland livelihoods in important ways. In traditional Tarieng communities, there is not much tangible difference between the wealthiest and the poorest households. They use the same materials for house construction, and for their subsistence they all rely on swidden cultivation, forest food products, and animal husbandry. Every household can obtain rice through multiple means, including bartering, borrowing, and labour exchange. Internal mechanisms of mutual assistance and risk management are additional institutions and assets that allow the general well-being of the whole community. The main differences between wealthier households and the others lie in the number of offspring (translating into ownership of labour), an above average number of large animals such as buffaloes, and ownership of a few prestige goods such as jars and gongs.

It turns out that the wealthier households are usually the first to resettle. Then, due to their generally larger contribution to the village's economic life, their leaving significantly undermines traditional ties and mutual assistance mechanisms that characterize traditional communities. In contrast, the poorest segments of each community are usually more reluctant to resettle chiefly because they lack the human and financial resources to move. Ironically, in many cases where there have been multiple waves of resettlement, the first to settle in a new site, the wealthier households, have been financially and logistically supported by the state and given access to paddy land, whereas later migrants, wary and vulnerable, have received whatever was left, which generally means much less than the frontrunners. Resettlement policy thus works systematically toward increasing the gap between wealthy and poor Tarieng households.

Resettlement also directly jeopardizes the food sovereignty of resettled populations. One of the main predicaments of resettlement to the lowlands, where demographic pressure on the land is higher than in the uplands, is a shortage of agricultural land and resources. This situation often triggers conflicts between the host population and resettled newcomers over water, land, firewood, and various other resources. Many recently resettled communities initially felt that they had sufficient resources for their needs, but after a while, many reassess their situation and come to the conclusion that they, more than ever, face food insecurity and dependency on neighbouring communities and the state for survival.

In addition, resettlement of upland communities has a tremendous effect on traditional knowledge and biodiversity. In Laos, rice varieties are exceptionally diverse. Laos has been the source of almost half of the global gene bank for rice, and the greatest diversity is found in upland rice (Bouahom Bounthong, Raintree, and Linkhan Douangsavanh 2003). In Dakcheung district, the Tarieng grow several indigenous rice varieties that help farmers maximize returns on specific soils, taking into account slopes and the cropping timetable. More than ten rice varieties are routinely found in a single village. Resettlement, the ban on shifting cultivation, and the imposed planting of cash crops have caused the loss of several indigenous rice varieties that contributed to Tarieng food sovereignty, as well as leading to an erosion of knowledge about the world's rice germplasm.

Even when resettled, Tarieng villagers are not inclined to swap agriculture in favour of wage labour on coffee plantations and other forms of paid work. Interviews conducted in the Tarieng resettled communities in Nam Pha focal sites in the lowlands of Sanxay district revealed that, despite chronic food insecurity and lack of access to agricultural land, men do not want to leave their new settlement. This, despite the demand for seasonal wage labour being high in coffee-production areas on the Bolaven Plateau in Paksong district, Champasak province. However, in the early years after resettlement, there are only scarce opportunities in Sanxay district to absorb this emerging rural proletariat. It is probable that, unlike their elders, teenagers will more easily accept having to leave, fearless of transportation hardships and psychological distance, to fill seasonal market demand.

The social suffering and human distress found in many resettled communities is out of synch with the state's positivist discourse on the benefits of resettling. By revealing the contradictions between state discourse and the reality of resettlement, the experience of resettlement stimulates forms of contestation over the inadequacy of resettlement sites among villagers. The case of Dak Lieng Loung, a Tarieng village in Sanxay district, illustrates this phenomenon.

A first segment of Dak Lieng Loung village was resettled in 2003. Then, not knowing much at all about what had happened to the first wave of re-settlers, twenty-two additional households endeavoured to move in 2004. Seeing the poor conditions endured by those from the first wave, combined with the lack of food and water in the dry season, these twenty-two additional households decided to return to their upland village, one villager declaring that: "We'd rather be killed in our hills than die miserably in the plain." This powerful remark reveals both a sense of pride and rebelliousness; while also hinting at the poor relationship between the highlanders and the military. It reflects the highlanders' defiance toward the state and their fatalism as to the probable outcome of that defiance.

Some disgruntled resettled villagers return to their original sites when they assess that they will not be able to make a decent living in the valleys. But for a large majority of them, this option is unworkable. The costs of moving back to the mountains, erecting a new house, starting herds from scratch, and working fields and swiddens that have been abandoned for some years constitute daunting challenges to small farmers who have already exhausted their capital. Some can be luckier. If the bulk of upland Tarieng villages have indeed been resettled, a fair number of relatives are still living upland and can provide some support in the form of reciprocity and collaboration.[9] On the other hand, on rare occasions, entire villages can be officially authorized to return permanently to their ancient settlements. In the specific case of swidden cultivators resettled from Kalum to Thateng and Lamam districts in the 1990s, out of thirty-seven villages resettled, seven villages have since been authorized to return to their former villages in Kalum district. Provincial authorities have acknowledged the hardship, high mortality rate, and social suffering commonly emerging in these resettled communities (Daviau 2003b). In this case, a helping hand was outstretched by the former provincial governor, himself an ethnic Ngkriang from Kalum district. The fact is that under certain circumstances, when no threat is felt, the Lao state may be prepared to accept that resettlement does not guarantee a successful transition to permanent farming, as theorized by orthodox models. Indeed, Tarieng resettled communities, like many others in the Annam Range, continue to rely on rotational swidden cultivation under the very gaze of the state that simply turns a blind eye. Lowland houses often remain empty as their Tarieng inhabitants have left to go farming in the uplands of Dakcheung and Sanxay district.

In terms of "everyday forms of peasant resistance," the Tarieng display a wide range of practices suiting their needs. In resettled communities, customary leaders are still managing village life and access to land and resources, and carry on solving conflicts based on customary law despite the availability of Party members and mass organizations in every village. There is still a regular flow of people toward unauthorized regions in lowland Laos and Vietnam. Hunting, collecting protected species in conservation areas, "counterproductive" animal sacrifice, border-crossing to conduct seasonal farming, purchasing and selling wage labour, accessing health care, and so on, combine with the constant underestimation, in the face of state agents, of numbers of domestic animals and the importance of agricultural yields. These are all forms of peasant struggle against external regulation to shape ethnically relevant, sustainable livelihoods. Some Tarieng communities that converted to paddy cultivation also display a form of symbolic traditionalism by keeping up animistic rituals that are only a remnant of the past. Sang village for instance, still conducts the upland rice-planting ritual despite the fact that households no longer cultivate upland rice. Since there are no upland rice fields, villagers symbolically plant a few grains of upland rice in an area within the village space. The occurrence of this ritual, presided over by the female shaman, far from being merely a form of cultural inertia in the face of rampant modernity, testifies on the contrary to a will to preserve the cultural memory and may be read, I argue, as a form of resistance to the symbolic and religious standardization promoted by the state along with the resettlement programs. Direct confrontation with the authorities is rarely an option.

Conclusion

In Michel Foucault's terms, the domineering regime of the Lao state, with its disciplinary technologies, contributes to consolidating a form of panopticon set up at the national level since the Revolution in 1975 that penetrates every stratum of the Lao administration. The Khumban Phathana strategy, or Village Development Clusters, is an essential part of the state's national development discourse. It legitimates the resettlement of Tarieng populations, and their economic redefinition following neo-liberal ideology. This process involves discourse refashioning, notably via the alteration of the Lao language, to put in place a regime of truth that has, over the last three decades, become hegemonic.

In the case of the Tarieng, and likely in the cases of many other highland non-Lao minorities in Laos, despite this constant pressure to change, and perhaps also because of it, individual and collective forms of (mainly covert) resistance take place. This case study shows that the tight control by the Lao People's Revolutionary Party and the constant surveillance by mass organizations all the way down to village, even household, level do not always suffice to significantly determine how people will think, react, and make a living. Individuals, households, communities, and sometimes even civil servants display forms of agency and resistance in order to maintain a certain degree of local autonomy and to preserve the core of their identity.

All the same, traditional livelihoods are increasingly threatened by the state policy of resettlement, compounded by the increase in foreign investment in the highlands, which entails state and foreign control over more and more land – plantations, mining concessions, hydropower schemes, infrastructure development. The fate of the Tarieng is intimately linked to the commitment of local governments to blindly implement national policies and to the extent to which local state agents can adopt a more pragmatic stance about the impacts of neo-liberal policies on highland people. The Lao state has definitely reduced the space available to highland minority groups to exercise their agency, but this space is not totally absent. The Tarieng will pursue diverse forms of negotiation, contestations, and resistance to continue to do what they have always done: adapt their livelihoods and maintain forms of autonomy in the face of powerful outside influences and predatory states: in this case, between neo-liberal dogmas and a socialist ideology reaching them from both sides of the Laos-Vietnam border.

Notes

1 I worked in Dakcheung district as a development aid agent in 2001-2 and conducted field studies on resettlement issues for the French NGO Action Contre la Faim (ACF) in Dakcheung district, Sekong province, and in Sanxay district, Attapeu province, in 2004-5, and for the Governance and Public Administration Reform (GPAR), UNV-UNDP project in Dakcheung district in June 2007.
2 For regions earlier overtaken by communist fighters, this curtailment of freedoms and values started as early as the 1960s.
3 Phoumi Vonvichit was a core member of the Central Committee and the Politburo. He worked for the Department of Education when he wrote the *Vayakorn Lao* in 1967. After 1975, he was named second deputy prime minister and minister of education, sports, and

religious affairs. He retired from political life at the Fifth Party Congress, in 1991 (Stuart-Fox and Kooyman 1992, 111-12).
4 State information is often self-promotional, covering such topics as the state of implementation of the Socio-Economic Development Plan since the last party congress, described in terms of numbers of animals, seeds, tools, and assets provided to the communities by the government or international agencies. Also broadcast are coming events and regulations.
5 For instance, in every provincial capital one can find a bronze of former leader Kayson Phomvihane displayed with stylized lotus petals, a potent Buddhist symbol. See Evans (1998).
6 This type of stigmatization is still displayed in internal government documents, such as in Sekong province Socio-Economic Master Plan 2020 (Sekong Province 2008, 7): "ປະຊາຊົນທີ່ອາໄສຢູ່ເຂດພູດອຍສ່ວນຫຼາຍເຮັດແບບກະແຈກກະຈາຍຕິ່ນຕໍ່ແມ່ນຖາງປ່າເຮັດໄຮ່,ຊີວິດການເປັນຢູ່ແມ່ນຜິດເຕື່ອງ,ຮີດຄອງ. ປະເພນີທີ່ຫຼ້າຫຼັງຍັງຄອບງຳສ່ວຍຫຼາຍ" [villagers that live in remote areas practise disorderly slash and burn; their livelihood is precarious; their customs are backward and are still strongly followed], my translation.
7 The notion of transition, when applied to the cases of Eastern Europe and Russia, refers to the transition from a planned to a market economy, thus referring to the marketization process. But in the case of Laos, we witness the passage from a subsistence-based economy to a market economy. As underlined by Rigg (2005), roughly 80 percent of the Lao population lives in rural areas, of which two-thirds are part of the subsistence economy. Accordingly, "command has always been more an ideological wish of the leadership than a tangible local reality" (Rigg 2005, 12).
8 Rotational shifting cultivation (or swiddening) is a form of agriculture that involves rotating crops regularly around semi-permanent settlements, allowing time for fallow. This customary form of cultivation allows much more sustainable soil and forest recovery than so-called pioneer cultivation, which uses soil at one site until exhaustion before relocating settlements (Grandstaff 1980).
9 Dak Lieng Loung and Moun Kao villages, which resettled in Tad Seng subdistrict, both have more than twenty households still remaining in the former location.

References
Alton, C., and Houmphanh Rattanavong. 2004. Service delivery and resettlement: Options for development planning. Final report, Livelihood study, 30 April. Vientiane: United Nations Development Programme/ECHO.
Bouahom Bounthong, J. Raintree, and Linkhan Douangsavanh. 2003. *Upland Agriculture and Forestry Research for Improving Livelihoods in Lao PDR*. Vientiane: National Agriculture and Forestry Research Institute of Laos, Ministry of Agriculture and Forestry.
Chagnon, R., and B. Van Gansberghe. 2003. *Governance and Participation in Laos*. Stockholm: Sida, The Asia Department.
Chou Norindr. 1982. Political institutions of the People's Democratic Republic. In *Contemporary Laos: Studies in the Politics and Society of the Lao People's Democratic Republic*, ed. M. Stuart-Fox, 39-61. New York: St. Martin's Press.
Daviau, S. 2001. *Resettlement in Long District, Louang Namtha Province, Lao PDR*. Vientiane: Action contre la Faim. Unpublished report.
–. 2003a. *Cultural and Technical Study of Traditional Animal Husbandry, Kalum District, Sekong Province Lao PDR*. Vientiane: Action contre la Faim.
–. 2003b. Resettlement in Long district, Louang Namtha province, update 2003. Vientiane: Action contre la Faim. Unpublished report.
–. 2005. Développement, modernité et relocalisation: Étude de cas de la zone focale de la Namma, district de Long, province de Louang Namtha Laos [Development, Modernity and Resettlement: Case study of the Namma focal site, Long district, Louang Namtha province]. Mémoire de Maîtriseé [Masters thesis], Department of Anthropology, Université de Montréal.
Doré, A. 1982. The three revolutions in Laos. In *Contemporary Laos: Studies in the Politics and Society of the Lao People's Democratic Republic*, ed. M. Stuart Fox, 101-15. New York: University of Queensland Press.

Enfield, N.J. 1999. Lao as a national language. In *The Politics of Ritual and Remembrance: Laos since 1975,* ed. G. Evans, 258-90. Chiang Mai: Silkworm Books.
Evans, G., ed. 1998. *The Politics of Ritual and Remembrance: Laos since 1975.* Chiang Mai: Silkworm Books.
Évrard, O., and Y. Goudineau. 2004. Planned resettlement, unexpected migrations and cultural trauma in Laos. *Development and Change* 35(5): 937-62.
Foucault, M. 1975. *Surveiller et Punir.* Paris: Tel Gallimard.
Goudineau, Y., ed. 1997. *Resettlement and Social Characteristics of New Villages: Basic Needs for Resettled Communities in the Lao PDR.* 2 vol. Vientiane: UNESCO/United Nations Development Programme/Orstom.
–, 2000. Ethnicité et déterritorialisation dans la péninsule indochinoise: Considérations à partir Du Laos. *Autrepart* 14: 17-31.
Government of Laos. 2001. Political report, Eighth Party Congress, presented by Khamtay Siphandone, 12 March.
–. 2003. *La loi de l'Administration Locale de la République démocratique Populaire Lao.* Vientiane, 21 October 2003. Unofficial translation.
–. Committee for Planning and Cooperation, Department of General Planning. 2002. Guidelines for Development Planning at the Village/Khumban, District and Provincial Level. Revised draft.
Grandstaff, T. 1980. Shifting Cultivation in Northern Thailand: Possibilities for Development. *UNU Resource Systems Theory and Methodology Series,* no. 3, UNU, Tokyo.
Johnson, A. 1989. Horticulturalists: Economic behaviour in tribes. In *Economic Anthropology,* ed. S. Plattner, 49-77. Palo Alto, CA: Stanford University Press.
Khamtay Siphandone. 2006. Political report of the president. Eighth Party Congress, March 2006.
Khonesavanh Latsaphao. 2007. Villagers agree to aluminum factory in Xekong. *Vientiane Times,* 3 August 2007.
Rigg, J. 2005. *Living with Transition in Laos: Market Integration in Southeast Asia.* New York: Routledge.
Scott, J.C. 1985. *Weapons of the Weak: Everyday Forms of Peasant Resistance.* New Haven, CT: Yale University Press.
–. 1990. *Domination and the Arts of Resistance: Hidden Transcripts.* New Haven, CT: Yale University Press.
Stuart-Fox, M., and M. Kooyman. 1992. *Historical Dictionary of Laos.* Asian Historical Dictionaries, No. 6. Metuchen, NJ and London: The Scarecrow Press.
Sekong Province. 2008. Socio-Economic Development Plan 2020. (In Lao language.)
Stuart-Fox, M. 1991. Foreign policy of the Lao People's Democratic Republic. In *Laos: Beyond the Revolution,* eds. J. Zasloff and L. Unger, 187-208. New York: St. Martin's Press.
–. 1997. *History of Laos.* Cambridge: Cambridge University Press.
Thayer, C.A. 1983. Laos in 1982: The Third Congress of the People's Revolutionary Party. *Asian Survey* 23(1): 84-93.
Verdery, K. 1991. Theorizing socialism. *American Ethnologist* 18(3): 419-39.
Zasloff, J., and L. Unger, eds. 1991. *Laos: Beyond the Revolution.* New York: St. Martin's Press.

4

Oral Histories of Livelihoods and Migration under Socialism and Post-Socialism among the Khmu of Northern Laos

Olivier Évrard

Migration and relocation play important roles in development policies and especially in local livelihood strategies. Here, I draw on oral histories and biographical methods of investigation to analyze how specific individuals express their agency while seeking to improve their livelihoods. I focus on two men from the Khmu ethnic group in Nalae district, Luang Namtha province in Northern Laos.[1]

The Study of Postwar Migrations in Northern Laos

Northern Laos has been the site of much political and ethnic turmoil in recent decades. Two Indochina wars (from 1946 to 1954 and from 1959 to 1975), followed by three decades of socialist rule, have enforced migration and set up new inter-ethnic contexts and complexities.

The fighting in both wars was bitter, long, and complex, creating divisions not only between ethnic groups but also within them. The terrain of northern Laos made for a warfare of raiding, air strikes, and patrols, with conflict occurring at the local scale over a number of years. First, the French, then the American-backed royalists, and then the eventually victorious Communist Pathet Lao forces allied selectively with some highlanders and fought continuously with others. When they finally took power in 1975, the Communists asserted their control over the highlands.

Huge migrations took place in the countryside during these periods, involving most villages in some way or another. Some inhabitants fled the combat or bombing zones or moved to escape possible retaliation by the Communist regime. Others sought access to new opportunities and land in the plains, or, since the 1970s, resettled in the lowlands under official government development schemes. Indeed, since the 1960s, more than 50 percent of highland villages have disappeared in northern Laos (Évrard 2006). Instead, people have gathered in new, bigger, and often multi-ethnic localities, usually on the edges of Laos' main plains or along newly built roads into the highlands (see also Daviau, this volume).

Several reports and academic studies have analyzed the social and economic consequences of resettlement in Laos (Goudineau 1997; Chamberlain 2001, Chamberlain 2007, Baird and Shoemaker 2007). These works have proposed typologies of displacement and explained the political and ideological contexts that sustained them (Évrard and Goudineau 2004). This chapter does not challenge these typologies but seeks to redress an imbalance; namely, the study of highlanders' migrations in Laos, as in other neighbouring socialist countries, has often been set in terms of macro versus micro approaches. That is, resettlement plans are juxtaposed against villagers' autonomy: techniques of control and discipline versus strategies of resistance and negotiation. There is a need here for a biographical method that can emphasize both structure and agency at individual and collective levels. Typologies of displacement in Laos are useful, but they can never account for the experiences, motivations, strategies, and constraints that a single individual might experience when undergoing these changes. These factors effectively shape an individual's life and livelihood, and it is important to ask how these changes were experienced.

Second, it is also important to understand the intellectual context in which migration takes place. These intellectual themes do not focus solely on the constraints, strategies, or itineraries but also, and most often, on how new ideologies and discourses (such as those regarding the nation-state, development, wealth, and poverty) are embedded in (and/or transformed by) local perceptions of identity, ethnicity, kinship, time, and space. In this attempt, I am inspired by Andrew Hardy, who, in his book on postwar migration in Vietnam, calls for an "ethnographic-style holistic approach" to historical migrations that could set "information about individual lives in a framework informed by flows, not only of migration, but of time, landscape, bureaucracy, ideology" (Hardy 2003, 21). Turning to Laos, only a few anthropologists have thus far adopted this approach, including Vatthana Pholsena (2006) and Pierre Petit (2006, 2008).

I also draw on the conceptual framework set up by Yves Goudineau (2000) in his work on resettlement and ethnicity in Laos. Within this framework, the current migrations of highland groups in Laos are understood as processes of deterritorialization (leaving a territory and a way of life) that preclude and sometimes parallel multi-level experiences and discourses of reterritorialization: not only settling in a new environment but also accepting and integrating into the cultural references that are bound up with it (Évrard and Goudineau 2004, 938).

Discourses on Poverty and Marginality: The Case of the Khmu

Research for this chapter was carried out among the Khmu people of Nalae district, in the Nam Tha area of Laos. The Khmu comprise 11 percent of the total population of Laos. They are an autochthonous population in northern

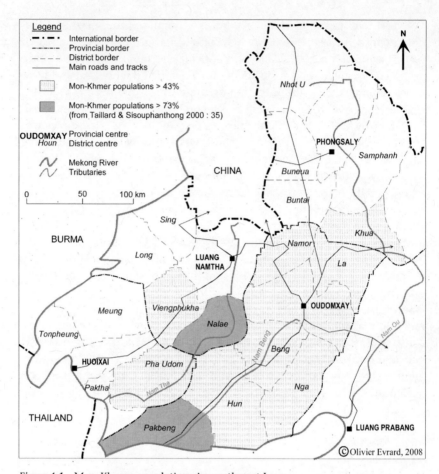

Figure 4.1 Mon-Khmer populations in northwest Laos.

Laos and are the largest minority in the country. In some areas, they even constitute overwhelming local majorities (see Figure 4.1), especially around the Nam Tha valley in northwestern Laos, where they comprise up to 80 percent of the total population – even without considering the mixed villages where some of them live alongside Lao people. Despite their demographic significance, the Khmu are seldom mentioned in the ethnographic literature. When they are, they usually appear as a marginalized people whose traditions and way of life represent a kind of coarser version of those of the Tai-speaking groups (see also Mellac, this volume) and who are on the road to complete assimilation by the latter.[2]

In the current development-related discourses of Lao institutions and foreign aid organizations, Khmu people, as for most Mon-Khmer groups, are often presented as being poorer than other populations.[3] Most of them indeed experience more difficult living conditions than lowland populations, but it is not always clear how this poverty is explained. Often the state and its representatives blame the traditional agricultural methods of the Khmu (usually consisting of forms of shifting cultivation and subsistence agriculture). Another common explanation is that Khmu cultural practices (such as spirit worshipping or animal sacrifices) prevent villagers from understanding and following official development expertise (Évrard 2006, 313-14).

Khmu culture and history is often portrayed as uninteresting and vanishing, on the one hand, or backward and an obstacle to development, on the other.[4] A narrow definition of their livelihoods focuses only on agricultural and subsistence-based activities, and, in official discourse, nearly nothing is said of the networks created, for instance, through the integration of Khmu people into political and administrative activities at the regional level or through their labour migration to the cities of Laos or Thailand.

In other words, Khmu people are twice marginalized: economically and conceptually. That is why I intend in this chapter to primarily give a space to alternative voices, to provide an emic point of view based on "inside" views from Khmu people themselves about their contemporary history and ways of life. The two oral histories or biographies presented below are only short summaries of longer discussions held with these two men.[5] Yet, they are representative of the diverse livelihood activities that have emerged within communities experiencing the typical dilemmas over agriculture, politics, and livelihoods of Khmu neighbourhoods. Although they are just two individuals, they can be seen as representative examples and personal stories in their own right. These biographies are used to introduce more general thoughts and remarks on the perpetuation and transformation of the ways of Khmu life and mobility during the last four decades. The men's personal histories show that a better understanding of rural livelihoods in Laos can be gained from a social history of the war and postwar periods and from a dynamic approach to culture.

Ta Kouan, a Former Provincial Governor[6]

Ta Kouan Keomany was born in 1940 in Ban Mokkoud, a Khmu village in the hills east of the Nam Tha River, in today's Nalae district. At that time, many male teenagers would leave their villages for a few months or years to earn money in Thailand or the Lao town of Luang Prabang. But in 1951, politics intervened. Vietnamese soldiers entered Ta Kouan's village "when the first cucumbers planted with the rice in the swiddens [were] ripe" (roughly the end of August). The soldiers told villagers not to pay taxes to the French colonizers or to the *lam*.[7] Villagers became involved in resistance activities against the French, and Ta Kouan became an aide-de-camp to Communist Neo Lao Issara (Free Laos Front) in 1954.[8] In 1959, Ta Kouan became a soldier and travelled to Luang Nam Tha, Oudomxay, Phongsaly, Samneua, and

Hanoi, where he undertook political training. These were happy years for Ta Kouan, although in 1966 US forces bombed his home village. Yet, according to Ta Kouan, people had "a good life; there were no thieves, no social problems like today."

The Communist victory came in 1975. Upper Nam Tha was renamed Nalae district, in Luang Namtha province. Ta Kouan was asked to set up the new district office *(samnak müang Nalae)*. He settled there with his wife and six children, along with five other Khmu households originally from the same area as him. In 1980, Ta Kouan and his family moved to the plain of Luang-namtha, where other Khmu families from Nalae had begun to settle as early as 1962. There, they cleared the forest and established the new provincial administrative centre of Luang Namtha province.

Ta Kouan's political career grew. In 1982, he became governor of Luang Namtha province and replaced Khamvong, another Khmu man from the same village as him, who had been governor since 1973. Ta Kouan travelled to meetings and conferences in Vietnam, China, Burma, Russia, and even, in 1983, to Berlin. Then, after the loosening of socialism in 1986, various international projects started in Luang Namtha. The first involved a Thai-owned sawmill. Many Khmu men from Nalae came to work at the mill and settled with their families in a new village nearby. Ta Kouan distributed cattle from the government to these Khmu villagers who had migrated from the hills.

Some Western aid projects expressed interest in the Nalae area but were repelled by the lack of good transport (at that time, Nalae was the only district in the province that was not connected by road to the prefecture). In 1996, Ta Kouan helped the provincial administration hire a Chinese company to build a road, and he also actively lobbied the main development agencies working in Luang Namtha province to start projects in his native area. Ta Kouan eventually retired from his government post in 1998 and began planting hevea trees in collaboration with Chinese traders.

Unlike many Khmu men, Ta Kouan does not display shame or embarrassment about his Khmu identity. Indeed, he happily and proudly shares his knowledge of Khmu traditions while insisting that his native area is probably one of the most "traditional" among the Khmu. However, he also criticizes its inhabitants, who refuse to quit their native village and settle downhill. "There is no future in the hills" he said, "people have to understand that they won't receive any help there."

Ta Müang, a Life in Between

Ta Müang was born in 1949 in the Khmu village of Ban Saphut, in the hills west of the Nam Tha River, in Nalae district. This village was close to the fighting between Royalists and Communists during the war, and both sides treated villagers with suspicion and constantly requisitioned rice and other resources. Ta Müang became a primary school teacher but was accused of being a Royalist by the Pathet Lao in 1977 and was sent for "political re-education" (called seminars, or *samana*, in Lao language) in Attapeu, southern Laos. He stayed in the south for thirteen years, marrying a woman from Saravane and eventually working in a sawmill.

In 1990, Ta Müang was allowed to return home. In 1991, he settled in Ban Oudom, near Hueysay, a trading town on the Mekong River opposite Chiang Khong in Thailand. He chose this location for a variety of reasons. Most villages in his home area had been resettled, and he had relatives in Hueysay. Furthermore, his wife, a lowland Lao, did not want to live among Khmu people in a remote place. Finally, Ta Müang was already used to living in cities; in 1970 he had spent six months with his brother in Lampang, in northern Thailand, where they had both worked as waiters.

After eight trips between his native village and Hueysay, he settled at the end of 1991 (just after the harvest) in Ban Oudom, a multi-ethnic locality made up of resettled Lamet, Lao, Tai Dam, and Khmu families, near Hueysay airport. Land in this new location was scarce. Ta Müang paid one buffalo and four thousand baht for three *rai* of paddy field *(na)* and four *rai* of garden *(suan)* (one *rai* is roughly 0.16 hectares).[9]

Ta Müang needed wood to build his house. At first, he bought wood from a nearby Hmong village. But a friend of his worked at the provincial forestry department and informed him each time the local administration was granting wood quotas to villagers. In 1998, he started building the stilts and upper part of his house, and in 2001, he started putting bricks and cement on the ground floor with money his brother sent him from Lampang.

Ta Müang had four children with his wife before getting divorced in 2000. His wife left for Lampang, where she married a Khmu migrant. She took one of the children with her. The three other children stayed with Ta Müang and attended secondary school. Ta Müang's oldest daughter married a Khmu man; she now owns a market stall in Nalae district. In 2004, Ta Müang began to work for a company building a road linking Hueysay to Luang Namtha. He currently earns 3,000 baht each month from supervising car parking, working seven days a week, from 8 a.m. to 5 p.m. This job bores him, but the money lets him support his children. He wants to visit his brother and sister-in-law in Lampang when he has saved enough funds.

At first glance, it would appear that Ta Kouan and Ta Müang do not have much in common. Ta Kouan has power, prestige, and money; he owns a big house and collaborates with Chinese companies. Khmu people from Nalae still contact him for advice and support. Conversely, Ta Müang was treated as an enemy by the new regime, possibly because of his relationships with Khmu people living in Thailand, and was exiled for thirteen years in the remote south. He then lived modestly as a farmer with the support of his connections in Hueysay and his brother in Lampang. However, despite such contrasts, these two biographies are two sides of the same history. They are alternative experiences of (and discourses on) war and deterritorialization under both socialism and post-socialism.

Reversed Experiences of War and Deterritorialization

Ta Kouan's and Ta Müang's biographies are good examples of how members of different Khmu subgroups can experience dissimilar personal itineraries, resulting in quite different livelihoods. The Khmu populations of the upper Nam Tha are divided into several subgroups (or *tmoys*): the Khmu Lue and Khmu Rok east of the river, and the Khmu Kwaen and Khmu Yuan on the west (see Figure 4.2). Ta Kouan belongs to the Rok subgroup, while Ta Müang was born in a Khmu Yuan village. These groups have different territories based on their historical relations with Tai chiefdoms (see Évrard 2006, 2007). The fighting in the Indochina wars reiterated these intra-ethnic divisions. The Khmu Lue and Rok mostly sided with the Communists (Lao and Vietnamese), while, conversely the Khmu Kwaen and Yuan mainly supported

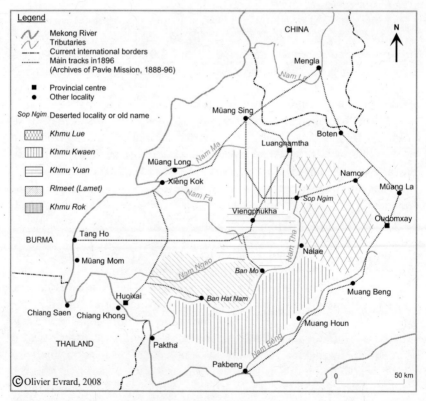

Figure 4.2 Khmu subgroups' areas *(tmoys)*.

the Royalist army backed by the French (1945-54) and later by US-funded paramilitary and multi-ethnic commandos.

In the more remote Khmu settlements – such as the Khmu Rok, east of the Nam Tha River – the villagers felt ethnic discrimination and exploitation under French colonization because of taxation and the power given to lowlanders. Accordingly, the villagers were happy to provide logistical support to Communist cadres and soldiers. The Communists offered a sense of nationalism free from cultural and ethnic prejudices, mixed with the promise of new opportunities and services.

Conversely, in Royalist areas, the Khmu (Kwaen and Yuan subgroups, west of the Nam Tha River) had a different history. Living at the border of several Tai principalities (Nan, Müang Sing, Chiang Hung), they were considered to be "guardians of the edges" and retained political autonomy during the pre-colonial period. They also benefited from numerous mule tracks and commercial networks in their territory. The Tai princes even gave titles of nobility to a few Khmu chiefs, who started using Tai clothing and pagodas to indicate their status. By 1900, the Khmu Kwaen welcomed the first French administrators into their territory (Lefèvre-Pontalis 1902) and maintained mostly good relations until the end of the French protectorate in 1954. Some also became involved with the pro-Royalist multi-ethnic commando groups (Khmu, Lamet, Lahu, Hmong, Yao) trained by US military advisers in guerrilla warfare and sabotage in the northern areas of Luang Namtha and even Yunnan province, in China. These paramilitary groups conducted several ambushes against Pathet Lao troops and even briefly recaptured Luangnamtha town at the end of 1967, before being eventually driven back by Lao and Vietnamese Communist forces.

Not all Khmu men west of the Nam Tha River supported the Royalists, however. Usually, only a few men in each village became soldiers, and they did so mainly after a pragmatic analysis of local geopolitics, and sometimes for financial reasons, rather than because of their commitment to a political cause, as occurred with the Khmu Rok and Lue. Ta Müang's account of this period is clear on this point; villagers were harassed by both sides, and many wanted to stay neutral. However, old cultural and political differences between eastern and western *tmoys* were reactivated by the conflict. The new Communist state distinguished between *vilason* (heroes) and *satu* (enemies) of the revolution, which determined how villagers were treated by the local administrations during the next two decades. After the war, the Khmu Yuan and Kwaen often suffered deterritorialization and resettlement, while the Rok and Lue subgroups were, by 2000, still relatively autonomous in the highlands and, at the same time, well connected to the lowlands via familial and institutional networks.

Some Khmu fighting for the Communists were rewarded with official positions in the new administration. Ta Kouan was the first head *(cao müang)* of the newly created Nalae district; a relative, Khamvong, became governor of the Upper Mekong province, which was later divided into two new provinces, Luang Namtha and Bokeo, in 1983. In all the "liberated" areas of northern Laos (Luang Namtha but also Oudomxay, Phongsaly, and Huaphan), leaders with minority gained access to administrative and political positions, sometimes as soon as the early 1960s. They established new administrative centres and acted as "propagators" of the new way of life promised by the Pathet Lao.[10] They were eventually followed to the lowlands by some of their relatives, and participated in the collectivization process (see also Mellac, this volume).

Once in the lowlands, migrants used rice fields that had been abandoned by the Tai during the war or established new ones. For example, in Ban Namtchang, on the outskirts of Luangnamtha town, at least eight households (thirty people) came from Ta Kouan's native area (or *tasaeng sakaen*).[11] In Sakaen village, elders remembered that the first migrations occurred as early as 1954. After that, forty households left for Luang Namtha province and more than twenty for Nalae district, about 60 percent of the village's population in 1960. Slightly fewer people left the neighbouring villages of Mokkoud and Konkoud. Migrants received logistical and material support during their migration, including being carried by military trucks from Müang Hun and Müang Beng to Oudomxay and Luang Namtha. Meanwhile, some Khmu Rok took boats south and went to Hueysay. Similar stories are told by members of other ethnic groups, such as the Phu Noy in Phongsaly or the Alak and the Katu in Sekong. Ta Kouan's history, therefore, reflects a general pattern of migration by ethnic groups that is linked to ideology and upward social mobility, that started as early as the 1960s, and that affected most of the lowland areas.

By contrast, Ta Müang's history refers to a massive and brutal depopulation. On the Vieng Phu Kha plateau, Khmu villagers were usually physically forced to move. Unlike the ideological migrations mentioned above, these enforced resettlements occurred relatively late and quickly. The crucial event here is not the creation of the Communist regime in 1975 but the failed insurrection in the summer of 1977 in the small town of Viengphukha.

In July 1977, a group of eighteen Royalist commandos, mostly Khmu, arriving from military bases in Thailand through Xieng Kok, infiltrated the Viengphukha garrison and persuaded soldiers to turn against their officers. Their attempt failed, but in August, regular Lao troops backed by Vietnamese forces launched a vast security operation in villages of the region. The whole Khmu Kwaen area was depopulated. The most important villages (especially where the *tasaeng* head resided) of the more densely populated Khmu Yuan area were resettled. Most of the Khmu villages along the banks of the Nam Tha River today, or along the road near Viengphukha city, were resettled under these circumstances. Unlike the Khmu Rok or Lue migrants, these people who had been forcibly removed received neither government nor foreign aid, and most experienced hardship. Moreover, anyone suspected of having links with "counter-revolutionary forces" was arrested and sent to "re-education camp" – many among them were people such as Ta Müang, who were not directly involved in armed groups but who worked as local teachers, headmen, or traders, or whose relatives had been involved with Royalist troops (which was briefly the case of Ta Müang's brother). After these forced resettlements in 1977, people continued to migrate from the region until 1985, as traditional upland matrimonial and commercial networks had been disrupted and people felt isolated and impoverished. Many went to the outskirts of Hueysay, where they mixed with other war refugees, sometimes creating multi-ethnic localities.[12]

In sum, the two oral histories or biographies presented above provide a good illustration of how the division of the country into two opposing camps during the war led to a crystallization of existing intra-ethnic solidarities among the Khmu of northwestern Laos. These local histories still influence contemporary livelihoods through access to land, relations with local officials, and experiences of the "development" process. The conditions of life may not seem so different from one subgroup *(tmoy)* to another, but a deeper analysis reveals different historical conditions and dissimilar discourses. Some *tmoy* suffered directly from the new social and political order, while others have been able to take advantage of it.

Since the 1990s, economic and political contexts have changed. Laos has officially adopted a market economy (Pholsena 2006, 5) but has kept its political organization highly centralized. These transformations are reflected locally in easier mobility (including the reopening of international borders and improved road infrastructure) and more international aid and private investment. Resettlement still occurs, and some highland villages continue to be merged. These changes have reduced social gaps between Khmu subgroups because they have been relatively unfavourable for those who benefited from the war and socialism, while they have, conversely, assisted people who were previously treated as enemies.[13] Accordingly, some Khmu Rok villagers now feel disillusioned, but the Khmu Yuan are more optimistic than they were before.

Resettlement under Post-Socialism: The Discourse of Necessity and the Feeling of Betrayal

The Pathet Lao once insisted that they had to "bring development to the mountainous areas" (Évrard and Goudineau 2004, 944). Now, highland villages are moved to the lowlands. This reversal occurred in the early 1990s with the tacit approval of aid agencies that had begun to play an increasingly important role in the national economy. The rationale behind resettlement is to gather highlanders in the plains or in the foothills where land is available and services can be provided at lower costs. Official discourses especially emphasize the need to eradicate shifting cultivation, which is presented as the main cause of poverty and as an obstacle to "permanent and sustainable activity" *(chatsan asib khong ti)*. Each district has to evaluate and map out its capacity to develop wet-rice agriculture, cash crops production, and other new activities, such as crafts or tourism. If the highland population exceeds the technical capacity of the district, the province orders the surplus population to relocate to other districts.

Nalae district demonstrates the effects of this new policy (see Figure 4.3). Between 1975 and 1995, most resettlement in Nalae affected the left bank

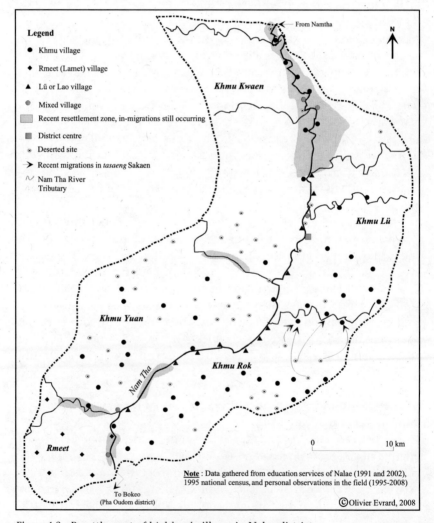

Figure 4.3 Resettlement of highland villages in Nalae district.

of the river and was motivated by security concerns (70 percent of migrants were either Khmu Kwaen or Yuan; Évrard 2006, 324). The mountainous areas west of the river were nearly emptied of people during that period. In the east, however, Khmu Rok and Lue villages remained on their traditional sites, even if some households did migrate to the plains of Luang Namtha and Oudomxay. After 1995, resettlement continued but in a different context. First, the local government gathered highland populations in so-called focal zones, selected for agricultural potential. Some model villages were created with foreign aid, though they were mostly short-lived. Second, the local government started resettling Khmu Rok populations in the eastern part of the district, which further depopulated the uplands. In 1996, there were more than seventy upland villages in Nalae district; by 2006, there were only sixteen, representing a decline from 65 to 20 percent of the total population of the district.

Ta Kouan – the ethnic leader who gained a high position within the party, whom we met earlier – actively supported collective resettlement as a tool for rural development. In Ta Kouan's native area, collective resettlement started in 2002. In the first months of 2003, more than two hundred families left for Vieng Phu Kha district. The local government announced that sixteen other villages (or 4,200 people in 710 households) were to be moved by 2005, including the seven villages of the *tasaeng* Sakaen. By 2005, six of these had moved, including two villages (Sakaen and Kanha) that received German bilateral assistance to help construct piped water systems. But despite this assistance, many villagers cannot yet sell rice surpluses because there is no road, and the market is now further away than before.

Two other neighbouring villages (Mokkoud, Ta Kouan's native village, and Konkoud) were resettled and merged on the foothills in 2006 with even less success (see Figure 4.4). Unlike Sakaen and Kanha villages, which had acceptable land for building a village, Mokkoud Mai ("the new Mokkoud") has no flat land, limited access to water, and floods during the rainy season. The local government promised a new road on the basis of "food for work" – considered exploitative by locals – as well as water pipes from international aid. Many households still keep some old upland fields, a three-hour walk from the new site. Some also keep their old dwellings, which they consider their real homes. Often, young adults move between the two sites, while many elders continue to live in the uplands. The previous headman, Tao Ploh, once told me: "Our head is downhill, but our stomach is still uphill."

This situation creates tension between villagers and encourages individuals to look after themselves. Two kinds of attitudes prevail. More reluctant people, who are often the oldest, argue that the new site is unsuitable and describe how the administration has made empty promises in the past. They want to persist in upland settlement through cattle breeding and cash crops. They do not understand why some nearby Khmu villages were allowed to

Figure 4.4 After several years of bargaining with the administration, Mokkoud and Konkoud villages merged and resettled downhill in 2006 against the promise of receiving help for water supply and road construction. *Photo by author*

stay upland whereas they were not. More pragmatic people, as well as the youngest, simply want to move downhill to gain access to public services. However, these people now feel betrayed by the administration because the new site is so difficult. A few households have already left for Luangnamtha, to join relatives or seek work in larger settlements.

When Ta Kouan talks about his native village, Mokkoud, it sounds like a scathing attack on "traditionalist" villagers who refuse to move downhill and whose nostalgia of bygone days condemns the younger generation. This discourse is common among high-ranking officials (especially those from minorities) who claim that villagers' cultural backwardness and resistance to government has caused their poverty. At the district level, local administrators are often fatalistic and sometimes cynical. They know the government has no alternative vision of upland rural development and that it lacks sufficient resources anyway. However, they also know that high-ranking officials

Figure 4.5 "Strengthen friendship between all the ethnic groups to unify the [Lao] society." Poster displayed in Bun Tai district, Phongsaly province. *Photo by B. Brunetti*

who insist on resettlement rarely appreciate the impoverishment it causes. They sometimes use international aid as a way to offer benefits to resettled villages, even if they are unsure it will make a difference.

Despite its overall contribution to the Lao economy, foreign aid has little ability to affect resettlement.[14] The guidelines adopted by the main institutions involved, such as the World Bank and the Asian Development Bank, are mainly concerned with involuntary resettlement from development projects such as dams and roads. These guidelines appear less efficient when applied to a "settling process" (Évrard and Goudineau 2004, 947). In most cases, it is impossible to assess the extent to which migration is voluntary or involuntary because there are always diverse motivations and constraints for each individual.[15] For example, in Ban Konechan, the first model village of Nalae district, villagers said they relocated because "one called them, asked them to try" *(eun ma haet kan totlong)* but immediately afterward added, "because we were experiencing difficult conditions of life" *(pova tuk yak)*. There was no direct coercion, only the prospect of a different and supposedly better life supported by the state and close to an already established administrative centre mostly inhabited by other Khmu people.

Even those foreign aid projects in a good position to influence the practices and planning of the local administration have managed only to slow down resettlement, rather than changing its outcome. In Nalae, the German bilateral cooperation Deutsche Gesellschaft für Technische Zusammenarbeit (GTZ), opposed large-scale resettlement between 1995 and 2000 and sought to install schools, piped water, and veterinary support in some upland villages. Yet, it appears these actions did not prevent resettlement of those villages.[16] GTZ then reduced its involvement in the district, as did other NGOs. New Chinese private investors then came in to establish rubber plantations, and much aid was still received indirectly through donations or loans from the European Union or the Asian Development Bank.

Ta Kouan's biography provides us with the elements required for a social history of state building and internal colonialism in Laos. The Lao state adopted a new political framework for rural development policies at the beginning of the 1990s, moving from a socialist and self-sufficiency ideology to a market-oriented approach sustained by foreign capital and technical means. Simultaneously, there has been a change in discourse regarding the participation of highlanders in economic development. They (or at least some of them) were heroes of the revolution, with many recruited to participate in the collectivization program in the lowlands; they now appear to be poor and isolated farmers who need to be taught how to find the path to development.

Of course, the reality is far more complex and carefully balanced. Many upland livelihoods are still viable, and highlanders contribute greatly to the food security of migrant households. However, dominant state discourses hide, or even deny, interdependency between hills and plains and refuse to consider alternative models of livelihood and development.[17] The Khmu villagers who still live upland are now presented as marginal remnants of a disappearing past. They also have to model their attitude on this image or else be stigmatized as backward and uneducated by members of their own ethnic group who have already settled in the lowlands (Ta Kouan, for example). For them, "post-socialism" has the bitter taste of disillusion: they could once change their life, now they try to enhance it.

Khmu Labour Migration Networks

Ta Müang's case offers different perspectives on contemporary Khmu livelihoods. For him, "post-socialism" has meant that the state now exerts less control over his life and mobility. He returned to his native region after his long exile in the south. The reopening of the border with Thailand gave him an economic opportunity (his current job in a Thai-Lao venture company) and allowed him to communicate more easily with his brother in Lampang, from whom he received financial support to buy land and build a house in Hueysay. Ta Müang is not an isolated case: Many villagers in the resettled Khmu villages near Hueysay have relatives living on the other side of the

Mekong River and migrate temporarily – mostly illegally, and during their teenage years – to earn cash. In effect, the old migratory networks between Laos and Thailand are now being reopened after being closed for nearly two decades (Walker 1999).

Khmu people (mostly men until the last decade) have a long – though often ignored – history of temporary migration to lowlands in Luang Prabang but also to northern Thailand and Burma (Lefèvre-Pontalis 1902; Lebar 1967; Évrard 2007). The origin of such migrations is unclear, but Mon-Khmer people from northern Laos (and especially from Nam Tha) used to travel during the cold season to barter rice and forest products for salt, clothes, and prestige goods such as bronze drums, gongs, swords, and silver bars. They were also recruited into the armies of Thai princes during wartime. It seems that the Khmu came to see temporary migration as a means of gaining prestige and social mobility and of compensating for temporary economic difficulties such as a bad harvest, indebtedness, or illness in a household.[18]

It is also unclear when the Khmu started to sell their labour in the lowlands on a large scale. Labour migrations increased sharply in the late nineteenth century following the development of the teak industry by foreign (mostly British) companies in northern Siam (now Thailand) and Burma. At the end of the nineteenth century, numerous Khmu people crossed the Mekong each year to work in teak plantations, factories, or elephant camps in Chiang Rai, Chiang Mai, Lamphun, Lampang, Phrae, and Nan. Some were also employed as gardeners or assistants by Thai patrons in large cities. Between the two world wars, these labour migrations were less numerous because of both the economic crisis and the slowdown of the teak exploitation. But following the industrialization of Thailand after the Second World War, the need for cheap labour grew and companies started to diversify their activities to tobacco plantations, turpentine factories, and import-export activities. For instance, when Ta Müang's brother, Taen Nyi, was engaged by the Lampang branch of the Danish East Asiatic Company (EAC) in the early 1950s, he was fourteen years old and had worked one year already in a tobacco factory near Chiang Khong. The EAC exported turpentine (called *slék* by the Khmu and *krang* by the Thai) since the 1930s and had also begun to import motor cultivators from Pakistan. At that time, the Lampang branch of the EAC was employing six Khmu men, four of whom came from the same area as Taen Nyi.

Migratory networks were easy to access then. Khmu middlemen known as *nay roy* recruited young men for Thai patrons. They travelled as far as Phongsaly in northern Laos, but most migrants came from the Nam Tha area and especially from the west banks of the Nam Tha River. The *nay roy* took them from their villages to their new workplaces and sent them back to their native villages at the end of their contracts. As compensation, they kept the first salaries of the young migrants for themselves. *Nay roy* were considered wealthy men and often had two houses (and often even two wives), one in Thailand, another in Laos. Most migrants returned to their villages after one or two years, but a substantial number settled permanently in Siam. Some, such as Ta Müang's elder brother, did not want to return to their previous life: They married Thai women and were integrated into Thai settlements. More recently, some migrants have married Khmu women also living in Thailand, or sometimes women from other ethnic groups. In these cases, they usually live in multi-ethnic villages. A last case is those migrants who did not marry but, nonetheless, never returned home. For them, migration was a failure or was chosen in order to avoid a previously difficult situation. These people often stayed alone in disused factories or slums outside Thai cities.

Statistics on these labour migrations are scarce and fragmentary. Some are to be found in the archives of the French consular agencies that were established in Nan, Phrae, Chiang Khong, Chiang Mai, and Chiang Rai after 1893.[19] A document from 1937 indicates that between 1932 and 1936, 2,800 Khmu men from Laos registered in the three consulates of Chiang Rai, Lampang, and Nan – 300 per year, more or less. Given that many migrants did not register, these figures are probably low. Moreover, the number of migrants was lower in the 1930s than at the end of the nineteenth century, at the peak of the teak industry. Discussions with elderly Khmu migrants in Laos and in Thailand showed that, for the villages of the west bank of the Nam Tha River in Laos (Khmu Yuan and Khmu Kwaen), about 30 to 50 percent of young men spent some time in Siam or Burma during their bachelor years at the beginning of the twentieth century (though this rate was lower elsewhere, and among the Khmu Rok especially).

Transnational migratory networks were disrupted by the war in the 1950s and 1960s, and then nearly completely shut down after the closure of the border between Laos and Thailand in 1975. Following the closure, Khmu migrants were viewed with suspicion on both sides of the Mekong. Labour migrations still occurred as many Khmu fled Laos and settled in Thailand (especially in the Chiang Khong and Vieng Kaen districts of Chiang Rai province). Full temporary migrations resumed in the 1990s, but once again, reliable statistics are scarce. Data given by the immigration office in Chiang Khong offer some insights, but individuals might inadvertently be counted several times and there is no mention of ethnicity. Other surveys in home villages are few and take time to complete. One survey in the Khmu village of Mokachok, near Ta Müang's house, shows that 24 young people (from a total population of 135 households and 678 inhabitants) left the village between January and August 2007 to work temporarily in Thailand. According to the head of the village, other Khmu villages had comparable rates. The figures are lower for other and more remote villages in Vieng Phu Kha

Figure 4.6 "The army needs the people like the fish needs water." Poster near Muang Hun central market, Udomxay province, November 2009. *Photo by author*

and Nalae districts, but even there, substantial numbers of unmarried young people still migrate to sell their labour.

Reliable figures are lacking on these questions, but biographies of migrants collected in Hueysay, Chiang Khong, and Lampang provide useful insights.[20] These biographies indicate that the organization of the migration has changed over time. People now rely on roads, buses, and mobile phones, rather than the *nay roy* system. Young migrants look for jobs by calling friends already working in Thailand. They usually leave Laos in groups of two to four people; before, these groups could be fifteen or more. Some migrants even go alone and look for a job haphazardly by themselves, visiting factories or restaurants, or gathering at certain points in the town. They also make contact with older migrants, especially those who did not return to their native area. In Laos, village headmen act as a modern-day *nay roy*, though they themselves do not travel. Instead, they provide migrants with contacts in Thailand and keep (unofficial) records of who leaves and returns. Some also collect money from migrants before their departure and after their return as a compensation for their silence and unofficial collaboration.

Although better roads have made travelling easier, the new political context tends to make migration more insecure. Migrants usually get a border pass on the Lao side, through their village headman. This document allows them to stay three days in the Chiang Khong district only. The luckiest are able to apply for longer work permits and visas with the support of their company or patron. Many just stay in Thailand illegally. Their travels consequently tend to be geographically restricted. The origin of migrants today also tends to be more limited, with most coming from villages settled (or, more precisely, resettled) near the banks of the Mekong after the war.

Many of the jobs done by migrants are similar to activities done fifty years ago. Some older activities have nearly disappeared (such as timber extraction, mahout work, or the production of *slék*), but some remain, including working in sawmills, rice mills, and ceramic factories, and working as gardeners, cooks, and waiters. Many migrants, both young and old, also sell their labour on a daily basis, working in maize fields in Vieng Kaen, loading trucks and boats in Chiang Khong, or carrying ice, rice, or maize in Lampang. Their daily wages may be one to three hundred baht (roughly from US$3 to 10) depending on the kind of work. Monthly salaries vary from three to eight thousand baht (US$90 to 310). Many young people coming directly from Laos usually sleep and eat at their working place.

The social value and livelihood importance of migration, however, are now quite different. Khmu migrants in Thailand used to convert their savings into prestige goods such as bronze drums or gongs or silver coins (several shops specialized in this trade in Chiang Khong), which were used for ritual purposes in their own society. Today, migrants invest in wood (for houses) and paddy land (which is scarce in resettled villages in Laos), as well as pay for special expenses such as medical care or education fees. In other words, wealth now relates to a house or an individual, not a lineage; it moves quicker than it used to; and the social value given to displaying the kind of wealth acquired through migration does not follow the same old ritual channels. It seems that migration now contributes more significantly toward basic needs than it used to, and it provides a useful contingency plan in the event of emergencies or the need to raise cash quickly.[21]

Finally, women are much more involved in migration than before. They started migrating in the 1990s and now account for about 40 percent of Khmu labourers in Thailand. Women work in factories, restaurants, shops, and guesthouses or as maids. This growth in female migrants probably results from better access to primary education and transportation networks; a greater expectation of women to meet the financial needs of their families in resettled localities; and an absence of young unmarried men in their villages. When asked, most women preferred not to discuss risks such as human trafficking or prostitution associated with migration, but these topics obviously generated anxiety. Many restaurants, bars, and karaoke shops have opened in northern Laos along the new road from Hueysay to Luang Namtha (which is part of a regional highway linking Yunnan to Thailand). These establishments mostly employ Khmu (and Rmeet) women. Some women then join migration networks in Thailand without always knowing where they are being sent or for which kind of work. There is also an emerging discourse on the "beauty" of these women among lowland men (both Lao and Thai).²² Although the eroticization of the minorities is quite common in Asia, such a phenomenon is very recent for northern Mon-Khmer linguistic populations and has probably resulted from female labour migration.

Conclusion

The personal histories of Ta Kouan and Ta Müang provide us with contrasting but complementary insights into contemporary livelihoods of Khmu populations in Laos. Their oral histories reveal structural patterns (such as subgroups) that have influenced how these populations have encountered the immense changes effected during and after socialism. Looking at these personal histories allows us to resist what Tim Forsyth and Jean Michaud (this volume) call the "anonymity" encouraged by mainstream analyses of upland livelihood and post-socialism in Southeast Asia.

In contemporary Laos, current debates on the concept of poverty are often based on two opposing approaches (Rigg 2005, 20-42). The first approach sees poverty as the result of a missed opportunity or, in the words of officials such as Ta Kouan, of a cultural backwardness that prevents people from accessing development. The second approach sees poverty as a phenomenon generated by development and social change such as land allocation or liberalization of the economy. Even though these approaches are different, they often sustain the same misleading idea that poverty is easier to understand in the highlands than in the lowlands because upland livelihoods are simpler and embedded in smaller social spaces. I hope that the two biographies presented here clearly show that highland livelihoods, and highlanders, are far more complex and resourceful than this representation suggests.

Highland livelihoods are complex, as are those in the lowlands. Highlanders are not simply experiencing a single transition based on greater integration with the lowlands but, rather, various and complex processes of deterritorialization and reterritorialization involving both material and symbolic aspects. Grasping this complexity means conducting multiple levels of analysis, including delving into both the present and recent history. As a tentative methodology, I suggest that we need to pay attention, for each particular case, to three aspects of livelihoods. The first is the ecological and social niches, acknowledging that these are varied and can change according to land uses or economic activities. The second is the social (and possibly interethnic) networks, as well as the verbal and symbolic categories highlanders mobilize to improve their conditions of life or to negotiate with local administrators. The third aspect is the ambivalent meaning of "development" and "globalization" from the viewpoint of highlanders. As shown with resettlement dynamics in Laos and labour migrations to Thailand, becoming more integrated with economic opportunities can provide benefits but also create or perpetuate spaces of exclusion and insecurity.

Notes

1 In this chapter I use Luang Namtha as the name of the province and Luangnmtha as the name of its administrative center. For the river that crosses this province, I use the spelling "Nam Tha." Accordingly, I write "Vieng Phou Kha" for the district or area but "Viengphukha" for its main city. I would like to thank Jean Michaud, Tim Forsyth, Guido Sprenger, and Pierre Petit, as well as the anonymous reviewers, for their comments on earlier versions of this chapter.
2 "Tai-speaking groups" refer here to everyone belonging to the Tai-Kadai linguistic family, be they located in Thailand, Laos, Vietnam, Burma, or China.
3 Although Mon-Khmer groups represent around 20 percent of the total population in Laos, they account for 53 percent of the population considered as poor by the Lao authorities (Chamberlain 2006, 27).
4 See, for instance, the work of the American missionary and linguist William Smalley (1965) or the Marxist approach of the Vietnamese ethnographer Dang Nghiem Van (1973). However, more balanced and scientifically relevant approaches are found in the work of Franck Proschan (1997, 2001), for instance, as well as in the numerous volumes and articles published by the team of linguists and folklorists at the Scandinavian Institute of Asian Studies (Lindell, Samuelsson, and Tayanin 1979; Lindell et al. 1982; Lindell and Tayanin 1991; to name a few). For a critical review of the ethnographic literature on the Khmu, see Évrard (2008).
5 This chapter is based on fieldwork conducted between 1995 and 2008 among Khmu populations in northwestern Laos and, since 2006, also in northern Thailand.
6 In Khmu language, "*ta*" refers to grandfather (either paternal or maternal) as well as to any male ancestor. By extension, this word is also used to address any man who has acquired an elder status through descent or prestige.
7 A *lam* was an administrative position (often hereditary) in Tai polities. The *lam*, sometimes called *pho lam* (*pho*, father, protector, patron; and *lam*, translator, go-between), were appointed by local Tai rulers to help rule the population of the valley basin *(müang)*. The *lam* had power over tax collection and the settlement of disputes. They constituted a kind of parallel power that facilitated relations between the ruler and his vassals.
8 The first nationalist and colonialist movement in Laos was named Lao Issara. Created in 1945 by Prince Phetsarath, it included two of his half-brothers, Prince Souvanna Phouma and Prince Souphanouvong, and other members of the aristocracy. Following internal dissent and France giving Laos formal independence, the Lao Issara was dissolved in 1949. In 1950, Prince Souphanouvong allied with the Vietnamese Communists and created the Neo Lao Issara (Free Laos Front), which was renamed Neo Lao Hak Sat (NLHS, the Lao Patriotic Front) in 1955. The resistance government was named Pathet Lao – the name by which the revolutionary movement became known. Pathet Lao members then spread Marxist-Leninist ideology among, and provided basic military training to, the rural population, especially in the highlands. According to Stuart-Fox (1986, 20) "by 1953, twenty-seven major zones of operation had been established throughout Laos, mainly in frontier areas inhabited by tribal minority peoples, among whom Pathet Lao recruitment was particularly effective." See also Deuve (1984).
9 Four thousand baht was equivalent to US$160 in 1991.
10 The territorial and administrative reorganization of the country after 1975 led to the creation of new provinces (Oudomxay in 1975, Luang Namtha and Bokeo in 1983) and new districts (Nalae, Long). New administrative centres were also built and marked the will of the new regime to transform physically and symbolically the old *müang* system (Évrard 2006, 318-20).
11 After 1975, and until the end of the 1990s, a *tasaeng* was an administrative subdivision of the district that usually carried the name of the village where the head of the *tasaeng* was living. Ban Mokkoud, Kouan's native village, belonged to the *tasaeng* Sakaen (*crkaer* in Khmu language), as did six other villages, including Sakaen itself.
12 For instance, the village of Mokachok, which lies a few hundred metres from Müang's house, is one of the four Khmu villages settled on the outskirts of Hueysay. This village

currently has 135 households (680 people), which historically came from two distinct areas: 13 households came from the Pak Tha area as war refugees in 1977, and 51 households arrived between 1977 and 1980 as segments of different villages (more than 10) located on the Vieng Phu Kha plateau (Khmu Yuan and Khmu Kwaen subgroups) either by road or by river. Later on, the population increased, with the influx of immigrants from Vieng Phu Kha and Nalae joining the first settlers. Similar stories account for the creation of the other neighbouring Khmu villages of Nam Ho Tay (225 households, mixed with Lue), Ban Nam Phu (70 households), Ban Huey Din Chee (30 households), and Ban Maenyang (30 households).

13 The *tmoy* affiliation is becoming an increasingly meaningless category because of the migration to and gathering of highlanders in the lowlands.
14 Foreign development aid represents 18 percent of gross domestic product and 80 percent of public investment (UNDAF, 2002).
15 For a recent debate on this question see the article by Holly High (2008), the response to it by Baird et al. (2009), and the reply by Holly High (2009). Holly High rightly calls for a narrative approach to resettlement in Laos that takes the aspirations of the people, as well as their disappointment and their local negotiations with the administration, into greater account. However, her text is sometimes overly polemical and lacking in ethnographic and historical thoroughness, especially with regard to the Northern part of the country.
16 Some of the lowland villages where GTZ worked will also have to be resettled soon because of a dam project in the lower Nam Tha valley.
17 There is more than cynicism here. Such an attitude also refers to imaginary conceptions of the relations between lowlanders and highlanders, and between them and the state. This imagination is a mutual process, since lowlanders and highlanders (especially Mon-Khmer linguistic groups) share common though sometimes conflicting "grammars" of identity and alterity (see Sprenger 2004).
18 This social mobility was then linked to old patterns of economic and political interdependence between lowland and highland populations, as well as to the ritual economy of the highland villages. Prestige goods obtained through contacts with the outside world were traditionally used during marriages and funerals to perpetuate and reinforce the links between the wife-givers and the wife-takers on the one hand, and between the living and the ancestors on the other hand. The same pattern is found among the neighbouring Rmeet, known as Lamet by the Lao (Izikowitz 1951; Sprenger 2005, 2007).
19 The French registered Khmu migration to ensure it was only temporary and did not severely depopulate northern Laos, where their labour was needed by the colonizers.
20 A total of sixty-three interviews between September and December 2007.
21 For a discussion of changes in the social meaning of wealth among the Lamet in Laos, which largely applies also to the Khmu, see Sprenger 2007.
22 Personal field notes as well as personal communication from Guido Sprenger. In Bolikhamsay province, Pierre Petit (2006, 36) notes that among the lowland Lao, having sexual relations with a Khmu woman is said to bring good luck.

References

Baird, I., and B. Shoemaker. 2007. Unsettling experiences: Internal resettlement and international aid agencies in Laos. *Development and Change* 38(5): 865-88.

Baird, I., K. Barney, P. Vandergeest, and B. Shoemaker. 2009. Internal resettlement in Laos. *Critical Asian Studies*, 41(4): 605-14.

Chamberlain, J. 2001. *Participatory Poverty Assessment*. Vientiane: Asian Development Bank and National Statistics center.

–. 2006. *Participatory Poverty Assessment II*. Vientiane: Asian Development Bank and National Statistics Center.

Dang Nghiem Van. 1973. The Khmu in Vietnam. *Vietnamese Studies* 36(2): 62-140.

Deuve, J. 1984. *Le royaume du Laos: Histoire événementielle de l'indépendance à la guerre américaine* [The kingdom of Laos: Factual history from independence to American War]. Paris: École française d'Extrême-Orient.

Évrard, O. 2006. *Chroniques des cendres: Anthropologie des sociétés khmou et relations interethniques du Nord Laos* [Chronicles of the ashes: Anthropology of Khmu societies and interethnic dynamics in Northern Laos]. Paris: IRD (coll. A Travers Champs).
—. 2007. Interethnic systems and localized identities: The Khmu subgroups in north-west Laos. In *Social Dynamics in the Highlands of Southeast Asia: Reconsidering* Political Systems of Highland Burma *by E.R. Leach*, ed. F. Robinne and M. Sadan, 127-59. Leiden: Brill.
—. 2008. Atténuation et perpétuation des frontières ethniques: Notes sur la taïsation des populations khmou du Laos [Lessening and perpetuation of ethnic borders: Notes of the Taization of Khmu populations in Laos]. In *Nouvelles Recherches sur le Laos* [New Research on Laos], ed. M. Lorillard and Y. Goudineau, 533-57. Paris: Publications de l'Ecole Française d'Extrême Orient.
Évrard, O., and Y. Goudineau. 2004. Planned resettlements, unexpected migrations and cultural trauma. *Development and Change* 35(5): 937-62.
Goudineau, Y., ed. 1997. *Resettlement and Social Characteristics of New Villages: Basic Needs for Resettled Communities in the Lao PDR*. 2 vol. Vientiane: UNESCO/United Nations Development Programme/Orstom.
—. 2000. Ethnicité et déterritorialisation dans la péninsule indochinoise: Considérations à partir du Laos [Ethnicity and deterritorialization in the Indochinese Peninsula: Considerations from Laos]. *Autrepart* (14): 17-31.
Hardy, A. 2003. *Red Hills: Migrants and the State in the Highlands of Vietnam*. Copenhagen/Honolulu: NIAS Press/University Press of Hawai'i.
High, H. 2008. The implications of aspirations: Reconsidering resettlement in Laos. *Critical Asian Studies* 40(4): 531-50.
—. 2009. Complicities and complexities: Provocations from the study of resettlement in Laos. *Critical Asian Studies* 41(4): 615-20.
Izikowitz, K.G. 1951. *Lamet: Hill Peasants in French Indochina*. Göteborg: AMS Press.
Lebar, F. 1967. Observations on the movement of Khmu into north Thailand. *Journal of Siam Society* 55(1): 61-79.
Lefèvre-Pontalis, P. 1902. *Voyage dans le Haut-Laos et sur les frontières de Chine et de Birmanie*. Mission Pavie, Vol. 5. Paris: Ernest Leroux. Published in English in 2000 as *Travels in Upper Laos and on the Borders of Yunnan and Burma*. Bangkok: White Lotus.
Lindell, K., R. Samuelsson, and D. Tayanin. 1979. Kinship and marriage in northern Kammu villages: The kinship model. *Sociologus* 29(1): 60-84.
Lindell, K., and D. Tayanin. 1991. *Hunting and Fishing in a Kammu Village*. Lund: Nordic Institute of Asian Studies and Curzon Press.
Lindell, K., D. Tayanin, J.O. Svantesson, and H. Lundström. 1982. *The Kammu Year: Its Lore, Its Music*. Lund: Scandinavian Institute of Asian Studies and Curzon Press.
Petit, P. 2006. Migrations, ethnicité et nouveaux villages au Laos [Migrations, ethnicity and new villages in Laos]. *Aséanie* 18: 15-45.
—. 2008. Rethinking internal migrations in Lao PDR: The resettlement process under microanalysis. *Anthropological Forum* 18(2): 117-38.
Pholsena, V. 2006. *Post-War Laos: The Politics of Culture, History and Identity*. Singapore/Leifsgade/Chiang Mai: NIAS Press/ISEAS/Silkworm Books.
Proschan, F. 1997. We are all Khmu, just the same: Ethnonyms, ethnic identities and ethnic groups. *American Ethnologist* 34(1): 91-113.
—. 2001. People of the gourd: Imagined ethnicities in highland Southeast Asia. *Journal of Asian Studies* 60(4): 999-1032.
Rigg, J. 2005. *Living with Transition in Laos: Market Integration in Southeast Asia*. New York: Routledge.
Smalley, W. 1965. *Ethnographic Notes on the Khamu*. Reproduced by US AID Mission to Laos. Original manuscript: *The Khamu: Final report to the National Research Council*, Bangkok, 27 April 1965.
Sprenger, G. 2004. Encompassment and its discontents: The Rmeet and the lowland Lao. In *Grammars of Identity/Alterity: A Structural Approach,* ed. G. Baumann and A. Gingrich, 173-91. New York: Berghahn Books.

–. 2005. The way of the buffaloes: Trade and sacrifice in northern Laos. *Ethnology* 44(4): 291-312.
–. 2007. From kettledrums to coins: Upland identity and the flow of valuables in northern Laos. In *Social Dynamics in the Highlands of Southeast Asia: Reconsidering* Political Systems of Highland Burma *by Edmund Leach*. Vol. 18, Handbook of Oriental Studies, Section 3: Southeast Asia, ed. F. Robinne and M. Sadan, 161-85. Leiden: Brill.
Stuart-Fox, M. 1986. *Laos: Politics, Economics and Society*. London: Pinter Rienner.
Taillard, C., and Bounthavy SiSouphanthong. 2000. *Atlas of Laos: Spatial Structures of the Economic and Social Development in the Lao People's Democratic Republic*. Copenhagen/Chiang Mai: NIAS/Silkworm.
UNDAF [United Nations Development Assistance Framework]. 2002. *United Nations Development Assistance Framework: The Lao People's Democratic Republic*. Vientiane: UNDAF.
Walker, A. 1999. *The Legend of the Golden Boat: Regulation, Trade and Traders in the Borderlands of Laos, Thailand, Burma and China*. Richmond: Curzon Press.

5
Of Rice and Spice: Hmong Livelihoods and Diversification in the Northern Vietnam Uplands

Claire Tugault-Lafleur and Sarah Turner

Ethnic minority Hmong in upland northern Vietnam have taken advantage of cultural connections, differential access to resources, and fluctuating consumer demands to sustain and diversify their livelihoods over recent times. Although traditionally horticulturalists practising swidden-based subsistence agriculture, Hmong in the northern Vietnam highlands are now increasingly sedentarized peasants, focusing for the most part on rice production as their staple crop or, in dryer areas, on maize production (Corlin 2004; Turner and Michaud 2008). These livelihoods are supported by the collection of forest products such as fuel wood, herbal medicines, wild animals, and honey. Hmong have always been engaged in commerce to a limited extent, maintaining contacts with inhabitants of neighbouring valleys and beyond to exchange goods. From the 1800s, this took the form of opium production for a number of households until opium poppy cultivation in Vietnam was banned by Decree 327 in the early 1990s. Felling timber was an additional commercial opportunity, until it too was prohibited during the same period (DiGregorio, Pham Thi Quynh, and Yasui 1996). Constantly flexible and adaptive to such changing contexts, some Hmong have more recently entered the small-scale trade of highlander textiles, engaged in local tourism activities, and expanded their trade in forest products, most notably cardamom (Turner 2007).[1]

This livelihood diversification takes place against a backdrop of policy directives and cultural (mis)understandings established and reproduced by the socialist government of Vietnam and lowland Vietnamese. Since reunification in 1975, Vietnam's lowland lawmakers have been committed to integrating highland minority societies into the Việt nation, the Communist state, and the national economy. This integration has been carried out via the extension of infrastructure into the highland regions, education in the Vietnamese language, and economic reorganization that reaches the so-called margins of the country. Despite such attempts, Hmong highlanders have remained relatively autonomous in both their socio-political organization and economic production since their settlement in the Vietnam highlands around the 1820s (Michaud and Turner 2000). These ethnic minorities continue to be poorly understood among the lowland Vietnamese majority, often portrayed as "backward" (van de Walle and Gunewardena 2001; Sowerwine 2004a). A lowland/highland, superior/inferior dualism has prevailed since pre-colonial times, a dualism rendered more obvious during the French colonial period when "the people and landscapes of the highlands became concomitant subjects of the classificatory and scientific management schema of the colonial state to be labelled, settled, and systematically 'developed'" (Sowerwine 2004a, 127-28). This labelling, settling, and "development" has continued since independence. In part, this dualism persists because lowland Vietnamese (Kinh) consider highlanders as "peoples without history," since few upland groups have indigenous written archives, yet they are living in a country where remembering and celebrating the past is of the utmost importance (Tapp et al. 2004; Scott 2009).

This chapter focuses on Hmong livelihoods in the northern Vietnam highlands. More specifically, we ask, how has Đổi Mới – the series of country-wide economic reforms that began around 1986 – impacted Hmong livelihoods? And are there now new forms of livelihood diversification occurring in these highland Hmong communities? Investigating Hmong livelihoods in Sa Pa district, Lào Cai province, the chapter builds on field research into Hmong livelihoods and non-timber forest products by Tugault-Lafleur in 2006, and regularly since the late 1990s by Turner.[2]

We adopt an actor-oriented approach to livelihoods in order to emphasize significant contextual and cultural influences on Hmong livelihoods. As discussed in Forsyth and Michaud's Chapter 1, there is now a common recognition within development studies of the need to understand assets and vulnerabilities (the presence or absence of forms of capital – human, physical, natural, financial, and social), strategies (how people deploy or exploit existing assets), and access or barriers to resources (defined by social relations, ideologies, and institutions) (see Chambers and Conway 1992; Ellis 2000; de Haan and Zoomers 2005).[3] Specifically, individual and household livelihoods are shaped by "local and distinct institutions (e.g., local customs regarding access to common property resources, local and national land tenure rules) and by social relations (gender, caste, kinship and so on), as well as by economic opportunities" (Ellis 2000, 6). These factors change frequently and, hence, both individual and household livelihoods are continuously reshaped so that "various elements may change from season to season or from year to year, as assets are built up and eroded and as access to resources and opportunities change" (Hapke and Ayyankeril 2004, 232).

If households are to overcome these uncertainties and fluctuations, their livelihoods must be responsive and adaptable. The concept of sustainable livelihoods captures this flexibility and is defined by Chambers and Conway

(1992, 6) as a livelihood that can "cope with and recover from stress and shocks, maintain or enhance its capabilities and assets, and provide sustainable livelihood opportunities for the next generation; and which contributes net benefits to other livelihoods at the local and global levels and in the short and long-term." Such a framework is useful since it emphasizes the need to examine "long-term flexibility" (de Haan and Zoomers 2005, 31) in livelihoods, and how access to different types of capital can change over time.

Critics of standard livelihoods approaches, however, are concerned that such approaches focus too much on material access and ability, and not enough on less obvious cultural, social, and political influences (Kanji, MacGregor, and Tacoli 2005). Critics have therefore called for more inclusive actor-oriented approaches that recognize context-specific cultural, historical, gendered, and spatial dynamics of livelihoods (Bebbington 1999, 2000; Arce and Long 2000; Long 2001). As such, actor-oriented approaches are useful, as they focus attention on social relations among individuals embedded within local socio-economic, political, and cultural systems, as well as emphasizing the voices and experiences of individual actors' own knowledge of "development" and modernity (Bebbington 1999; Arce and Long 2000).

Historical Hmong Livelihoods

The Hmong are the only highland minority group found today in all six countries sharing the mainland Southeast Asian Massif, namely Vietnam, Thailand, China, Burma, Cambodia, and Laos. Of the many highland groups that emigrated south from China into the Vietnamese highlands, the Hmong are probably among the most recent migrants (Culas and Michaud 2004; Michaud 2006). Belonging to the Miao-Yao linguistic group, they tend to inhabit the highest landscapes over one thousand metres, with highly fragmented dwelling patterns. With fifty-four officially recognized ethnic groups in Vietnam, including the lowland Vietnamese (Kinh), the Hmong are one of fifty-three ethnic "minorities"*(các dân tộc thiểu số)* that together make up about 13.8 percent of the country's population of around 83 million (Socialist Republic of Vietnam 1999). Given their migration history, the Hmong are predominantly members of highland transnational ethnicities, and, in Vietnam, they have maintained or developed economic practices, political approaches, and cosmologies that reflect their distinctiveness from the majority Kinh (Michaud and Turner 2003). As will be seen throughout this chapter, Hmong values regarding livelihoods, forest commodities, traditional medicines, and different food sources highlight specific world views and perceptions that are not in line with those of the Kinh majority.

Lào Cai province, the contextual setting of this chapter, shares a border with Yunnan province, China (see Figure 5.1). At the time of the 1999 census, within Sa Pa district alone, where many of our interviewees live, seven ethnic

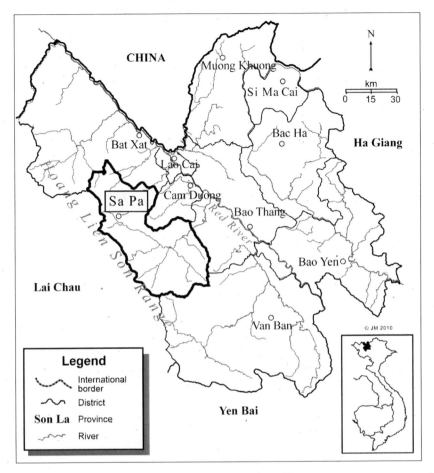

Figure 5.1 Sa Pa district in Lào Cai province, northern Vietnam.

minority groups were officially recorded as resident with over ten individuals – in descending population size, the Hmong, Yao, Tày, Giáy, Mường, Hoa, Thái; along with the majority Kinh. The Hmong totalled 19,827 individuals, or about half of the district's total population of 37,905 (Socialist Republic of Vietnam 1999).

Hmong livelihoods are entwined with recent political events and wars in this Chinese-Vietnamese border zone. The First Indochina war between the Việt Minh and Indochina's French colonial rulers catalyzed a series of reforms within the country's political economy (Hardy and Turner 2000). In the 1950s, the collectivization process – with all land owned and managed by the state – began in the northern region. Officially, only a small residential land plot and family garden could be privately operated, with all remaining lands managed by cooperatives or run as state enterprises (Corlin 2004). Yet, collectivization was never efficiently implemented in mountainous areas, partly because of the persistence of cultural prejudice, superstitions, and fear of highland minority cultures among Kinh lowlanders, which meant few Kinh were willing to settle permanently in the highlands to oversee collectives (ibid.). Numerous projects were thus abandoned, leaving highland minorities more or less free to engage in small-scale trade with local and regional markets (Michaud 1997).

During interviews, Hmong elders explained that they continued their traditional farming practices during this period, chiefly undertaking swidden agriculture, from which they derived various foods, including tubers, dry rice, and several varieties of maize. The opium poppy remained an important source of cash, along with the trade of precious woods such as *Fokienia hodginsii* (Fujian cypress), with lowland Kinh.[4] Hmong elders also recalled trading forest products and vegetables. For example, Mai Yia (14/6/06) explained that in the 1970s her parents travelled several days on horse or by foot to the Lào Cai city market to sell chillies and root crops; while Lia (3/6/06) in Lao Chải commune (shown in Figure 5.2) remembered her parents regularly selling wood to Kinh traders.

The socialist period was punctuated by border conflicts, including the 1979 Sino-Vietnamese War, which marked a period of intense poverty and hunger for ethnic minorities in the region.[5] An elderly Hmong woman, Cham (13/6/06), recalled that during the war many Hmong, herself included, collected various wild forest foods, such as roots, mushrooms, and insects. She explained, "sometimes, we did not have any rice to eat for three or four days, so we had to go to the forest to get wild tubers." Another elderly Hmong woman, Lam (10/7/06), said of the border war: "People were very hungry, and my family and I went hiding in the forest because there were a lot of soldiers with guns in Sa Pa. Everybody was very scared. We stayed in the forest a long time and ate only leaves, mice, and frogs." Indeed, forests played a key role in securing livelihoods during the socialist period – in times of war and peace – by providing protection and subsistence foods.

Recent Political Restructuring
Đổi Mới, the Vietnam state's economic renovation that instigated numerous reforms from the mid-1980s onward, as well as more recent government policies and programs, have altered how access to resources is mediated, impacting directly on Hmong livelihoods. Hmong interviewees generally felt that although state forest and land allocation policies from this period were often discriminatory, and development projects were sometimes ill-conceived, changing market conditions offered new livelihood opportunities, albeit not always that advantageous (see Tran Duc Vien et al. 2006).

New property arrangements and forest classification systems, as well as recent reforestation initiatives, have impacted Hmong households in terms

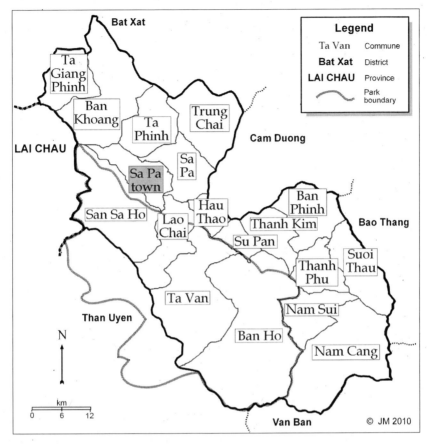

Figure 5.2   Sa Pa District and Hoàng Liên National Park.

of access to different livelihood opportunities. One idiosyncrasy that makes these options even more complex for those living in Sa Pa district is that about three-quarters of the district is located within Hoàng Liên National Park (see Figure 5.2). This park has been designated a protected forest since 2002, and all households within the park are prohibited from collecting plants and animals, lighting fires, or grazing animals within park boundaries (Hoàng Liên National Park director, personal communication, 26/5/06; Le Van Lanh 2004). Households living within the park do not own legal title to their land and cannot participate in reforestation compensation schemes such as the Five Million Hectares reforestation program.[6]

Hmong interviewees in Sa Pa district frequently voiced their disapproval of the bans on logging, opium cultivation, and forest-product gathering that have reduced their access to historically important sources of cash income, as well as to products used in their everyday lives. Members of the poorest

Hmong households, who cannot grow or purchase enough rice to see them through the year, continue to trade wood illegally with private Kinh traders. For instance, Lim (28/6/06), an elderly Hmong woman, reported that one of her sons occasionally cuts forest trees for wood, but only "very far away in the forest, close to Séo Mí Tỷ [a hamlet with difficult road access, located deep in the national park]." Lim worried that the authorities might arrest her son but noted that they have little alternative to make ends meet.

Rural development programs in these highlands have generally shifted away from agricultural extensification to intensification (with the introduction of hybridized rice and maize seeds), in addition to diversification initiatives. For example, in the late 1990s, Hmong households in the Sa Pa, Tả Phìn, and Trung Chải communes of Sa Pa district were given fruit seedlings (mostly plums) for additional income generation.[7] When the seedlings were initially distributed, competition was low and prices high. Yet, as the trees began to bear fruit a few years later, local markets were flooded with plums, prices fell, and many Hmong abandoned this commercial production. With no infrastructure for fruit processing, and strong competition not only among themselves but also from plum growers in Bắc Hà district to the east, local Hmong faced a limited market. It was not long before most of those in Sa Pa district who were involved decided that the low prices gained did not warrant the time and labour spent.[8]

Infrastructure development programs in the highlands have improved road access for numerous highland hamlets, connecting them more easily to other hamlets and larger towns (see Rambo 1995; Vu Thang Long 2003; World Bank n.d.). Moreover, the reopening of the Chinese border in 1988 after the Sino-Vietnamese War, with concomitant easier (legal) access for local residents to cross into China at several border posts, has facilitated cross-border trade (Schoenberger and Turner 2008). Access to markets has therefore grown. In Sa Pa town, a group of Hmong women have taken advantage of increased road and market access to participate in trading old and refashioned embroidered textiles to foreign tourists, or to Kinh traders managing ethnic craft shops in the town (Turner 2007). Similarly, selling forest products such as wild orchids, honey, and mushrooms helps some households earn sufficient cash to buy additional rice, maize, and other goods. Recent reforms have therefore created opportunities, while adding to the complexities of current-day Hmong livelihoods, detailed next.

Current Hmong Livelihoods

Despite new trading opportunities, terraced rice production remains at the core of the majority of Hmong livelihoods, constituting the staple food (if soil conditions and topography allow), complemented by upland fields for maize, cassava, and other crops; livestock; horticultural gardens; and forest products (see Vuong Xuan Tinh 1997a, 1997b). Focusing on such activities,

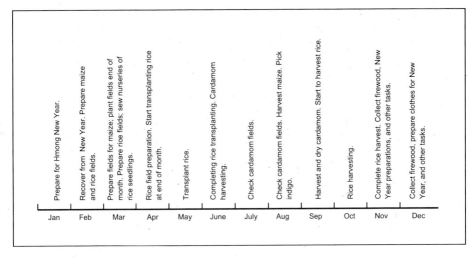

Figure 5.3 Typical Hmong household labour calendar in Sa Pa district.

a typical annual labour calendar for Hmong households in Sa Pa district is depicted in Figure 5.3.

Because of high elevations and cool temperatures in the district, only one rice crop is produced per year. From March to April, rice paddy fields are ploughed and fertilized with manure, forest leaves, and/or chemical fertilizers. Ploughing is considered the most physically demanding task and is usually completed by men. In the same time period, mothers and daughters then help sow the seeds in nursery plots as the first rains begin. Young rice seedlings are then left to grow until late April or early May, before being transplanted. The transplanted seedlings grow throughout the rainy season, from May until the end of September, when the harvest begins.

Villagers grow and experiment with different rice seeds to maximize yields and taste. Households use different proportions of seeds, but most either store them from the previous year, exchange seeds with family and friends, or, as is increasingly the case in recent years, buy high-yield varieties (HYVs) at subsidized prices from government distribution centres. Shu (15/7/06) described how villagers in Lao Chải commune grow "short" HYV government-subsidized rice, alongside "long" traditional varieties. Villagers choose the HYV seeds because of the higher productivity and shorter maturing time, but most also keep old local varieties because they prefer their taste. Individuals thus take advantage of new rice breeds selectively, balancing the ecological limits of the land they cultivate and their taste preferences.

Dry (non-terraced) rice has historically been an important crop in Sa Pa district, but our interviewees noted that it is less abundant nowadays. The age of different Hmong hamlets appears to play a role in the quantity of dry rice being planted, with Lu (6/6/06) from San Sả Hồ commune explaining that households in her hamlet continue to plant dry rice on mountain slopes because they have more land available than in older settlements. Lu explained how her family plants dry rice along with wet rice so that they can consume the dry rice from June to September, when wet rice supplies from the preceding year are diminishing. Highlighting the heterogeneity of local livelihood decision making, Lu added that families in Cát Cát and Lao Chải hamlets – older settlements – do not have suitable land left for dry rice because the population densities there are considered too high for this type of land use.

Maize is usually a subsidiary crop in the Hmong food system, though it forms a core part of the daily diet for those living in steeper and/or rockier terrain, such as Bản Khoang and Tả Giàng Phình communes. Maize is planted on steeper slopes, where wet rice cultivation is difficult or impossible. It is also a feed for livestock and acts as food insurance in case of other crop failures. As with rice, households usually cultivate several maize varieties with seeds kept from the year before. Seeds are also received from extended family, friends, or neighbours or sometimes new hybridized seeds are bought from the government.

In addition to rice and maize, Hmong may have swidden fields in which they grow tubers or other root vegetables, such as cassava. However, since swiddening is frowned on by government officials, especially within the national park, some Hmong households are abandoning these fields and turning to focus on cardamom production (detailed below), raising livestock such as cattle or buffalo, or collecting wild forest products to sell in the Sa Pa market. As in other parts of Asia, many Hmong now view rice paddy farming as a more secure guarantee of food production than dry rice and swiddens. Yet, at the same time, dry rice and maize are valuable food safety nets in case of other crop failures.

Small gardens provide other supplementary foods, including mustard greens, string beans, taro, pumpkins, cucumber, and ginger, all used for cooking, as well as hemp and indigo, used in the production of clothes. Women are usually in charge of these gardens and of the fabrication of clothes from hemp. A few households have a medicinal garden too, discussed in more detail below.

Finally, livestock is an important asset for Hmong households, a form of monetary insurance and a symbol of social status and wealth. Buffaloes are raised primarily for ploughing fields and for sacrifice at important funerals, while chickens, pigs, ducks, and goats are used for household consumption and rituals. Horses are occasionally owned for transportation and ploughing. When a household needs cash quickly, chickens and ducks can usually be sold to Kinh or Giáy shopkeepers in the commune, while chickens are also used to pay healers or shamans when a family member is sick.

Figure 5.4 A Hmong household's fuel wood collection in San Sả Hồ commune. Photo by authors

Hmong Use of Forest Products

Despite restrictions in the Hoàng Liên National Park, Hmong household members explained to us how they make trips to forests (both inside and outside the park) to gather firewood (Figure 5.4) and a broad range of forest products to complement their subsistence needs. Firewood collection is a year-round activity performed by all able-bodied Hmong household members, including young children. Women and children typically collect firewood from nearby forests around their homes, or in swidden fields, whereas men transport wood from forest areas further away. The collection of dead wood in the Hoàng Liên National Park is tolerated by park authorities, though householders can be charged a hefty fine if caught cutting live wood there. As a result, some families now plant small bamboo groves near their homes for fuel wood.

Construction materials are harvested (usually illegally) directly from the national park and from other forests nearby to build houses and other infrastructure, such as fences, irrigation canals, pigsties, and house furniture. In Hầu Thào commune, Shio (13/7/06) explained that district officials have told Hmong families that they are forbidden to cut trees, used in the past for constructing homes, yet she noted that regardless, many families continue to do so for house construction, as no alternatives have been suggested.

Like many other highland minority groups throughout the Southeast Asian Massif, the Hmong in Sa Pa district have an extensive knowledge of edible forest products. These are commonly harvested opportunistically when labour is not required in the rice fields. Some products follow seasonal patterns, whereas others are collected throughout the year. For instance, bamboo shoots are collected during the rainy season, from early March until June; while mushrooms are generally more abundant after a few days of heavy rainfall regardless of the season. Wild honeycombs and small animals are also harvested throughout the year, predominantly by men.

Nevertheless, Hmong interviewees commented that, since the 1980s, these wild foods have become increasingly difficult to access, especially because of the creation of the Hoàng Liên National Park, adding stress on poorer Hmong households that often rely on these goods to complement their diet or to provide cash income.[9] Many families said they collected these products less often than in the past because of the perceived low return on their labour. One elderly woman, Lam (10/7/06), explained, "now, you need to walk for a very long time [before you can find anything]. Before, the forest was much closer, we did not have to walk very far ... Now, very few people go to the forest because it is dangerous [as you might get caught]." Mai Yia (14/6/06) reported that in Tả Van commune, only a small number of hamlet members spend time collecting forest products, commenting that these harvesters are usually members of the poorest households, who need extra cash to supplement their rice production. In Sin Chải hamlet, Lu (6/6/06), a young mother, visited the forest regularly to harvest mushrooms and bamboo shoots, selling them to a Kinh vegetable trader in Sa Pa town market. Lu knew the trade was risky because of its illegal nature but, she explained, she needed the money to buy rice for her family during the "lean" months (June to September):

> One day I went to Sa Pa with my friend to sell bamboo shoots. Just before entering town, the police stopped us and got very angry when they saw what was in our baskets. I had a basket full of fresh bamboo shoots to sell and they took everything away! This has happened two times already to my friend. So now when we go to sell, we have to leave very early in the morning, when it is still dark and the government is asleep.

Members of a few Hmong households have also secured a small market niche for wild orchids. Demand for these has developed in Sa Pa town from lowland Kinh tourists who visit for brief weekend getaway trips (Michaud and Turner 2006). However, collecting orchids is considered highly laborious, and only a few young Hmong men engage in it. On Sundays, these men – usually from Sa Pả and Hầu Thào communes, both fairly close to Sa Pa town – carry orchid plants on long sticks into the town. Interestingly, these

Figure 5.5 A Hmong healer in her medicinal plant garden. *Photo by authors*

Hmong seldom sell the orchids directly to consumers, selling them instead to Kinh private traders.[10]

Given the constraints of resource scarcity, poor market prices, and park restrictions, many Hmong interviewees saw the trade in wild foods and plants as unprofitable and risky. Wild foods have played a more important role in the past, during times of famine and insecurity, but today this food trade is important only for the poorest households with insufficient access to rice paddy land, and for those with important emergency needs, such as hospital treatment costs.

Medicinal plants, however, play a different role. With both practical and symbolic functions for Hmong households, wild medicinal plants provide individuals with ready access to traditional health care products. Hmong medicinal practices include both shamanism and botanical medicine, depending on the source of the disease, and are distinct from traditional Vietnamese medicinal practices – often considered by Hmong interviewees to be barbarian and similar to Western medicine (see Cooper 1998; Corlin 2004). Some forest plants are collected by households for medicinal purposes;

others are collected by specialized local healers (see Figure 5.5). Hmong healer Zhia (15/7/06) uses medicinal plants to cure health troubles, including postpartum problems, headaches, injuries from work in the fields or forest, and being inhabited by evil spirits. In Hầu Thào commune, another healer, Lan (13/7/06; 4/4/09), reported using some two hundred plant species from the forest. In addition, in Lao Chải commune, Chau (5/6/06) explained how many Hmong fear Vietnamese medicine because they worry that Kinh doctors will amputate limbs without listening to the patient. She stressed that Hmong medicine is different because "we believe that a person's illness is caused by a *dab qus* [wild spirit] which needs to be chased away. One way is to give the offering of a chicken or a pig to the hungry spirit so that he will leave the soul of the person" (see Fadiman 1998). Herbal medicines thus sustain Hmong health cosmologies, which stand in contrast to the dominant Vietnamese health care paradigm.

Cardamom
For an increasing number of Hmong, black cardamom *(Amomum aromaticum)* represents an important source of cash income that requires relatively little labour compared with rice and maize and that does not compete with other seasonal labour requirements (see Figure 5.3). Cardamom grows wild in the Hoàng Liên National Park and surrounding forest but has recently been intensively cultivated under the shade of trees by ethnic minorities (chiefly Hmong and Yao) in Lào Cai province and other northwest provinces. Because of its high value-weight ratio and increasing market demand, along with government policies banning opium production and logging, many Hmong individuals have been planting and harvesting cardamom under the forest canopy more intensively since the 1990s. In Lao Chải and Tả Van communes in Sa Pa district, families reported producing, on average, between 70 to 100 kilograms in 2005, roughly valued at 5.6 million Vietnamese dong (US$350) per family.[11] Although some informants reported yields as low as 20 kilograms, other households in San Sả Hồ and Bản Khoang communes recounted sometimes harvesting and processing up to 150 kilograms per year, the highest yield noted being 200 kilograms for one household in San Sả Hồ commune.[12]

Cardamom plays a strategic role in helping households cover seasonal food deficits. In June and July, when some households begin to rely more on maize or dry rice, those with access to cardamom can use cash from advance credit sales to buy extra commodities.[13] In Sin Chải hamlet, Moua (28/5/06) explained how she uses profits from cardamom to buy extra rice, as well as various items including vegetables, meat, salt, cooking fat, monosodium glutamate, and occasionally small treats for her children. Income from cardamom is also sometimes used to purchase other household items such as clothing, blankets, cooking pots, light bulbs, and oil. In the same hamlet, another informant, Cho (7/6/6), uses his proceeds to buy building materials, fertilizer, and HYV rice seeds. His female cousin Lu (6/6/06) noted:

> When the cardamom comes, we bring a lot of it to give back to the Kinh people because we get food from them before the cardamom is ready. If you have some money left, people use it for buying animals like pigs and chicken ... Some also use that money to make their houses stronger because we're not allowed to cut trees in the forest anymore. Many use it to buy some clothes for the New Year for children. If you are wealthy, some are able to buy things like televisions and radios.

Cardamom therefore allows Hmong to gain income at opportune periods of their seasonal food calendars. Additional returns are also sometimes used for ritual and ceremonial purchases, which help strengthen kin as well as community relations; this income can also be used to pay a bride price and to buy new clothes for the Hmong New Year.[14]

Comparing Access, Assets, and Opportunities
Comparing two Hmong households allows us to further grasp the heterogeneity of these livelihood portfolios, while delving into their complexity. Here we compare the household livelihood portfolios for Hoa (4/6/06) and Tao (16/6/06), interviewed in Lao Chải and Bản Khoang communes respectively. Figures 5.6 and 5.7 portray these families' different sources of income, in both cash and in kind.[15] Here, we draw on Ellis' (1998, 4) definition of income as

> the cash earnings of the household plus the payment in kind of the household that can be valued in market prices. The cash earnings refer to items like crop or livestock sales, wages, rents and remittances. The in-kind component of household income refers to consumption of on-farm produce, payments in kind (for example, in food), and transfers or exchanges of consumption items that occur between households in rural communities.

In-kind, non-cash income for these households comes from wet and dry rice, maize, garden vegetables, food, feed, and medicine from the forest, as well as from swidden crops. Cash income can include money earned by selling livestock, forest products (including cardamom), and handicrafts; wage labour (such as on construction sites in Sa Pa town); and guiding tourist treks. The focus here is on considering the emic, or self-defined values, of different components. The different percentages in the pie charts in Figures 5.6 and 5.7 therefore indicate the importance of each activity to household survival, in the views of the interviewees after in-depth discussions. Hence, wet rice is given high significance because of the centrality of this crop to

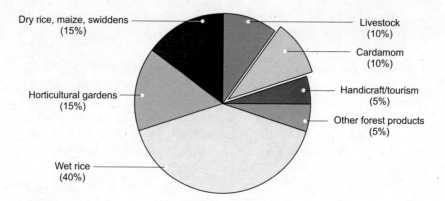

Figure 5.6 Livelihood portfolio for Hoa's household, Lào Chải commune.

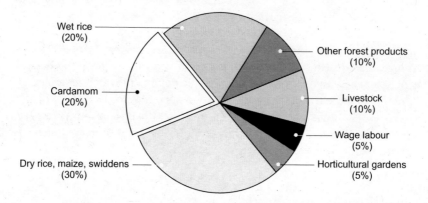

Figure 5.7 Livelihood portfolio for Tao's household, Bản Khoang commune.

Hmong food regimes, even though the market price for wet rice might be much lower than cash income received from cardamom sales.

Figure 5.6 shows the livelihood portfolio for Hoa's household. In 2006, Hoa and her husband had five children and lived in Lào Chải commune, one of the first Hmong settlements established in the district (Hoa 4/6/06). The population density in this commune is now higher than that of others nearby, resulting in greater pressure on nearby ecological resources. However, Lao Chải is also thought to have fertile land and contains many rice paddy fields. At the same time, it is located far from the forest in comparison to many other communes in Sa Pa district, and Hoa's husband has to walk a full day to reach their two cardamom fields. In 2005, he produced seventy kilograms of cardamom, or about 10 percent of the total household income. Hoa's household is fortunate to have enough rice for the year, and estimated their paddy land to contribute approximately 40 percent to the total household income. In contrast, dry rice, maize, and swidden provide only 15 percent of the family's income. Indeed, Hoa's household stopped growing dry rice in 2002 when her husband started to buy HYV wet rice and maize seeds from the government. Hoa's household also gains some 10 percent of its income from two buffaloes, chickens, and ducks; and 15 percent of income from a garden providing plentiful vegetables for their daily meals.

In terms of market accessibility, Lao Chải is relatively well connected to Sa Pa town via a paved road. Between June and September, when rice fields require less labour, Hoa walks to Sa Pa market twice a week to sell handicrafts. Her income from this trade varies a great deal, and she regards this revenue source as a "lucky additional extra," rather than as secure and regular. Consequently, wet rice production accounts for the largest proportion of livelihood income, being the staple dietary food for this family year-round, whereas incomes derived from cardamom and tourist handicrafts are considered more discretionary.

In comparison, Figure 5.7 illustrates the livelihood portfolio for Tao's household in Bản Khoang commune. As noted earlier, variations in ecological settings and access to economic opportunities account for some of the differences in the composition of Hmong livelihood portfolios. The steep topography and rocky terrain in Bản Khoang commune makes rice paddy farming difficult, and fewer people have settled in this valley (Tao 16/6/06). Hmong in Bản Khoang cultivate mostly dry rice and maize for subsistence foods, occasionally supplemented by swidden crops such as cassava and potatoes. In contrast with Hoa's case, wet rice accounts for only 20 percent of Tao's income. Instead, maize, dry rice, and other swidden crops occupy some 30 percent. Tao explained that cardamom provides his household with the vast majority of its cash earnings. In 2005, Tao collected two hundred kilograms of dry cardamom from his three fields – far more than Hoa's family in Lao Chải commune – accounting for 20 percent of his family's income. In addition, living near the forest, Tao walks for only one or two hours before reaching his three cardamom fields, scattered in the forest.

In contrast to Hoa, Tao's wife does not make handicrafts. With a poorly paved road prone to slippages linking the commune to Sa Pa town, a motorised trip can take up to two or three hours. Trips are rare (once a month at most), and thus textile trading is difficult. Instead, Tao occasionally does waged construction work for a Kinh man in Sa Pa, staying in town for a few days as necessary.

Comparing the livelihood portfolios for Hoa's and Tao's households highlights the different levels of access, assets, and opportunities these households have that, in turn, shape the heterogeneous livelihood activities developed by each. For example, differences in natural capital concerning terrain and soil quality influence livelihood decisions. Tao, in Bản Khoang, has greater access to forest and cardamom fields; yet at the same time, because of the mountainous terrain, his family relies more on dry rice, maize, and swidden. On the other hand, Tao's household has more difficulty gaining physical access to the market, whereas Hoa is able to undertake new marketing opportunities to supplement her family's livelihood portfolio.

Conclusion: Local Agency and Livelihood Diversification

A diversification of livelihood strategies is often at the core of attempts to create sustainable livelihood opportunities (Moser 1998; Eakin, Tucker, and Castellanos 2006). Diversification can increase livelihood security by mitigating risks and allowing individuals or households to withstand exogenous and endogenous shocks and stresses, while enhancing overall resilience. This process might be achieved by undertaking new income opportunities, by planting new crops in an effort to enhance food security, or by attempting to create or alter a mixture of agricultural, livestock, and off-farm activities (Chambers and Conway 1992; Rigg 2006). Global market integration also results in a multitude of new and often unparalleled challenges for rural families, in turn resulting in further diversification (Eakin, Tucker, and Castellanos 2006). Indeed, this has been brought to our attention by authors such as Bouahom Bounthong, Linkhan Douangsavanh, and Rigg (2004, 615), who contend that the *fluidity* of rural livelihoods has, for the most part, been ignored to date and that "the extent to which livelihoods are being constantly reworked, particularly when the wider economic context is fluid, is often underplayed."

Hmong livelihoods in Sa Pa district are clearly flexible and fluid, over both temporal and spatial scales. Under socialism, rather than being tightly organized around agricultural collectivization schemes, the highland livelihoods of Hmong households tended to remain reliant on kinship structures, being largely subsistence-oriented and based on swiddening. Logging and opium production provided households with a limited cash income, while forest products were relied on as emergency foods in times of famine and war. Since Đổi Mới, new economic policies and regulations have reformed customary land use and access to forest resources. These government interventions – such as the creation of a national park, and laws banning logging and opium production – have directly affected Hmong access to resources, land use rights, and market integration.

Contemporary Hmong livelihoods, however, indicate several diversification strategies. Households have intensified certain crops, such as wet rice and maize, utilizing government subsidized HYV seeds, while also diversifying their cash incomes via trade in cardamom and, to lesser extents, handicrafts and tourism. Differential access to local markets, distances to forests, and local climate and topography are also important, influencing their assessments of a range of viable options, resulting in a diversity of livelihood strategies.

Yet, we must not assume that Hmong households are becoming completely integrated into the market. Our findings suggest that Hmong willingness to participate in the market is discriminating – as they carefully choose economic opportunities that best fit their needs and belief systems. For instance, unlike the Yao, the Hmong have been reluctant to sell traditional herbal medicines to tourists in Sa Pa town.[16] One Hmong healer, Lan (13/7/06), explained:

> We cannot bring the medicine and sell it to just anybody in the market because the spirits will be angry and this is very bad for the sick person. The spirits are very important for making people feel better. When somebody is sick, you cannot just go buy medicine ... you need to go see somebody to help you. For one problem, you have to take many different plants.

Another Hmong female elder, Lam (10/7/06), elucidated:

> We never sell our herbal medicine to the Vietnamese [Kinh]. If some people do, they sell only the dried medicine and a special tree bark and cut it into very small pieces. If not, the Vietnamese people will go to the forest and harvest it themselves.

Hmong informants consistently reiterated that fresh herbal medicine should only ever be given or exchanged between friends, family, or healers, and should *never* be sold to traders. Fresh medicinal plants and botanical knowledge hold intrinsic spiritual value in Hmong health cosmologies. Despite increasing market demand for these goods, Hmong are keeping their herbal medicine knowledge outside the formal market system. This example highlights how Hmong in Sa Pa district are currently diversifying their livelihood portfolios selectively. Indeed, "flexibility around a solid, culturally embedded core appears to be an important characteristic feature of Hmong livelihoods in Sa Pa district" (Turner and Michaud 2008, 182).

These choices are made even more evident by the Hmong view, in contrast to their beliefs about traditional medicine, that cardamom is a cash crop. As such, they are more than willing to sell most of what they harvest to Kinh and Giáy intermediaries, keeping only a small portion for their own needs. At the same time, though, not all Hmong households are rushing into this economic activity and many are cautious of the difficulties surrounding its cultivation and trade, such as climatic variations, disputes with neighbours over field rights and crops, and the illegal nature of much of the local cultivation (see Tugault-Lafleur and Turner 2009). Hence, we argue that Hmong are both embracing *and* resisting new livelihood prospects offered by the growing market integration of the highlands in ways they deem appropriate. Cultural values and meanings central to Hmong understandings of different forest products, as well as relationships between ethnic groups (as seen, for example, in the Hmong refusal to sell certain medicinal plants to Kinh), combine to influence decision-making processes. Hmong forms of market integration are therefore selective, reflecting the choices, conditions, and constraints of the local cultural, political, and economic environments.

Consequently, the case of the Hmong in Sa Pa district indicates the importance when employing a livelihoods approach of not becoming trapped into utilizing an equation through which positive outcomes for those involved are measured only in terms of economic indicators, often poorly defined, such as poverty and wealth. Using an actor-oriented approach provides space for non-material aspects of livelihoods, including actions that are strongly influenced by local cultural and social frameworks, to be incorporated into interpretations of livelihood decision making, while remaining cognizant of the importance of the broader political and economic context. Such an approach places local people at the centre of attention, allowing for better understandings of everyday decision making and activities. In so doing, we begin to gain a more nuanced appreciation of how Hmong adapt to, negotiate, and resist local and larger-scale political and economic forces.

Notes

1 Ethnonyms used in this text follow the most widely accepted international usage, based on ethnolinguistic divisions. In Vietnam however, the Hmong are officially named "H'mông" or "Hmông," while the Yao are called the "Dao" (pronounced Zao) (see Condominas 1978; Dang Nguyen Van, Chu Thai Son, and Luu Hung 2000).

2 We appreciate that livelihood strategies diverge between individuals and households and do not mean to cover all variations here. Rather, we explore a range of strategies and diversification processes. To do so, we completed conversational interviews with Hmong, Yao (Dao), Giáy, and Kinh farmers and small-scale traders in Sa Pa district; semi-structured interviews with People's Committee representatives both in Sa Pa district and in the provincial capital, Lào Cai city; and oral histories with numerous long-term residents in Sa Pa district, including male and female Hmong and Kinh. All names are pseudonyms. The interviews conducted with Hmong households were conducted in Hmong with the help of local interpreters; interviews with lowland Kinh were conducted in Vietnamese with or without interpreters.

3 Sometimes referred to as the "asset pentagon," the five capitals – human, physical, natural, financial, and social – shape the foundation of livelihood analyses (Carney 1998; Bebbington 1999). Natural capital, or environmental resources, constitute non-renewable resources such as minerals and soils as well as renewable resources such as nutrient cycling and ecosystem services (Bury 2004). Physical capital refers to human-produced infrastructure, including buildings, transportation, and electrical services. Financial capital includes accessible supplies of cash, such as earned income, pensions, remittances, and transfers from the state. Human capital concerns capabilities such as skills, education, ability to labour, and health (Ellis 1998). Social capital refers to the linkages, trust, and social networks utilized by individuals or groups to "get by" or "get ahead" (Portes 1998; Woolcock and Narayan 2000; Turner and Nguyen An Phong 2005). For critiques of the "asset pentagon" see Conway et al. (2002) and Toner (2003).

4 *Fokienia hodginsii* is a valuable timber used in construction, furniture making, and especially coffin construction in Vietnam, also containing essential oils (Tordoff et al. 1999).

5   In 1979, Chinese forces invaded Vietnam's northern frontier to protest Vietnam's incursions into Cambodia and treatment of ethnic Chinese in Vietnam. As people fled the invasion, many livelihoods were disrupted by the widespread damage to infrastructure, including bridges, roads, electricity, schools, and hospitals (Donnell 1980). In 1988, the Vietnamese state officially reopened the border, followed shortly after by the normalization of Sino-Vietnamese relations in 1991.
6   The ambitious Five Million Hectares reforestation program (also known as Program 661), launched in its first phase in 1998 by the forestry department, aimed at reforesting Vietnam's so-called "barren lands," covering an estimated area of 12 or 13 million hectares (Poffenberger and Nguyen Huy Phon 1998). The vast majority of these reforestation activities have taken place in the north and central highlands, the regions with higher numbers of ethnic minorities (McElwee 2001; Neef 2001; Sowerwine 2004b).
7   Similar projects occurred in other upland northern provinces, including in Bắc Kạn (Alther et al. 2002).
8   A parallel can be made here with the notable collapse in the worldwide price of coffee from 2000 following a massive surge in the numbers of lowland Vietnamese growing coffee in the central highlands, strongly promoted by the state and international development organizations. A number of these farmers are now opting to grow other crops (Ha Dang Thanh and Shively 2007).
9   "Poor people" were defined by Hmong interviewees as those who did not have enough rice from wet rice harvests to meet household consumption needs between annual harvests.
10 In 2006, we counted approximately twenty orchid traders (all Kinh) based in Sa Pa town. These orchid traders also sometimes deal with traders based in larger lowland cities, including Hải Phòng, Hà Nội, and Hồ Chí Minh City.
11 Cardamom market prices are for the dried fruit.
12 Sa Pa district's unpredictable weather makes cardamom yields fluctuate widely. Cardamom usually matures at the end of the rainy season and may be damaged by intense rain and cold. In Tả Van commune, cultivator Kao (23/6/06) reported losing almost half of his production in 2005 because of incessant cold, drizzling rain that destroyed most of the plants. Strong storms can also play havoc with harvest yields.
13 From June to August, Hmong will often promise part of their production to local store owners, who extend them credit (see Tugault-Lafleur and Turner 2009).
14 It is a Hmong custom to pay a bridal price, with the husband-to-be traditionally required to pay a certain amount of cash or goods (traditionally silver, nowadays more often cash) to the family of the bride (Culas and Michaud 2004).
15 Numerous methodological challenges are associated with measuring the total household income in the Hmong context. First, it is difficult to use market values for products, as they often do not reflect Hmong perceptions. Second, activities often overlap: trips to swidden fields often include collecting fuel wood or herbal medicines. Accordingly, these percentages are rough estimates of mean income share by activity.
16 For a more detailed description of the commercialization of medicinal plants among the Yao, see Sowerwine (1999, 2004a).

References

Alther, C., J.C. Castella, P. Novosad, E. Rousseau, and Tran Trong Hieu. 2002. Impact of accessibility on the range of livelihood options available to farm households in mountainous areas of northern Vietnam. In *Đổi Mới in the Mountains, Land Use Changes and Farmers' Livelihood Strategies in Bac Kan Province, Vietnam,* ed. J.C. Castella and Dang Dinh Quang, 121-46. Hanoi: Agricultural Publishing House.

Arce, A., and N. Long. 2000. Reconfiguring modernity and development from an anthropological perspective. In *Anthropology, Development and Modernities: Exploring Discourses, Counter Tendencies and Violence,* ed. A. Arce and N. Long, 1-31. London: Routledge.

Bebbington, A. 1999. Capitals and capabilities: A framework for analyzing peasant viability, rural livelihoods and poverty. *World Development* 27(12): 2021-44.

–. 2000. Reencountering Development: Livelihood transitions and place transformations in the Andes. *Annals of the Association of American Geographers* 90(3): 495-520.

Bouahom Bounthong, Linkhan Douangsavanh, and J. Rigg. 2004. Building sustainable livelihoods in Laos: Untangling farm from non-farm, progress from distress. *Geoforum* 35(5): 607-19.

Bury, B. 2004. Livelihoods in transition: Transnational gold mining operations and local change in Cajamarca, Peru. *Geographical Journal* 170(1): 78-91.

Carney, D. 1998. *Sustainable Rural Livelihoods: What Contributions Can We Make?* London: UK Department for International Development.

Chambers, R., and G. Conway. 1992. *Sustainable Rural Livelihoods: Practical Concepts for the 21st Century.* Brighton: Institute of Development Studies.

Cooper, R.G. (1998). *The Hmong.* Thailand: Artasia Press.

Condominas, G. 1978. L'Asie du sud-est. In *Ethnologie Régionale 2*, ed. J. Poirier, 283-374. Paris: Gallimard, Encyclopédie de la Pléiade.

Conway, T., C. Moser, A. Norton, and J. Farrington. 2002. Rights and livelihoods approaches: Exploring policy dimensions. *Natural Resources Perspectives* 78: 1-6.

Corlin, C. 2004. Hmong and the land question in Vietnam: National policy and local concepts of the environment. In *Hmong/Miao in Asia*, ed. N. Tapp, J. Michaud, C. Culas, and G.Y. Lee, 295-320. Chiang Mai: Silkworm Books.

Culas, C., and J. Michaud. 2004. A contribution to the study of the Hmong *(Miao)* migrations and history. In *Hmong/Miao in Asia*, ed. N. Tapp, J. Michaud, C. Culas, and G.Y. Lee, 71-96. Chiang Mai: Silkworm Books.

Dang Nguyen Van, Chu Thai Son, and Luu Hung 2000. *Ethnic Minorities in Vietnam.* Hanoi: The Gioi Publishers.

de Haan, L., and A. Zoomers. 2005. Exploring the frontier of livelihood research. *Development and Change* 36(1): 27-47.

DiGregorio, M., Pham Thi Quynh Phong, and M. Yasui. 1996. *The Growth and Impact of Tourism in Sa Pa.* Honolulu: Center for Natural Resources and Environmental Studies, East-West Center.

Donnell, J.C. 1980. Vietnam 1979: Year of calamity. *Asian Survey* 20(1): 19-32.

Eakin, H., C. Tucker, and E. Castellanos. 2006. Responding to the coffee crisis: A pilot study of farmers' adaptations in Mexico, Guatemala and Honduras. *Geographical Journal* 172(2): 156-71.

Ellis, F. 1998. Household strategies and rural livelihood diversification. *Journal of Development Studies* 35(1): 1-38.

—. 2000. *Rural Livelihoods and Diversity in Developing Countries.* Oxford: Oxford University Press.

Fadiman, A. 1998. *The Spirit Catches You and You Fall Down: A Hmong Child, Her American Doctors and the Collision between Two Cultures.* New York: Farrar, Straus and Giroux.

Ha Dang Thanh, and G. Shively. 2007. Coffee boom, coffee bust and smallholder response in Vietnam's Central Highlands. *Review of Development Economics* 12(2): 312-26.

Hapke, H., and D. Ayyankeril. 2004. Gender, the work-life course and livelihood strategies in a south Indian fish market. *Gender, Place and Culture* 11(2): 229-56.

Hardy, A., and S. Turner. 2000. Editorial: Migration, markets and social change in the highlands of Vietnam. *Asia Pacific Viewpoint* 41(1): 1-6.

Kanji, N., J. MacGregor, and C. Tacoli. 2005. *Understanding Market-Based Livelihoods in a Globalising World: Combining Approaches and Methods.* London: International Institute for Environment and Development.

Le Van Lanh. 2004. *Hoang Lien National Park.* Hanoi: Sa Pa Tourism and Information Center, National Culture Publishing House.

Long, N. 2001. *Development Sociology: Actor Perspectives.* London: Routledge.

McElwee, P. 2001. Parks or People: Exploring Alternative Explanations for Protected Areas Development in Vietnam. Paper presented at the Conservation and Sustainable Development Conference – Comparative Perspectives, New Haven, CT, August 2001.

Michaud, J. 1997. Economic transformations in a Hmong village of Thailand. *Human Organisation* 56(2): 222-32.

—. 2006. *People of the Southeast Asian Massif: Historical Dictionary.* Lanham, MD: Scarecrow Press.

Michaud, J., and S. Turner. 2000. The Sa Pa marketplace, Lào Cai province, Vietnam. *Asia Pacific Viewpoint* 41(1): 84-99.
–. 2003. Tribulations d'un marché de montagne du nord-Vietnam [Tribulations of a mountain market in Northern Vietnam]. *Études Rurales* 165-66: 53-80.
–. 2006. Contending visions of Sa Pa, a hill-station in Viet Nam. *Annals of Tourism Research* 33(3): 785-808.
Moser, C.O.N. 1998. The asset vulnerability framework: Reassessing urban poverty reduction strategies. *World Development* 26(1): 1-19.
Neef, A. 2001. Sustainable agriculture in the northern uplands: Attitudes, constraints and priorities of ethnic minorities. In *Living with Environmental Change: Social Vulnerability, Adaptation and Resilience in Vietnam*, ed. W.N. Adger, P.M. Kelly, and N.H. Ninh, 109-21. London and New York: Routledge.
Poffenberger, M., and Nguyen Huy Phon. 1998. National forest sector. In *Stewards of Vietnam's Upland Forests*, ed. M. Poffenberger, 1-17. Berkeley: Asia Forest Network Center for Southeast Asia Studies, University of California Berkeley.
Portes, A. 1998. Social capital: Its origins and applications in modern sociology. *Annual Review of Sociology* 24: 1-24.
Rambo, T. 1995. Perspectives on defining highland development challenges in Vietnam: New frontier or cul-de-sac? In *The Challenges of Highland Development in Vietnam*, ed. R. Rambo, R.R. Reed, Le Trong Cuc, and D. Gregorio, 21-30. Honolulu: East-West Center.
Rigg, J. 2006. Land, farming, livelihoods, and poverty: Rethinking the links in the rural south. *World Development* 34(1): 180-202.
Schoenberger, L., and S. Turner. 2008. Negotiating remote borderland access: Small-scale trade on the Vietnam-China border. *Development and Change* 39(4): 665-93.
Scott, J.C. 2009. *The Art of Not Being Governed: An Anarchist History of Upland Southeast Asia*. New Haven, CT: Yale University Press.
Socialist Republic of Vietnam. 1999. *Census of Vietnam*. General Statistic Office, Hanoi.
Sowerwine, J.C. 1999. New land rights and women's access to medicinal plants in northern Vietnam. In *Women's Rights to House and Land: China, Laos and Vietnam*, ed. I. Tinker and G. Summerfield, 131-45. Boulder, CO: Lynne Rienner.
–. 2004a. The Political Ecology of Yao (Dzao) Landscape Transformations: Territory, Gender and Livelihood Politics in Highland Vietnam. PhD diss., University of California, Berkeley.
–. 2004b. Territorialisation and the politics of highland landscapes in Vietnam: Negotiating property relations in policy, meaning and practice. *Conservation and Society* 2(1): 97-135.
Tapp, N., J. Michaud, C. Culas, and G.Y. Lee, eds. 2004. *Hmong/Miao in Asia*. Chiang Mai: Silkworm Books.
Toner, A. 2003. Exploring sustainable livelihoods approaches (SLAs) in relation to two interventions in Tanzania. *Journal of International Development* 15(6): 771-81.
Tordoff, A., S. Swann, M. Grindley, and H. Siurua. 1999. *Hoang Lien Natural Reserve: Biodiversity and Conservation Evaluation 1997/8*. London: Society for Environment and Exploration.
Tran Duc Vien, S.J. Leisz, Nguyen Thanh Lam, and A.T. Rambo. 2006. Using traditional swidden agriculture to enhance rural livelihoods in Vietnam's uplands. *Mountain Research and Development* 26(3), 192-96.
Tugault-Lafleur, C., and S. Turner. 2009. The price of spice: Ethnic minority livelihoods and cardamom commodity chains in upland northern Vietnam. *Singapore Journal of Tropical Geography* 30(3): 202-34.
Turner, S. 2007. Trading old textiles: The selective diversification of highland livelihoods in northern Vietnam. *Human Organization* 66(4): 389-404.
Turner, S., and J. Michaud. 2008. Imaginative and adaptive economic strategies for Hmong livelihoods in Lào Cai province, northern Vietnam. *Journal of Vietnamese Studies* 3(3): 158-90.
Turner, S., and Nguyen An Phong. 2005. Young entrepreneurs, social capital and *Doi Moi* in Hanoi, Vietnam. *Urban Studies* 42(10): 1693-1710.

van de Walle, D., and D. Gunewardena. 2001. Sources of ethnic inequality in Vietnam. *Journal of Development Economics* 65: 177-207.

Vu Thang Long. 2003. Transport Development to Improve People's Life, Vietnam. *Economic News* 21: 18.

Vuong Xuan Tinh. 1997a. *Food System of the Hmong People in Ha Giang Province, Vietnam*. Paper presented at the Food Culture Conference in Southeast Asia, Seoul.

–. 1997b. *Looking for Food: The Difficult Journey of the Hmong in Vietnam*. Paper presented at the Anthropological Perspective on Food Security conference, Madison, Wisconsin.

Woolcock, M., and D. Narayan. 2000. Social capital: Implications for development theory, research, and policy. *World Bank Research Observer* 15(2): 225-49.

World Bank. n.d. Vietnam: Support to Ethnic Minority Communities in Remote and Mountainous Areas – Program 135, Phase 2 Support Operation. http://web.worldbank.org Accessed 19/8/08.

6
Hani Agency and Ways of Seeing Environmental Change on the China-Vietnam Border

John McKinnon

In the southeast of Yunnan province, in southwest China, supported by a participatory research project, members of two ethnic minority Hani villages have mobilized themselves to regain control over ritual land use practices. In these villages, local Hani farmers' land uses were traditionally in accordance with local beliefs and rationalities; yet these practices were then subordinated and discredited under socialism. Now, in a so-called post-socialist era, farmers' primary interests have been captured by the market. This chapter illustrates how a group of highlanders, using their ethnically specific agency, have handled the pressures placed on their livelihoods by different regimes and outside agents and have made their own developmental decisions, for better or, one can argue, for worse.

This chapter stems from concerns that first came to my attention in the highlands of northern Thailand. There, in 1975, I was appointed as an adviser to the then-troubled Tribal Research Centre in Chiang Mai, a post I held until 1979. In my work during that period I defended shifting cultivation and attacked the "forest fetish" at a time when planting forests was being promoted as the best, if not the only, rational way to protect the national watershed (McKinnon 1977, 1). In subsequent years, I returned to Chiang Mai as a researcher working for the French Institut de Recherche pour le Développement (1986-88) and, later, as an academic. It was my belief then, as it is now, that we must bring bearers of indigenous and scientific knowledge together (McKinnon 1989) in an appropriate, participatory, and interactive way (McKinnon 2003, 2005).

Over the thirty years since then, much has changed. First, the value of indigenous knowledge has been increasingly recognized. Second, there has been a rise of highlander, community-based organizations in Asia, and a growth of participatory techniques to engage local peoples in both research and development planning. The importance of recognizing the dynamic nature of contemporary livelihoods and the need to focus on the specifics of each situation rather than drawing general conclusions has been increasingly highlighted. Placing indigenous cultural discourses centre stage can promote dignity as much as it makes available the content of indigenous knowledge; it can also focus attention on political aspects that further the ability of environmental activists to provide support. Such approaches present us with a complex view of a world about which our understandings were once monopolized by outside colonial authorities, missionaries, bureaucrats, development specialists, and indeed, academics.

A specific event in northern Thailand propelled the project on which this chapter focuses. The event in Thailand, and later in China, led me to want to bring together bearers of indigenous and scientific knowledge in a participatory, interactive manner. The event in question occurred when I was engaged with the Highland Inter Mountain Peoples Education and Culture in Thailand Association. A Karen *lue pakha,* namely a Karen ethnic minority ceremony to propitiate and manipulate the spirits that frequent the area around the *taa de do* (forest shrine), provided me with an opportunity to experiment with a short exercise using participatory techniques of engagement, alongside the use of maps and photographs (McKinnon 2003, 64-84). The aim was to better understand how change occurs for ethnic minorities, and it became clear that people who were considered to live in relative isolation were remarkably willing to adapt new ways and novel forms and images in order to express themselves. Using similar methodologies in the China context, I then wanted to focus on how changes imposed by a socialist state might impact an indigenous society and its members' livelihoods. I wished to better understand: How do people in such a context cope with urbanization, marketization, and globalization? And how do people retain (or modify) their identity? The Karen study in Thailand suggested that references to the past provided the "moral stuff" that villagers could use to resist management by outsiders, while taking onboard contemporary signs, symbols, and techniques to enhance both their credibility and confidence to run their own affairs. Would the same be found in China?

As part of the search for a suitable field site, I presented a paper at the Second International Hani Akha conference held in Chiang Mai and Chiang Rai, Thailand in May 1996, subtitled "A project in search of a partner." It was there that I met Mr. Li Qibo, the Hani director of the Hani-Lisu Honghe Institute for Minority Studies, Yunnan province, China, who offered to host a joint field exercise. His work on Hani terraced fields and their environmental constraints was presented at the same conference (Li Qibo 1996), and his critical treatment of the way "traditional [Hani] production patterns have been broken ... and replaced by other forms" (Li Qibo 1996, 3) echoed the Karen experience that I had witnessed in Thailand.

Li Qibo took a critical stance to Hani contemporary resource management, which he believed ignored the old practices he had learned as a young man and which he credited to the wisdom of his ancestors. Working with data collected by his research institute, he reported "big changes," including a rapid increase of population, the felling of forest, increased erosion, and increasing water shortages, which to him suggested that traditional knowledge and skills relating to conservation and tenure arrangements were being undermined (see also Yin Shaoting 2001; Corlin 2004). Li Qibo argued that, before the 1949 Communist victory (or "Liberation") and the introduction of formal collective ownership of forest and land, resource protection measures were based on indigenous forms of customary tenure. These forms were

> clearly determined by various local and clan rules and agreements. Within the scope of the power of a specific village, some forests and land were commonly owned by the entire village; some were mutually owned by clans; and some were owned by individual families. Except for individually owned portions, land and forest use was decided by village and clan rules [and those who wanted usufruct rights] had to go through specific procedures to [gain access]. (Li Qibo 1996, 10)

Over the last several decades, he continued,

> in keeping with changing times, the Hani area traditional consciousness has faded, [and] old production arrangements have been replaced by other forms [of management]. Today, traditional methods only have a definite place within the scope of religious beliefs. (Li Qibo 1996, 10)

In discussions, Li Qibo added that local Hani villagers still consciously protected the village "sacred forest." Yet, these special groves now represented only a remnant of the protective up-slope forest. Hani religious beliefs had become detached from a wider concern for the environment and no longer played a significant functional role in overall livelihood decisions, natural resource assessment, management, and individual farming practices. Li Qibo wanted to see what an independent group of researchers might find out – whether they would confirm his findings or provide a quite different interpretation.

The Study

The resultant research exercise that took place in two adjacent Hani villages in Yunnan during 1999 and 2000 was undertaken using participatory learning and action (PLA) tools and methods, supplemented with participatory geographic information systems (GIS) (which at the time we called Mobile Interactive GIS, or MIGIS). Each village appointed a team of men and women to represent them that included both young and older people. These Hani research teams not only provided information, but continued to own the information that was being gathered and analyzed through a range of participatory techniques.[1] The first objective of our joint study was to establish a symmetrical relationship between overseas researchers, researchers in China, and local villagers.[2] Did we achieve such a partnership? While most local Hani villagers responded to us outsiders (both overseas and Chinese researchers) in what appeared to be an open and familiar way, drawing us into their confidence and sharing their concerns; we must, of course, question how much of this was merely "public transcript," and how much was the unavoidable "hidden transcript"? (Scott 1990). Many must have remained guarded and out of sight, and indeed, an independent fourteen-day evaluation of our work carried out in 2005 (Zheng 2005) indicated that not everybody had understood what we were doing. Nevertheless, it was extremely rewarding for all involved when, presented with the findings, Hani villagers said, "This is what we made, it is our product" (ibid., 61).

The information and interpretations of livelihood change analyzed here are taken either directly from information Hani farmers volunteered in participatory learning and action (PLA) exercises, interviews, and casual conversations, or from data that the outside research team collected with local Hani farmer assistance.

Study Villages

The study villages of Shangshapu and Xiashapu are located in the Badong sub-catchment at the headwaters of the Amo Jiang River in Yunnan, which in Vietnam becomes the Sông Đà (Black River). These two Hani villages lie within the administrative area of Sanmeng township, some eighteen kilometres from Daxing, the administrative centre of Lüchun County, Honghe Prefecture, in the steep hill country typical of the Ailao and Wuliang mountains. To the southeast lie some of the most inaccessible wet highlands in the world. To the southeast, annual precipitation on the peaks exceeds four thousand millimetres. The two villages lie within a relatively sheltered area where annual monsoon precipitation drops to just over two thousand millimetres. In an average year, the rain is enough to germinate and maintain early growth of a single crop of hill rice and maize. Yet, if there is a summer drought followed by a poor rainy season, annual precipitation may drop to fifteen hundred millimetres.

Although the region lies just within the Tropic of Cancer, the elevation of the study area (twelve hundred to two thousand metres) reduces the tropical effect, and people are not equipped to cope with extended cold periods. Albeit, winters can be cold. The lowest temperatures recorded over the past thirty years were below freezing (-1° to -2°C). Snow has been known to fall, and starting in late April or May, and even after the onset of the monsoon, heavy hail can damage field crops, as it did in 1998.

The two study villages sit below a ridge that runs on a northeast-southwest diagonal. At the time of our initial fieldwork in 1999, the upper village,

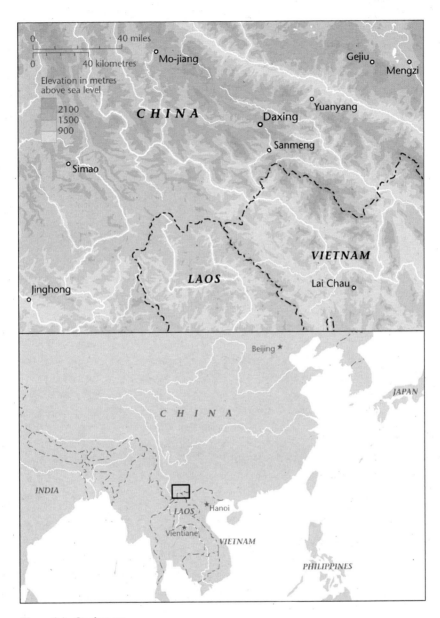

Figure 6.1 Study area.

Shangshapu, had a population of 178 people divided between 79 households. The lower village, Xiashapu, was slightly smaller, with a population of 140 living in 70 households. When the study was conducted, 28 percent of the combined population was fourteen years of age or younger, while less than 10 percent were fifty-five years of age or older. People were aware of the national family planning guidelines, but most parents ignored the (1986) prescribed limit of two children.

Both Shapu villages share a common past with the neighbouring communities of Xibidong, Badong, Puyi, and Pushan, and villagers come together for principal events. For example, when the important *tubhe* or Spirit Stone ceremony was held on Snake Day, in March 1999, a representative male from each household in all these villages attended. Being closely related does not preclude tensions and open disagreements, however, but there are customary procedures that can be followed to right wrongs.

In a purely material sense, like those in many other Hani communities in Lüchun County, the people of Xiashapu and Shangshapu are not well off. Administrative village statistics indicate that securing livelihoods is a struggle. A single and not particularly good indicator of this is average annual income. In 1998, while including an estimate of subsistence production, the average annual income was just over 700 yuan (US$80) per capita. An individual's net cash income is considerably lower. According to official Lüchun County statistics, in 1998, the per capita net income was 388 yuan for Shangshapu and 422 yuan for Xiashapu, just below the average for the county as a whole (434 yuan). Such statistics, of course, do not include all production for consumption, barter, and unrecorded exchange between villagers. If such factors were included, which undoubtedly amount to a significant portion of any household's livelihood, then this would notably alter the level of "poverty" of the subjects.

When we visited these two villages initially in 1999, local Hani were experiencing a bad year. Owing to a heavy hail storm, 40 percent of the total number of households in both villages did not have enough grain to last for more than five months, yet people talked of extending support to those who were less well off and seeing them through to the next harvest. Indeed, kinship is important and a wealth that is easily overlooked by outsiders attempting to understand livelihood strategies.

Unfortunately, membership in a resilient culture is not enough to guarantee a secure future, and within the villages there were single-parent households that found it difficult to make ends meet. There were houses in danger of collapse; mice and rats ate far into grain reserves, and food insecurity was a constant threat. Property was not entirely secure, and although residents of both villages had no complaints about antisocial behaviour in their own village, they did not necessarily trust the honesty of all residents in neighbouring communities. Livestock occasionally went missing, and accusations of poaching eels from flooded paddy fields and fish from ponds abound.

Since "Liberation" (the 1949 Communist victory), villagers had come to rely increasingly on officials to help them in times of trouble, yet this was not resulting in more secure livelihoods, as discussed shortly.

Local Hani Livelihoods before the Mid-1970s

Xiashapu and Shangshapu share a common origin. Both villages include people descended from the same founding ancestor, Li Awke, who arrived ten generations ago. Historically, each village was headed by a *tusi*, literally native *(tu)* officials *(si)*, who could be Hani, but were often Tai or a member of any ethnolinguistic group as long as he (hardly ever a "she") had a position of authority to start with, was willing to swear allegiance to the emperor and state, and would pay a proportion of revenues collected through tax as tribute to the Dragon Throne. This was a policy "of ruling barbarians through the barbarians." The *tusi* role was usually hereditary, and the legitimacy of the position was based on official letters and seals provided by the emperor. They were expected to maintain a military force and when asked, were expected to send troops to assist the emperor's army. The *tusi* were required to provide tribute in local products to the emperor. These local lords under both imperial and later the Republican government, remained relatively independent. The last *tusi*, Du Guo Tang, was based in the township of Long Shanli, some twenty hours' walk from Shapu in what is today Yuanyang County.

Despite the hierarchical nature of the political structure under which they lived, and the highly skewed nature of land ownership, the Hani shared an egalitarian ethos.[3] Ancestor worship was well-established in all households. Land could be formally bought and sold, or could change hands following customary land tenure. Wealthy families could increase the size of their farms by buying land from those who for personal reasons wanted to sell or had to sell to pay off debts. State officials and villagers widely accepted individual ownership of irrigated fields under permanent cultivation.

The exception to land ownership applied to forested land, which was claimed as part of a village estate known as *donghon* land. Land in this zone was released for use in a manner that followed specific, strict procedures laid down by a representative group of village elders who determined what building materials could be gathered and, depending on suitability, what land could be cleared and planted. This form of traditional governance allowed villagers access to land to grow low-yielding dry (non-irrigated) rice and other crops, such as millet, buckwheat, and maize. As many as a third of the total number of households secured the greater part of their food needs by working land as tenants or labour paid with food.

When fieldwork was undertaken in 1999, villagers were following the customary round of ceremonies that had existed before Liberation. Villagers drew up an annual calendar of celebrations followed widely by those who share Hani-Akha culture, as well as some specific local characteristics. The Hani New Year in October is followed by a ceremony to drive out bad spirits, erect a new village gate, and make offerings to the Dragon Tree and the Lord of the Land (November-December). In February, activities that mark the start of the new cropping year commence with the spring festival. This is followed by offerings to the Elephant Pool (a local ceremony maintained in the absence of elephants to keep them away!) and the Mountain Spirit.[4] The spirits of the land are then called back (late March) to participate in the renewal. In June, as the main surge of the monsoon arrives, the Swing festival is held (the Swing festival is marked by younger villagers building, and riding, a large wooden swing within each village). Stages in the growth and maturation of the single rice crop provide the focus for the remaining ceremonies.

Local Hani Livelihoods through Time

Liberation

As in several other remote parts of Yunnan, such as the Drung Valley in the west described by Gros (this volume), it took a while for the People's Liberation Army to arrive. Communist Party authorities did not make their presence felt until 1953, and Lüchun County was established the same year. Initially, little was done that impinged on the way people lived. Those old enough to remember recalled how things then changed for the better. In 1955-56, land reform was carried out. The relatively better off landlord class was dispossessed and agricultural land evenly distributed between households on the understanding that it would be worked cooperatively. Rice yields were good, 6,750 *jing* per hectare (3,375 kilograms per hectare). The gap between rich and poor – in terms of land – declined significantly. The opium tax was abolished along with poppy growing itself. Villagers were more optimistic than ever before and looked forward to a prosperous and healthy future.

It was with the advent of the Great Leap Forward (starting in 1958) that people first felt the full force of the utopian socialist ideology. The Great Leap was the state's attempt to achieve industrialization, modernization, and Communist enlightenment in a single authoritarian jump that people remembered as the time of the "great kitchen." Villagers were told to stop celebrating events listed on their annual ceremonial calendar and stop making offerings to both spirits and ancestors. It was a time of disruption, long hard days of work, and serious food shortages.

By 1962, the state began to relax pressure to conform to party-driven communal expectations. Family private life was restored. Ancestral altars were reconstructed, ceremonial offerings could be made, and families prepared their own food. Collective life continued but in a less intrusive way.

When the Cultural Revolution came along in 1966, the relative isolation of the village, as measured by its distance from a town of significant size, served it well. According to villagers born in the 1940s and 1950s, the Cultural

Revolution did not have a great impact on either village. By this time, villagers had become familiar with party demands and how to deal with them. They had learned to relinquish any show of independence that might challenge the authority of the collective or commune. In Xiashapu, the big Dragon Tree was abandoned and the ritual head or *milguq* secretly installed a modest replacement off the main path, where it could not be seen by visiting Red Guards. The demands of zealous visitors could be satisfied by being shown the old tree, with the remnants of a demolished protective wall around it. Ancestor altars were once again removed, but by silent consensus the celebration of important seasonal events continued in an appropriately muted manner – another good example of Scott's (1990) hidden transcript.

Challenges to Traditional Environment Management and Hani Agency

During interviews, the oldest Hani villagers talked about how a great deal of the forest land was first converted to agriculture during the 1950s and 1960s, principally to meet state collective targets (compare with Yin Shaoting 2001). These decisions were the first to ignore cultural guidelines but certainly not the last. At this time, irrigated terraces were built on lower-lying ground on slopes of up to twenty degrees, but the more spectacular terraces on steeper slopes between twenty-one and thirty degrees appeared later, from the 1970s onward. Following the land reforms of the 1980s, the most rapid expansion of land under cultivation took place on even steeper land (thirty-one to forty degrees), where pockets of the original soil horizon had, until then, remained undisturbed.[5]

According to research participants, the efforts of the state to suppress customary Hani religious practices – in this case, a complex and sophisticated form of animism – during the core socialist period (1953-80), only succeeded in fragmenting them and driving them underground.[6] Ritual heads remained quietly active; the party was neither so alert nor held in such high regard that it was ever able to entirely break the intimacy of proprietary knowledge guarded by elders. If any official watch that was mounted to flush out counter-revolutionaries succeeded, it has either been suppressed or forgotten. People prefer to remember that nobody was victimized and that requests for such information were dealt with in a manner consistent with subaltern behaviour across the region: smile and outwardly submit to authority. But as soon as the backs of the authorities are turned, go about your business as if nothing has happened.

By this time, Hani cultural guidelines relating to land management as a part of the Hani cultural legacy had been placed aside and fallen by the wayside. Even small, isolated religious and spiritual ceremonies were performed in such a way as to avoid scrutiny. Those who believed these were important enough to play the risky game of maintaining such practices kept their activities to themselves.

This came at a cost. Indigenous knowledge lost its public working consensus and coherence. Empirical wisdom relating to environmental assessment and land use conservation were displaced by the authority of a party based on a generalized Marxist-Leninist theory of modernization and science that ignored the competence and relevance of farmer "know how," that is, the specificity of place and the legitimacy of local "natural science." Science came to be based not on observation as much as on instruction and rhetoric: commonsense cause and effect was replaced by the need to do what you were told. Increasingly, mythologized themes were remembered, but the precise content of oral texts was lost. This fundamental loss of agency in all but language and less profound aspects of Hani tradition such as costume and cultural performance fundamentally undermined confidence. Indigenous leadership was diminished, and control over resource use was relinquished. People learned that it was better to be quiet and passive rather than to be politically active, and this withdrawal from day-to-day decision making weakened village self-governance. When ritual practices were revived, the critical link between religious practice, community coherence, and environmental protection had been broken. This is what Li Qibo meant when he wrote, "Today, traditional methods [of environmental management] only have a definite place within the scope of religious beliefs" (Li Qibo 1996, 10-11).

Li Qibo explained that when collective ownership was vested in the state, local Hani agency was taken away from the community. As the government then became more relaxed and people began to exercise more control over family life again, they were left with being the "colonized" Hani they had become, with fewer and only fragmented cultural guidelines to fall back on. Collective or state ownership had been designed as a constitutional arrangement to avoid alienation of poorer members of society. As such, it included strong conservation measures, but these came to be associated in people's minds not so much with good sense but with an integral part of party control. When the socialist collective relaxed its hold, the privilege of agency was not immediately reclaimed by traditional Hani leadership: individual farmers acted in pursuit of their own self-interest and that of their families. Farmers responded to increased economic freedom by exploiting land without considering ways to maintain the watershed. The consequences of this situation are explored below.

Post-Socialist Period

In the early 1980s, land that remained under socialist collective ownership was distributed to the farmers of Xiashapu and Shangshapu, increasing their ability to farm as they chose.

Tenure reform agreements passed in 1980 provided the model for individual tenure, while further reforms that followed in 1984-85 allocated forest land to households. Although this did not include outright ownership, the singularity of the idea had a large impact. After the reforms came into effect, those who developed irrigated terraces and canals claimed exclusive rights of usufruct.[7] Those who did not assist in clearing, construction, and maintenance of canals were excluded from their use. When applied to canals and access to water, the assertion of individual over communal rights ensured that tensions and potential conflict were not far behind. Yet, most importantly, the emergence of individualized tenure also meant that the responsibilities of the previous collectives went into recess.

At this time ninety-six people were living in Xiashapu. After taking into account land that was contributed to the collective in the 1960s, and past yields as a measure of soil fertility, the best agricultural land was distributed approximately as follows: 0.40 *mu* of irrigated paddy land per capita, and 0.50 *mu* of dry terrace land per capita. In Shangshapu, 128 people received approximately 0.22 *mu* of irrigated paddy land per capita, and 0.10 *mu* of dry terrace land per capita.

Swidden land along with remaining forest was also allocated to households. Between 1984 and 1985, the collective appeared to divest itself of any management and administrative responsibility associated with land use. The understanding may have been to return management to villages so that it could be administered in ways that followed cultural guidelines, but the allocation to individual households was unconditional.

In turn, villagers embraced these changes and welcomed the opportunities they presented. They felt free to criticize shortfalls in the government administration system and felt at liberty to practise their religion again. There was a resurgence of soul-calling cures and mediations that required the services of priests and shamans. Traditional festivals were celebrated openly without fear of criticism. Yet, it was certainly not a return to the past, and the few who remember the old *tusi* system are adamant:

> The system [today] is a whole lot better than it used to be. If you get into debt, people can't force you to sell your land. Even if you are poor, your livelihood cannot be taken away. Relatives can always be relied on to help those who cannot work for themselves. Now wealth is much more evenly distributed. (Shangshapu elder)

However, both villages continued to face serious challenges. In neither village was there enough land of sufficient quality to grow all the food required for household consumption. During our research, the project's hydro-geomorphologist was taken aback at the poor physical properties of recently cleared land on slopes of between thirty-one and forty degrees. This included heavily weathered slopes with sandy soils, and V-shaped valleys found in association with heavily jointed bedrock and jasperite. Once cleared and cultivated, if only for a short period, the former quickly becomes scree. The valleys, from which trees had been cut for firewood, had become waterways when subject to high volumes of rapid runoff, particularly vulnerable to active headwater and bank erosion. The extension of farming onto exposed marginal land was far from sustainable. Fortunately though, on more gentle slopes or where the original soil horizon with a high clay fraction remained undisturbed, even on steep slopes, it was possible to build the distinct high-yielding irrigated Hani terraces (McConchie and Ma 2003; McConchie and McKinnon 2004).

If the mainstay of household livelihoods cannot be agriculture due to limited suitable land, there remains the challenge of finding alternative sources of income. It is difficult for young people who do not speak Putonghua (the official name given to standard Mandarin and used here to refer to the Yunnan variant) to secure fair employment deals in nearby towns, and the chances are slimmer the further one travels from the village. Employment opportunities organized by state agencies tend to favour the majority Chinese Han rather than minority people. Then there is the challenge of population growth. Between 1980 and 2000, in disregard of the release in 1986 of party policy guidelines limiting the size of minority families to two children, the population of Xiashapu increased by 68 percent and in Shangshapu by 72 percent. Twenty-eight percent of the population was fourteen years of age or younger. As this age group matures, they will encounter difficulties in gaining access to land, employment, and sufficient food.

This was how the outside research team saw the situation in 1999, but how did the Hani see it? Li Qibo had identified similar issues in the Hani areas of Jiache district in Honghe County and in the Huangcaoling district of Yuanyang County, in which he had carried out survey work in the early 1990s, but his view, besides being a native Hani speaker, was a trained researchers' view. How did villagers see it?

Some villagers complained of problems with the erosion of topsoil, and sedimentation into waterways and onto irrigated terraces. Others described problems with the water supply and runoff, but most people did not want to be seen as taking a critical stance. In village meetings and interviews, it was clear that farmers had a wide range of observations. Generally, people wanted to assure us that, compared with the past, life was good and their outlook was optimistic. The performances of village religious practitioners, leaders, mill owners and operators, and the village committee were all seen as satisfactory. The performance of line service agencies and officials (those offering state-based services) were not highly rated, but there was neither consensus on this nor serious dissatisfaction. Considerable understanding was shown of what they expected agencies to do; for instance, the Foreign

Trade Bureau was singled out for critical comment because it promoted the planting of commercial crops such as cardamom, tea, and lemon grass, which had failed to provide the expected sustainable returns.

Market Economy

Since the movement away from economic socialism in the early 1980s, inhabitants of southeast Yunnan have become more and more involved with market activities. Opportunities to earn money were taken up by Hani villagers not only to supplement local food shortages but also to pay school fees and to buy a wide range of articles such as traditional silver ornaments, textiles, roofing, tools, clothes, lighters, tobacco, sugar, and other industrial products that were becoming available. As the old headman of Shangshapu told me, "People no longer want to work together. They just look for things that will benefit their own family." Cash crops were capturing great interest, but local experiences in this field have not always delivered the expected livelihood rewards.

The first commercial crop to be introduced to the villages in the early 1960s, approximately ten years after the demise of the opium poppy, was black cardamom, also known as brown cardamom or *tsao-ko (Amomum costatum)*. Adapted to relatively high altitudes, the plant was recommended to the collective by the Foreign Trade Bureau and was first planted under a high forest canopy in damp gullies above the village. The pods can be smoked to dry, kept for a long time, and sold at growers' convenience. But, like many collective ventures, it was not clear from the beginning who owned the crop and who would profit. Moreover, there were only limited areas in which to grow cardamom, and prices for it remained low. Cardamom was still grown in the early 2000s, but in contrast to the situation found by Tugault-Lafleur and Turner (this volume) in northern Vietnam, the harvest remains commercially insignificant. Most of what is harvested is used locally in cooking, as a medicine, or sold in handfuls to pharmaceutical shops in the nearby town.

Tea was introduced as a cash crop in 1988 and over the following year was systematically planted by a few individual farmers who were taught how to process it by local traders. During the 1990s, the number of people planting tea, and the quality of the crop, declined. Some farmers believed they were not growing the right variety and remained pessimistic about getting good advice on what to grow or where to get better plant stocks.

The third crop that has had, by far, the biggest impact on the land is lemon grass, *Cymbopogon citratus* or *flexuosus*. It was the last promising cash crop to arrive – in 1994 – and, as most of the remaining land available for cultivation was on the steeper slopes between thirty-one and forty degrees, this is where it was planted and where firewood was cut to run the stills to render lemon-grass oil. Farmers knew from experience that soils on these steep slopes could only be cultivated for short periods, and shrubs and trees regenerated slowly, if at all. However, this did not dissuade villagers from cutting firewood, clearing, and planting. At this time, herbal medicine practitioners in Western countries had made the oil popular, and it was also being used to make perfume. A market had developed in China, local buyers were looking for growers, and it was in short supply. At a local price of sixty yuan per bottle (sixty yuan per *jing* or US$11 per 0.6 kilogram of oil), the cultivation of lemon grass spread rapidly. Plant materials were obtained from friends in other villages, relatives, and in some cases purchased. For the people of Shapu, lemon grass had much going for it. It was easy to propagate by dividing root-stock; it was hardy; and once established, it required little care. In most cases, it provided a reasonable ground cover and could be harvested and processed any time money was needed.

Environmental Impacts of Cash Crops

Lemon-grass cultivation had many commercial advantages, as well as a considerable environmental impact (McConchie and McKinnon 2004). To plant it, watershed forest had to be cleared. Once established, it was physically difficult to remove, especially as some cultural practices restricted people from destroying plants that had contributed to their livelihood. Furthermore, a considerable amount of wood was needed to fuel the distilleries and extract the oil, which provided a further incentive for deforestation.

When the price of lemon grass dropped to between ten and twelve yuan a bottle, many farmers chose alternative cash crops. Better-off households no longer bothered to cultivate it, and the stills they had set up to process their own and other farmers' lemon grass were either dismantled or allowed to fall into disrepair.

On its own, the interest in lemon-grass oil production may not have been overly significant. However, when evaluated in the context of wider postsocialist changes, with cultivation already stretched beyond sustainable boundaries, the impact of lemon grass on the landscape was dramatic. An official land use map published in 1990, based on aerial photographs taken in the late 1980s, covered the study area (8.5 square kilometres). In discussion with the Hani research teams, the outside researchers in this participatory project decided to update the map.[8]

The original 1990 map showed that before lemon grass was introduced, forest (lighter grey) covered 58 percent of the total area. By 1999, the map drawn by the villagers showed that this forest cover had dropped to 22 percent (see Figure 6.2). This was not the only change. Over the same period, irrigated rice terraces (paddy) increased from 12 to 18 percent of the total area. Upland fields (waste grassland, darker grey; dry terraces and dry land), including gardens cleared for maize and upland rice, as well as lemon grass,

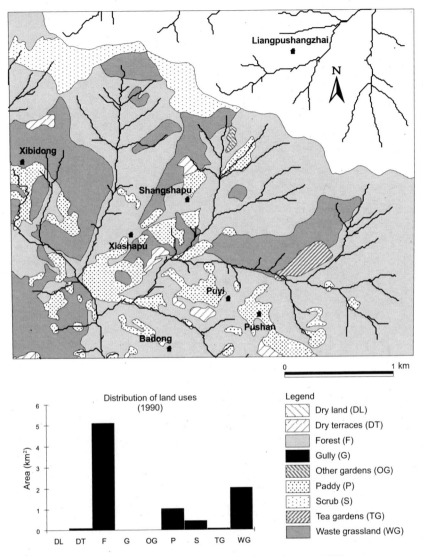

Figure 6.2 Land use in Shapu sector of Badong sub-catchment, 1990.
Source: McConchie

increased from 24 to 46 percent, and the remaining secondary re-growth from 6 to 14 percent.

These changes in land use and land cover will inevitably have implications for water and runoff, resulting in enhanced erosion and sedimentation. Indeed, at the time of our research in 1999, our field notes recorded that "erosion is a major problem. Over 30% of the ground is partially exposed.

138 *John McKinnon*

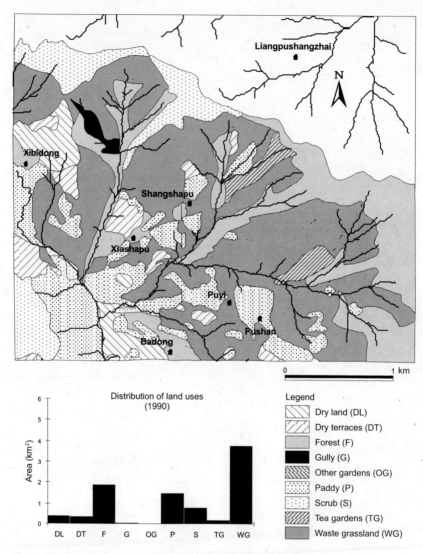

Figure 6.3 Land use in Shapu sector of Badong sub-catchment, 1999.
Source: McConchie

The relatively low cohesion of the material results in instability during the dry months as well as the rainy season. As a consequence irrigation canals, paddy fields and water supply systems are now at risk."

Extreme runoff events after high levels of rainfall are much less likely under continuous forest cover than on more exposed ground. Villagers were well aware of how extreme rainfall events affected steep forested and terraced land alike. They knew of major landslides that had torn terraces off hillsides and had even buried people in a sea of mud. It did not take too much imagination to extend what had happened to others as something that could also happen to them. Half the total land area in the Badong sub-catchment where these villages are located is characterized by slopes of more than 30 percent, of which half again has slopes of more than 40 percent. Hence, a severe or intense rainstorm followed by high volumes of runoff might put whole hillsides of irrigated terraces at risk (some 18 percent of the land area was irrigated terraces).

Elders, even *without* reference to extreme events, were of the opinion that the removal of much of the forest cover, especially that on steep land close to mountain streams and gullies, had over the past ten years created a number of potential environmental hazards. They did not share the vocabulary of the overseas researchers among the research team, but they did share our observations concerning geomorphological surface processes. Elders were of the opinion that the increase in storm runoff had reduced the discharge of springs that were now less likely to flow during the whole year, and they pointed to sedimentation on low-lying cultivated terraces and within streams as evidence of rapid runoff. Within recent memory, the water of several streams had been buried under stones and now flowed underground.

I should emphasize here that these findings relate to a specific geographical situation, and I am not attempting to generalize here. Clearly, an inspection of other research findings on upland agriculture and environmental impacts confirm that such effects are often limited to specific valleys or localities (see Calder and Aylward 2002; Bonell and Bruijnzeel 2004) and can even be seen in fully forested areas (Lee 1980; Forsyth and Walker 2008). These overviews agree, however, that however reluctant we may be to admit it (McKinnon 1977, 1989), sudden land use changes and increases in land use on forest margins or unsuitable land due to perceived livelihood opportunities (or indeed any reason) produce changes in local hydrology and soil movement.

Listening to Farmers Regarding Livelihood Change

As these overviews of upland livelihood change, land use, and hydrology show, it is often difficult to explain observed changes in terms of clear cause and effect. As part of our participatory research project, we held an open meeting of Hani villagers near the end of our time in the field, at which the research team presented the results of the joint research, using the maps and photos that had been assembled. This included the 1990 and 1999 land use maps discussed earlier. When these were revealed, they elicited sighs and remarks of surprise from the villagers at the scale of the changes. For example, a photograph showed an aggraded stream bed immediately below a field of lemon grass. Elders who had witnessed the transformation from forest to bare slopes, and who remembered when the stream flowed on the surface, spoke to the matter. Another image taken from a high point looking back up the Badong River clearly showed the advance of shingle and how it had covered low-lying terraces.

It was a very lively meeting. When it ended, the farmers who had tried to point out what was happening to the land around them due to local livelihood decision making and the consequences of turning a blind eye to the transformations were relieved that at last their story had been told. The old headman of Shangshapu was positively joyful, raising his hands above his head and with a broad smile exclaiming what could be translated as "yes, yes, yes!" over and over again. "Now they must see!" For Li Qibo, there was the satisfaction of seeing his research apparently triangulated (that was his interpretation at least) and, further, seeing how this interpretation could be shared with and appreciated by people who, in his mind, had previously seemed to be solely absorbed with the fortunes of their own families.

Whether the discussion of environmental concerns was accurate or not, in an unexpected way, the interpretation and discussion appeared to strengthen people's sense of community and their ethnicity as Hani by reminding them of what they already knew and of what they had been reluctant to acknowledge. In somewhat optimistic words, Li Qibo, a native Hani who started his life as a farmer and thus trusted he could speak with authority on these matters, considered that the occasion had stimulated people to think that "the thing most needed today is to strengthen environmental consciousness, revive the people's understanding, and cherish everything about nature"(Li Qibo 1996, 12).

This is all very well and heartening for those who find it easy to go along with such statements, but true reform requires more than a rush of blood to the head. As we have seen, sentiments can be expressed in fine words and religious practice performed as detached ritual. Neither words nor ritual traditionally associated with the environment necessarily have to lead to actions consistent with effective resource management.

Action plans – that had been facilitated by the visiting team and drawn up as part of the participatory exercises – were created and left in the hands of those with whom the information had originated, the village leaders of Xiashapu and Shangshapu, and both the Hani-Lisu Honghe Institute for Minority Studies and the Environment Protection Bureau that had mentored and participated in the exercise. But out of respect for Hani agency and their right to self-governance, it was not the business of the outside research team to advise and design any follow-up other than to provide copies of the results of the shared research in local languages to the research partners.

In June 2000, I returned to find out what had happened in Xiashapu and Shangshapu.[9] The Environment Protection Bureau had been involved in the villages, providing support for villager-initiated projects. Other projects had been initiated without the involvement of any outsiders. The headman of Shangshapu village, along with fourteen other elders, had put his authority and local knowledge to work and formed a watershed protection committee. Empowered by what they had been able to articulate from their localized point of view on the matter, they began to reclaim collective land that they considered too steep for cultivation and placed it under protection. All remaining forest, regardless of who had been issued with rights of usufruct, was declared part of a common reserve. A forest reserve agreement was also negotiated with each household to make sure that everybody agreed on what was involved and that they accepted that this agreement superseded the rights of individual tenure granted under the 1984-85 land reform exercise. Household heads confirmed their commitment to abide by the agreement by signing with a fingerprint.

The small amount of land claimed back, 10 *mu* (1.65 acres or 0.66 hectares), was immediately planted with Chinese fir seedlings (*Cunninghamia lanceolata* [Lamb.] Hook.) in conservation clusters on steep land.[10] Hani leaders told me that it was "the first act, for this generation and the next." This was accompanied by an offering to the Mountain Spirit and the calling back of the spirits of the forest and the land, followed four days later in a symbolic affirmation by each household at which a chicken was sacrificed to ensure good fortune. Environmental action and support for sustainable livelihood measures was once again linked to religious practice and Hani ethnic ways. It was initially reported that three thousand seedlings were planted, followed by a further five thousand.[11] Additionally, a levy of two yuan per household had been initiated and collected to pay the annual honorarium for the forest guards.[12] It was not possible to check to what extent these seedling estimates were exaggerated, yet the important thing was not the actual number of trees planted or that an official had been appointed to guard them, but that villagers had taken the initiative to assert community guidelines and authority over individual claims to land-based resources. As a culturally sanctioned step, it implicitly declared Hani agency in a way that had not been seen since pre-revolution days.

Other projects, however, undertaken by villagers or associated with them did not enjoy the same level of support. These included a steep tractor road down to Shangshapu that was opposed by Xiashapu and cut by the Environment Protection Bureau bulldozer (the path was already impassable by the time I arrived); a private walnut orchard planted by one of the research teams' bureau mentors who had secured land rights by marrying a young Xiashapu woman; and a commercial piggery in Xiashapu, an enterprise shared by a leading village family and county Environment Protection Bureau staff. The piggery had the capacity to house one hundred sows, and the idea was to buy feed from surrounding villages and sell breeding stock to local farmers and piglets into the restaurant trade. It is interesting to note, though, that in these cases, state-sponsored, as opposed to local, Hani-designed development options were less likely to be seen in a positive light. Crucially, the process of selection between what was opposed and what was accepted was clearly a locally grounded, ethnically informed process of developing and putting to use a local form of Hani agency.

Concluding Remarks

In simplistic terms, development aid is about intervening in the lives of others with the aim of eventually changing things for the better. However, generally, as the proverb states, "the road to hell is paved with good intentions." "Developers" think they know what is best for a local population; yet, what outsiders consider best may not be what the people for whom the assistance is intended really want. Although participatory grassroots approaches are designed to address this concern, they are frequently compromised. Outside agencies usually do not fund participatory exercises in order to get villagers to plan their own future. Sometimes the objectives of participatory exercises have been organized in advance. Even if this is not clearly stated outright, villagers do their best, usually successfully, to uncover what it is the development agency has in mind so that they can use their own will to massage the results to fit the expectation. This is precisely what the indigenization of modernity is about (Sahlins 1999).

Over the years and through the successive drastic changes of regime that China has known, the customary connections between indigenous Hani religious beliefs and environmental management in Shapu have been severely challenged but, visibly, not lost. The symbols of ritual were muted by several decades of concealment and demoted to a hidden transcript. Yet, oral histories of land management resurfaced later and referred explicitly to managing water as potency, the "basic productive force of the universe" (Tooker 1996). These discussions were crowded with spiritual references to the environment and reminded local villagers of what it meant to be Hani. As villagers saw an opportunity to become actively involved in the decision-making process concerning what was happening around them, through a participatory research project, they were also reminded that their survival in both a physical and spiritual domain – their ethnicity – meant they must activate their own agency and exercise their collective will rather than waiting to see what happens.

Combined with the economic and political liberalization occurring in China in recent years, which has opened zones of negotiation with the state and presented new economic opportunities, the participatory research project described here appears to have been an element contributing to triggering Hani people to acknowledge the consequences of what was happening around them and feel empowered to act on it. Acting on their own initiative, though not immune to outside influences from local elite, state representatives, and powerful neighbours, elders with popular support in both communities moved to introduce conservation measures in a Hani way. The whole exercise, I suggest, helped people cultivate confidence to assert their ethnicity and play an active role in determining their own future.

I am not suggesting in any way that the adoption by these Hani communities of conservation tree planting justifies the establishment of forests on a wide scale such as that promoted in the Go West scheme; likewise, I do not support monoculture plantations as a sustainable long-term solution to deforestation. But what is important to note here is that Hani villagers show an active will to make their own decisions about the development paths and livelihood choices they prefer to follow. Whether those paths are the best or the more fruitful ones available is a matter for another debate. Local, culturally rooted decision-making processes, those that had to be kept undercover during the stricter socialist period, are now being revived as the political and economic climate allows. Rooted in indigenous knowledge of the environment, local spirituality, and cultural interpretations of their life world, Hani are taking stock of the livelihood options available to them, and weighing up their options.

Acknowledgments

The author wishes to acknowledge NZAID for its financial support. I also wish to acknowledge the contribution made to the work by all members of the Hani teams from Xiashapu and Shangshapu, staff of the Lüchun Environment Protection Bureau, and the following: Mr. Li Qibo, director and staff of the Hani-Lisu Honghe Institute for Minority Studies; Dr. Ma Huan-Cheng, associate professor of Forestry and Soil Science, Southwest Forest College, Kunming; Dr. Cai Kui, director, Rural Development Research Center, Yunnan Institute of Geography, Kunming; and in Wellington, Ms. Jean McKinnon, KINSA Associates, and especially Dr. Jack McConchie, Opus International Consultants Ltd., who prepared the maps and conducted the hydro-geomorphological research presented in this chapter.

Notes

1 See McKinnon 2010 for a detailed description of the participatory methods and processes that took place.
2 The principal members of the research team are named in the Acknowledgments.
3 See Johnson (1989) and Cancian (1989) for a general discussion on peasant egalitarianism in economic behaviour.
4 The Mountain Spirit ceremony is like the Akha Water Divide Ceremony and was celebrated in 1999 at about the same time as the Lunar New Year (Tooker 1996). It was conducted on the banks of the Badong River to purify the water so that small amounts could be carried away and used in offerings. The ceremony involved several villages and, as Tooker (1996) observed for the Akha, it is not so much a local event as a ceremony focused on the watershed.
5 Land use profiles were reconstructed for 1950, 1980, and 1999 solely by the village research groups (McKinnon et al. 1999).
6 Traditional Akha-Hani ontology is based on animistic premises. However, I need to make it clear that, with Anthony Walker writing on the Lahu, I do not take this to "refer to some residual metaphysical system to which primitivity and antiquity must necessarily be attributed" (Walker 2003b, 116). Instead, I refer to a contemporary metaphysical perspective that holds (in theory at least) that all phenomena in the visible world comprise two, mostly conjoined, parts: material form and non-material or "spiritual" essence, to which may or may not be attributed a special name and attributes. See also Alting von Geusau (1986) for related attributes.

7 Usufruct is a means of property rights by which people claim ownership of crops or land on account of being in residence, or having used the land, for some years.
8 A base map drawn to scale showing the location of houses and the position of the Badong River and highland streams was initially prepared for the village teams. As part of the PLA exercise, the village teams were asked to add the boundary of their village estate and current land use. Interestingly, both teams immediately erased one stream, which they said had no obvious watercourse and could not be seen on the surface. They then proceeded to draw a detailed map of every field. The maps for each village were then put together and carefully generalized. With the help of village volunteers, the land outside the study area was then included, digitized at the Xiashapu schoolhouse field shelter, and projected onto a screen for everybody to see (see Figure 6.2). It was shown with photographs illustrating what was happening to the land around the villages.
9 I initially returned six months later to see what had happened, but could not complete the journey to Lüchun. Unseasonal heavy rain had caused whole mountainsides of Hani irrigated terraces to collapse and block the only road. For several hours, I watched kinsmen hoe through the mud covering the road, searching for the bodies of the family who had gone out at the height of the deluge to divert the increased volume of water entering the irrigation system. A whole family of farmers had lost their lives: buried, drowned, suffocated, and crushed in the slump of mud. Several such slips covered the road to Lüchun. The visit was abandoned.
10 This is a very small-scale initiative. To talk in more general terms, many academics and critical observers harbour strong reservations about monoculture plantation forestry for increasing water demand, diminishing biodiversity, and reducing agricultural land (Calder 1999; Walker 2003a). For these reasons, the Go West program in Yunnan, which particularly uses the strategy of coniferous monoculture replanting in Yunnan, has been criticized (for example, see chapters by Gros, Swain, and Sturgeon, this volume).
11 A subsequent independent evaluation carried out in 2003 found that at least half the seedlings had either died or were destroyed (Zheng Baohua 2005, 64). Replanting may well have been more successful had the alder *Alnus nepalensis* been provided.
12 Zheng Baohua's team from the Center for Community Development Studies, Kunming, and the Luchun Environment Protection Bureau found that this had not worked (ibid.)

References

Alting von Geusau, L. 1986. Dialectics of Akhazan: The interiorizations of a perennial minority group. In *Highlanders of Thailand,* ed. John McKinnon and Wanat Bhruksasri, 142-277. Singapore: Oxford University Press.
Bonell, M., and L.A. Bruijnzeel. 2004. *Forests, Water, and People in the Humid Tropics: Past, Present, and Future Hydrological Research for Integrated Land and Water Management.* New York: Cambridge University Press.
Calder, I. 1999. *The Blue Revolution: Land Use and Integrated Resource Management.* London: Earthscan.
Calder, I., and B. Aylward. 2002. *Forests and Floods: Perspectives on Watershed Management and Integrated Flood Management.* Rome/Newcastle: Food and Agriculture Organization of the United Nations/University of Newcastle.
Cancian, F. 1989. Economic behavior in peasant communities. In *Economic Anthropology,* ed. S. Plattner, 127-70. Palo Alto, CA: Stanford University Press.
Corlin, C. 2004. Hmong and the land question in Vietnam: National policy and local concepts of the environment. In *Hmong/Miao in Asia,* ed. N. Tapp, J. Michaud, C. Culas, and G.Y. Lee, 295-320. Chiang Mai: Silkworm Books.
Forsyth, T., and A. Walker. 2008. *Forest Guardians, Forest Destroyers: The Politics of Environmental Knowledge in Northern Thailand.* Seattle: Washington University Press.
Johnson, A. 1989. Horticulturalists: Economic behaviour in tribes. In *Economic Anthropology,* ed. S. Plattner, 49-77. Palo Alto, CA: Stanford University Press.
Lee, R. 1980. *Forest Hydrology.* New York: Columbia University Press.

Leepreecha, P. 2004. *Ntoo Xeeb:* Cultural redefinition of forest conservation among the Hmong in Thailand. In *Hmong/Miao in Asia,* ed. N. Tapp, J. Michaud, C. Culas, and G.Y. Lee, 335-52. Chiang Mai: Silkworm Books.

Li Qibo. 1996. *Hani Terraced Fields and the Ecological Environment.* Paper presented at the Second International Conference on Hani-Akha Culture, Chiang Mai and Chiang Rai, Thailand, 12-18 May 1996.

McConchie, J.A., and H.C. Ma. 2003. MIGIS – an effective tool to negotiate development interventions relating to forestry. *Journal of Forestry Research* 14(1): 9-18.

McConchie, J.A., and J.M. McKinnon. 2004. Empowering indigenous peoples and promoting collaborative natural resource management through mobile interactive GIS (MIGIS). In *WorldMinds: Geographical Perspectives on 100 Problems,* ed. Donald G. Janelle, Barney Warf, Kathy Hansen, 138-52. Dordrecht : Kluwer Academic Publishers.

McKinnon, J. 1977. *Shifting Cultivation: Who's Afraid of the Big Bad Wolf?* Paper presented at the seventy-seventh Seminar on Agriculture in Northern Thailand, Northern Agricultural Development Center and the Faculty of Agriculture, Chiang Mai, 8 April.

–. 1989. Structural assimilation and the consensus: Clearing grounds on which to rearrange our thoughts. In *Hill Tribes Today: Problems in Change,* ed. John McKinnon and Bernard Vienne, 303-59. Bangkok: White Lotus/Orstom.

–. 2003. Community culture: Strengthening persistence to empower resistance. In *Living at the Edge of Thai Society: The Karen in the Highlands of Northern Thailand,* ed. Claudio O. Delang, 64-84. London: RoutledgeCurzon.

–. 2005. Mobile Interactive GIS (MIGIS): Bringing indigenous knowledge and scientific information together – A narrative account. In *Participatory Approaches for Sustainable Land Use in Southeast Asia,* ed. A. Neef, 97-121. Bangkok: White Lotus Press.

–. 2010. Ways of seeing environmental change: Participatory research engagement in Yunnan, China with ethnic minority Hani participants. *Asia Pacific Viewpoint* 51(2).

McKinnon, John M., Cai Kui, Ma Huan-Cheng, Jack McConchie, and Jean McKinnon. 1999. *MIGIS Report Incorporating the PRA Reports for Xiashapu and Shangshapu, Luchun County, Honghe.* Unpublished field report, Kunming.

Sahlins, M. 1999. What is anthropological enlightenment? Some lessons of the twentieth century. *Annual Review of Anthropology* 28: i-xxiii.

Scott, J.C. 1985. *Weapons of the Weak: Everyday Forms of Peasant Resistance.* New Haven, CT: Yale University Press.

–. 1990. *Domination and the Arts of Resistance: Hidden Transcripts.* New Haven, CT: Yale University Press.

Tooker, D. 1996. *Irrigation Systems in the Ideology and Ritual Practices of Akha Shifting Agriculturalists.* Paper presented at the second international conference on Hani-Akha culture, Chiang Mai and Chiang Rai, Thailand, 12-18 May 1996.

Walker, A. 2003a. Agricultural transformation and the politics of hydrology in northern Thailand. *Development and Change* 34(5): 941-64.

–. 2003b. *Merit and the Millennium: Routine and Crisis in the Ritual Lives of the Lahu People.* New Delhi: Hindustan Publishing.

Yin Shaoting. 2001. *People and Forests: Yunnan Swidden Agriculture in Human Ecological Perspective.* Kunming: Yunnan Education.

Zheng Baohua. 2005. Empowering communities through mapping: Evaluation of participatory mapping in two Hani villages, Yunnan province, PR China. In *Mapping Communities: Ethics, Values, Practice,* eds. Jefferson Fox, Krishnawati Suryanata, and Peter Hershock, 57-72. Honolulu: East-West Center.

7
Land Reform and Changing Identities in Two Tai-Speaking Districts in Northern Vietnam

Marie Mellac

State-led land reform has impacted on identities and ethnicities among two Tai-speaking groups in northern Vietnam, the Tày and the Thái.[1] Indeed, Vietnam offers a fertile example of how customary land tenure systems can creatively mingle with very different, and sometimes contradictory, land policies promoted by successive and diametrically opposite political regimes: imperial, colonial, socialist, and market-oriented.

Land reform has always been a classic strategy of socialist regimes to build a more equitable society. The Indochinese Communist Party identified land reform as a key objective when it was formed in 1930 (Le Thanh Khoi 1978, quoted in Tessier 2003). During the war with the French, the promise of agrarian reform allowed the Communist Party to win the trust of peasants in the Red River delta. But when the Democratic Republic of Vietnam (DRV) started land collectivization at the end of the 1950s, some five years after China started its own collectivization, many peasants found this a difficult and challenging process because it radically changed how villagers were connected to their land.

For the government of North Vietnam (as the DRV was commonly known in the West), collectivization was not only a means of redistributing land; it was also part of a wider project to build a new type of society, including breaking individual links between people and the means of production. Invariably, this meant informing peasants that traditional property rights, or means of accessing land, were no longer allowed, and introducing newer, more collective, means of tenure. Quite quickly, agricultural land became managed by cooperatives, which farmers were supposed to join, as stated in the 1959 constitution (Article 14), "in accordance with the principle of voluntariness" (SRV 1995). New cooperative members were assigned different specialized activities, such as distributing irrigation water, keeping buffaloes, raising fish, and transplanting and harvesting crops. Accordingly, collectivization in North Vietnam was not simply a redistribution of land but a complete modification of the official (or legal) aspects of land tenure, understood as "the entire rules defining access, exploitation and control rights on the land and on the renewable resources" (Lavigne Delville 1998).

In 1976, one year after the fall of Saigon (Sài Gòn), the party launched the "Great Socialist Agriculture" to reinforce the process of collectivization and to speed up Vietnam's unification. But from this time, opposition to collectivization grew steadily. Collective agriculture was failing. In part it contributed to the serious economic crisis the country faced at the end of the 1970s. Accordingly, from the early 1980s, the government started, haphazardly, to decollectivize land. The first step was to create what is now understood as favourable conditions in which peasants could adopt individual farming practices on collectively owned land. By 1993, the second land law finally ended the role of cooperatives by withdrawing the last prerogatives they had on land distribution (Pillot and Yvon 1995). Under this law, land was allocated by the state to individuals on a medium- or long-term basis, and land use rights (not ownership) could be legally transferred, exchanged, leased, mortgaged, and inherited. However, at this stage, the state did not recognize in a formal way that the law ended the cooperatives because that would have represented a clash with socialist ideology. Moreover, some observers have claimed that decollectivization resulted in part from peasants' everyday resistance, which progressively led the Vietnam Communist Party leaders to recognize the failure of collectivization and to propose new contracts of production with peasant households (Kerkvliet 1997). The state therefore did not proclaim new, individual forms of land tenure because, as Bergeret (2002) notes, that would mean a loss of party legitimacy.

As a result, social and political aspects of land-based reforms are still very sensitive in Vietnam and are rarely discussed. The question of land, when discussed in official arenas, is mainly restricted to economic standpoints. Social aspects of land, when considered, are subordinated to economic ones. Indeed, land registration and individual land tenure are considered necessary institutions to facilitate agricultural investments by providing collateral for agricultural credit. These institutions are also intended to discourage land fragmentation and hence encourage the development of land markets (Sikor 2006). Consequently, Vietnamese land tenure has almost come full circle from the days of collectivization and is now moving toward encouraging modernization and capitalist standards of production.

In this chapter, I consider these recent transformations by analyzing how changes in land tenure have also affected ethnic identities. Such identities are not fixed and have to be understood, as stated in Chapter 1, as being produced in social contexts at all scales, including the national level. And they also are influenced and fed by differentiations and identification processes. I explore here the way in which the new state-led and -imposed land model (that is, individual tenure and land titling) influences social relations within each ethnic group, among neighbouring groups, and with political institutions. Specifically, do land reforms lead to a homogenization of society through the erosion of ethnic identities? Or is ethnicity still relevant for understanding rural society in highland Vietnam?

To answer these questions, I compare the experiences of two ethnic groups in northern Vietnam. The Thái (1.3 million in 1999) and the Tày (1.5 million) are the two largest groups of a dozen Tai-speaking peoples in Vietnam (a total of 3.8 million). The names of these two groups are the Vietnamese official ethnonyms (or exonyms, names given to an ethnic group from the outside), but they also happen to be their autonyms (names created and used by the people themselves), a relatively rare occurrence in the region. It can sometimes come as a surprise to people new to Southeast Asia that a few million Tai speakers live throughout northern Vietnam, explained by ancient migration paths from China into the peninsula.

This chapter looks at two cases studies, that of Chợ Đồn and Bản Lượt.[2] Chợ Đồn is a mountainous district 150 kilometres north of Hanoi (Hà Nội), in the Ba Bê Lake area of Bắc Kạn province. Chợ Đồn's population is typical of mountainous areas of North Vietnam, where Tai-speaking people represent 70 percent of the total population. Yao people (Dao in Vietnamese, also known as Mien, of the Miao-Yao ethnolinguistic family) account for 12 percent of the population, and lowland Kinh or Viet (Việt, of the Austro-Asiatic ethnolinguistic family) account for 9 percent. Bản Lượt is a Thái village in Mường Kim commune, Than Uyên district, Lào Cai province. The Thái here are unofficially subdivided between Black and White Thái (Câm Trọng 1978), though this study does not take this difference into account. Besides the Thái, Than Uyên district is inhabited by the Kinh, Hmong (H'mông, from the Miao-Yao ethnolinguistic group) and Khmu (Khơ Mú, from the Austro-Asiatic ethnolinguistic group).

These two cases allow a comparison of different ethnicities. The Tai speakers in Chợ Đồn belong to the Tày subgroup. Most of the Tày ancestors have settled in Vietnam's northwest for about two thousand years, whereas the Thái arrived from the ninth century (Lemoine 1997). The Tày have shared much of their history in the area with lowland Kinh people, and by the end of the nineteenth century had adopted similar social and administrative organizations. For example, Vietnamese ethnologists believe that the formal customary Tai practice of adopting collective land tenure at the village level disappeared in this region and was replaced a few centuries ago by individual property rights allowing family transfers, purchases, and sales based on patrilineal inheritance. The Thái, by contrast, dwelling further away from the delta, remained more independent from the Kinh and managed land at the village level in the customary collective way until the early 1950s. These

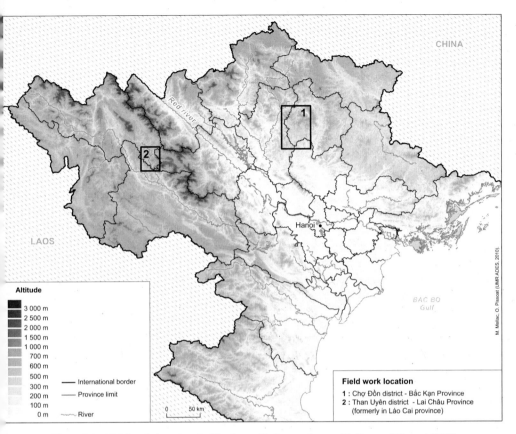

Figure 7.1 Fieldwork location in Northern Vietnam. *Source:* Mellac and Pissoat 2010

two groups may, therefore, have been affected differently by recent land reforms.

But first, it is useful to review how land titling has changed over time in northern Vietnam (Figure 7.1).

Land-Based Institutions in Northern Vietnam from Colonization to Decollectivization

Land-based institutions in northern Vietnam are the result of various influences and policy approaches adopted by diverse upland people, colonial authorities, and the Vietnamese state over time. Figure 7.2 presents an overview of overlapping influences at the central and local levels. Figure 7.3 summarizes the legal details of each model.

Local tenure systems in mountainous areas under colonization can be described as hybrid, complex, and dynamic. Such characteristics were the result of the extraordinary diversity and intricacy of the population in terms

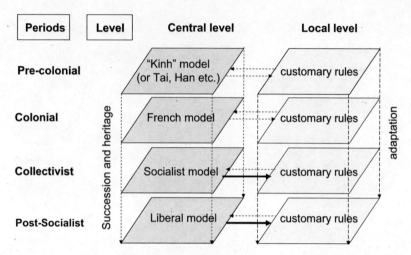

Figure 7.2 Overlapping influences of land-based institutions' models at local and national levels in Northern Vietnam. *Source:* Mellac

of both cultural and material practices. Agricultural practices, for instance, ranged from intensive rice cultivation conducted in valley bottoms, using complex irrigation networks, to extensive forest cultivations, either through individual activities or as part of group ventures. Land tenure was also influenced by constant struggles between the neighbouring powers of Laos, China, and Vietnam, occasionally Burma and Siam, and then France. Searching for order in such a complex mosaic is a perilous exercise. Spencer (1966), in his well-known essay "Shifting Cultivation in Southeastern Asia," lists dozens of systems of land use and tenure. Nonetheless, he argued that land tenure could be broadly divided between shifting cultivation (where land tenure is controlled by usufruct) and permanent-field cultivation such as irrigated paddy fields (controlled by private ownership). He also noticed that by the 1960s, the first form of ownership "retreated together to rougher country, to the more isolated reaches of inland territories, and to more remote locations off the main routes of political and cultural encroachment," whereas the second type "appeared in open lowland regions and around centers of urban influence, progressively replaced the first, though there has not always been a strict parallelism between them" (Spencer 1966, 98).

In reality, however, neither ethnicity nor types of agriculture are sufficient on their own to explain how different types of land tenure emerged over time. Land tenure also played a major part in the construction of the relations and distinctions between ethnic communities. Neighbouring groups shared at least a common understanding of their mutual systems. In some cases, when a group was politically and/or numerically dominant, the dominant land regime was extended to the dominated groups. For example,

Historical periods (North Vietnam)	National model (concerning/affecting land management)	Local situations (northern mountains)

Colonial period 1800-1953	**Central administration of land management:**
	• private property:
	  ▪ land registration and titling
	  ▪ land-based taxes
	  ▪ commoditization of land
		High local diversity:
		• central administration poorly enforced
		• customary rules: inclusive rights (land as a social product without monetary value)
		• mutual recognition of neighbouring institutions

Collectivist period 1953-86 1953-58: agrarian reform 1959-81: collectivization 1976: "Great socialist agriculture" 1981: • Chi Thi 100: individual contracts of production • first individual land allocation within the cooperatives	**Pyramidal and hierarchical organization of land management:** • land ownership: state (entire people) • land administration: administration units • restricted land use rights: cooperatives and state enterprises	**Apparent correspondence with the official standard:** • collectivization of the land • interethnic cooperatives • approximate calendars **High local diversity:** • lots of discrepancies with the official model • customary land rules and previous social organization still operating (spatial hinterlands, temporary systems, etc.)
Post-socialist period (socialist market economy) since 1986 1986: Đổi Mới 1988-89: • *khoan 10:* new individual contracts • *first land law:* new individual land allocation within the cooperatives 1993: *second land law* • new land allocation • individual land-use titles • exclusive land rights 2003: *third land law* • new land users (e.g., communities)	**Dual organization of land management:** • land ownership and administration: state • extended land use rights (including rights of transfer exchange, mortgage, and inheritance): cooperatives, state enterprises, individuals, exclusive (land use) rights, territorial nature of land rights	**Apparent correspondence with the official standard:** • land use rights allocation **High local diversity:** • lots of discrepancies with the official model • customary and collectivist land rules still operating

Figure 7.3 Land management and administration, situation at the national and local level from the colonial period to the post-socialist period.

in pre-colonial times, weaker groups such as the Khmu were forced to cultivate the paddy land belonging to the Thái ruling class (the noblemen or *tao*) and were only occasionally authorized to cultivate paddy land plots of their own.

French colonization added to this complexity. The French promoted a new type of land tenure based on their own model of private property and adopted a centralized system of administering land that was partly based on the Kinh's pre-existing management. But the colonists had neither the capacity nor the will to impose this system everywhere with the same intensity or speed, especially in the mountainous zones of the north. By the start of the twentieth century, however, northern regions were further integrated into central civil and military administrative systems, and Kinh representatives who had been vetted by the French authorities began progressively replacing local political leaders. At the same time, new rules were introduced. Land taxes, instead of head taxes, progressively penetrated the mountain regions and, accordingly, the French encouraged a system of individual land ownership as the only way to control land. In Thái areas, the French rejected collective land tenure systems, thinking that these systems strengthened the leadership of local chiefs (Abadie 1924). The French rejected all forms of shifting cultivation and considered permanent cultivation to be the only practice ensuring effective land control. Fallow land was identified as vacant and unowned and became registered as public domain. But progress was slow. In Lào Cai and Bắc Kạn provinces, land registration units had hardly appeared in the early 1940s, and soon after, the Second World War put a stop to the reforms. As Spencer put it, speaking for all of colonial Asia:

> Through all the colonial lands of southern and eastern Asia administrators worked from coastal points inland and up river valleys, establishing some variant of their European system of land control in such areas as could be brought under administrative supervision. Never did they complete the job of installing their own systems of land control, never were the untouched hinterlands systems fully codified and adjusted to the basic administrative system, and never was the concept of public domain made fully effective in all remaining territories. (Spencer 1966, 100)

The French system of land control is now seen to have contributed to widespread legal pluralism – the coexistence of multiple forms of land tenure from formal and informal jurisdictions. It is also considered an important reference for modern land legislation, both at local and national levels (Nguyen and Leroy 2005). But the French land regime, unfinished and spatially discontinuous, left lots of room for the pre-colonial land tenure systems to operate at the local scale.

The Socialist Land Tenure System

The socialist regime of the Democratic Republic of Vietnam (1954-76) keenly sought to unify the country through processes of agrarian and land reform. "Legal pluralism" never fully disappeared, but the socialist project was implemented, and the great majority of peasants cooperated with this. As mentioned, agrarian reform was such a popular reform that it largely sustained the launching of collectivization, a far less popular one. Initially, collectivization was, therefore, a relative success. As a contemporary author remarked:

> By the end of 1961, over 70 per cent of toiling peasants households of all national minorities, even the most backward ones, had joined agricultural cooperatives of a less advanced type (semi-socialist). From the outset, nearly all the rice fields and part of the livestock were managed by those cooperatives. This characterizes agricultural cooperation among the minorities. (Quang Canh 1968, 97)

But over time, collectivization did not succeed in boosting agricultural production or local development as hoped. Moreover, many peasants began to modify the official model. Below we explore how they did this.

Land was the property of the entire population, uniformly managed by the state (and theoretically, this is still the case today). The state held definitive rights of exclusion from and inclusion to land, delegating only rights for land use management. Land use management was organized in a top-down pyramid. Each administrative unit was allocated land use rights by the upper level and devolved part of the received rights to the lower level. Following this organization, each unit had restricted access to land and depended on the decisions taken at the higher level.[3]

Cooperatives, state enterprises, and state farms were the smaller official land users. These entities held the rights to allocate land and divide the production between workers' groups and brigades. One major difference between cooperatives and state farms and enterprises was the process that created them. State farms and enterprises were created and managed by administrative units or state bodies such as districts, provinces, or military units. Cooperatives, at their initial stages, were established on the basis of pre-existing social entities such as villages or hamlets. Later on, cooperatives were enlarged and restructured in order to break traditional social units, which was one of the core objectives of collectivization. But some of the main characteristics of the cooperatives, at least in mountainous and remote areas, continued to reflect village structures.

The main characteristics of the Chợ Đồn and Bản Lượt cooperatives can be described in terms of both time and space. Concerning time, it is noticeable that most of the cooperatives followed the official calendar with a recurrent interval. Moreover, despite this approximate timing, the main reforms were deprived of their substance in the process of their adoption. As such, large cooperatives in Chợ Đồn and Bản Lượt had, at best, only a short-term existence. In Bản Lượt, the initial cooperative created at the village scale grew quickly and gave birth to a two-village cooperative that was supposed to be a high-scaled one – that is, a more integrated one. Thus, this cooperative was permanently and strictly divided into two production units based on different villages. In Chợ Đồn, cooperatives took far more varied forms, but very few of them followed official requirements to break traditional social units. Indeed, research for this chapter showed that previous political and social structures were, in most cases, still very active.[4]

These traditional structures had consequences in terms of the spatial extent and organization of cooperatives. Unlike state enterprises and state farms, which had clear and restricted boundaries, mountainous cooperatives were not clearly delimited. In both regions, the cooperatives were built up around paddy land, which was the only permanently collectivized land, often surrounded by large, non-collectivized hinterlands between the different cooperatives. Furthermore, neither collective nor individually owned land were permanently delimited, and their extent varied over time.

These characteristics had important consequences on both land tenure and social and ethnic organization in the mountains. First, most farmers belonged to two groups: the cooperative and their original social group. This double system of belonging was complex and dynamic. In some cases in both Bản Lượt and Chợ Đồn, the two units overlapped, allowing the previous land regime to be largely maintained. In other cases, such as pluri-ethnic cooperatives (with no dominant group) or in cooperatives where paddy land was materially transformed by opening new paddy land or transforming irrigation networks, farmers were only remotely attached to their old structure and did not maintain the old land tenure system. These cooperatives were the last to disappear at the time of decollectivization.

The new collective arrangements also influenced social relations in other ways. Where there was a large availability of non-irrigated land surrounding villages, the collective administration allowed individuals or households with problems, such as shortages of food, to graze animals or to open new individually owned swiddens. Larger groups – comprising several households – were also allowed to cultivate non-irrigated land if villages had limited access to paddy. In Chợ Đồn, shifting cultivation was the only solution for sedentarized Yao people who had little paddy, or for cooperatives located on marginal land that was remote and/or at high elevation. For such activities, land rights and regulations were very similar to the pre-collectivist ones. Accordingly, cooperative members were engaged in a double land system, which was both recognized and respected by neighbouring groups. For instance, old servile groups, which previously had to pay tribute to dominant ethnicities, still had difficulties in gaining recognition. In Bản Lượt, Sa people (Khmu) benefited under collectivization because they did not have to pay tribute anymore, but they still did not obtain a full and definitive recognition of their rights from Thái on the paddy land they cultivated.

And finally, as I discussed elsewhere (Mellac 2009), the importance of cooperatives varied for different reasons. In Chợ Đồn, it was generally easier for Kinh people than for Yao people to become integrated within lowland Tày cooperatives and territories because of several common, mutually recognized cultural practices between lowland Tày and Kinh. Yao-Tày relations, on the other hand, were rendered more problematic, paradoxically, because they had lived close to each other for a long period but had specialized in different forms of agriculture. Ethnic identities played an important role in the evolution of cooperatives and the construction of territorial units both during and after collectivization. But it was also clear in Chợ Đồn that the ethnic proximity between Kinh and Tày differed depending on the initial size of cooperatives, which in turn were influenced by local politics and histories.

For example, the cooperatives and inter-ethnic relations were very different in the northern and southeastern communes of Chợ Đồn district. In the southeastern communes, small-scale cooperatives were created thanks to the fragmentation of rice field areas and to the small size and low density of villages and hamlets. These cooperatives never fully broke the relations between households and their land. They worked well when small numbers of non-Tày households were included. But they did not work very well when there were large numbers of non-Tày. In this latter case, newcomers had to create a new cooperative in an old Tày hamlet.

In the northern communes, the higher concentration of paddy land and large populations led to larger cooperatives and greater management difficulties. Moreover, paddy land and irrigation systems were deeply altered and were managed at a higher collective level than in southern communes. Both factors created tensions inside cooperatives, as well as within and between ethnic groups. Access to paddy land was more difficult for newcomers such that the northern Kinh always had more precarious livelihoods during collectivization than did those in the south. This situation encouraged the division of cooperatives following ethnicity. But full decollectivization led to numerous cases of resistance. As a result, large northern cooperatives were the last to be dismantled, and paddy land was the last to be recovered by Tày people. Later, this led to further difficulties in access to agricultural land for non-Tày.

It is also clear that communes with important political roles (for various reasons) in the new (socialist) system created larger cooperatives with a greater ability to transform both the social order and land tenure. In such communes, the inter-ethnic relations were managed under cooperative rules. This, in turn, produced tensions both within cooperatives and between communities, which resulted in strengthening the social identities of the communities.

In sum, as these examples show, cooperatives were important factors in constructing identities, and identities were a fundamental reference for the building and functioning of the pluri-ethnic cooperatives.

The Post-Socialist Regime

As Nguyen and Leroy (2005) noted, the advent of the Socialist Republic of Vietnam in 1976 coincided with the return to peacetime and resulted in a new form of social identity. During the wars against France, South Vietnam, the United States, Cambodia, and China, the state was able to present the threat of defeat as a national Vietnamese problem, for which it, the state, should take responsibility. In peacetime, the state lost its primacy and people began to identify more with lower-scaled organizations, such as households or villages. As soon as the threat was gone and the country reunified, the sacrifices the lower organizations had made for the state could no longer be easily justified.

Nguyen and Leroy explain the advent of decollectivization by pointing to the incapacity of the state to continue to legitimate its reform. Accordingly, the loss of state authority resulted in the progressive and careful implementation of a land regime that was very different from the socialist model.

Land reforms of the 1980s were conducted in two fundamental steps. First, from 1981 to 1993, reforms did not question the existence of the cooperatives. They remained the smallest land user officially recognized, but cooperatives were allowed to allocate land to households and individuals. New contracts (such as "contract 100" and "contract 10") under this system introduced direct (but not full) control of the harvest by individuals.[5] A direct link between land and households was thus progressively introduced (Bergeret 1995).

The second step started in 1993 with the second land law. The law legally recognized individuals and households as new land users and acknowledged new rights to exchange, transfer, lease, inherit, and mortgage the land use right.[6] Land was then allocated for a second time to households on either medium- or long-term bases (fifteen years for land planted annually; fifty years for land covered by perennial crops). With this law, cooperatives definitively lost their control on land.

Under this new system, as under the socialist regime before, land remained the property of the entire people, uniformly managed by the state. But a new dual structure was introduced, dividing the control over land between landholders and the state. On the one hand, this new legislation gave certain rights to landholders. On the other hand, it also gave the state an active role in safeguarding landholders' rights, enforcing limits on land use, and collecting land taxes. The new legislation, therefore, promotes exclusive rights in the sense that the law does not recognize any claims other than the estate of production held by landholders and a single estate of administration held by the state (Sikor 2006). The resulting situation is somewhere between the collectivist situation and the liberal model of private property, which considers individual property rights as opposable to a third party and not as rights exchangeable by way of compensation within a community.

One of the major changes of the post-socialist regime lies in the territorial nature of new rights for land and resources. Land is classified and divided into various categories that correspond to restricted activities and access. In return, access to resources is restricted according to various land categories. The whole territory is divided into these categories, from permanent cultivations to forest sanctuaries dedicated to wild animals surviving in remote forests. As Scott (1998, 2) argues, one of the crucial characteristics of a modern state is the attempt to give administrative order to nature and society, with the objective being to better manage them both and to better assume the "classic state functions of taxation, conscription, and prevention of rebellions." In decolonized Vietnam, collectivization was the first state-led attempt to order nature and society. Nowadays, the state is more likely to impose a liberal and market-oriented standardization, which, following the capitalist model, uses a geometrical perception of the land and sees individual tenure of fragmented land as the only possible category and means of managing and sharing resources.

A further important change was to make it easier to treat land and resources as commodities. Formally, however, this is not recognized by the state. A careful analysis of successive land regulations (the 1988, 1993, and 2003 land laws, for instance) shows that commodifying the means of production, such as land and resources, is legally restricted. The first large-scale allocations of agricultural land in 1989 and 1993 were designed to benefit solely the residents of administrative units at the commune level, rather than to allow commodity purchasing and reselling more generally. Successive laws also fixed maximum areas of land per user for each category of agricultural and forestry land. Land was not to be reclassified easily and had to be used for the specified purpose. For instance, one former definition of agricultural land defined it as the land cultivated without interruption for more than one year. As such, capitalistic accumulation or speculation of agricultural and forestry land are rendered difficult.

Moreover, land laws successively recognized an increasing number of land users. Under the 1993 land law, state farms, state enterprises, and cooperatives were joined by households and individuals as legitimate landholders. Later on, the 2003 land law recognized land use rights of private enterprises, overseas Vietnamese, and foreigners.[7] It also introduced a new category of "population communities," or villagers who have the same customary practices. In 2007, the government (and some international donors) openly favoured "communal" tenure (World Bank 2007), but such tenure remains relatively rare.

The allocation of land use rights to different users is complex and varies with the type of land. In simple terms, agricultural land was mainly allocated to households on an egalitarian basis under the supervision of cooperatives prior to (or in some cases soon after) the 1993 law. After this law was introduced, the newly created district cadastral units could produce land use titles. This system is also applied to forest land when such land is neither strictly protected nor allocated to forest enterprises, and hence a large part of forest land is considered to be under the usual state-led management scheme.[8]

The delimitation between forest and agricultural land is a very important and complex element of the present legislation (Mellac 2000). Defining the lines between agricultural and forest land has caused conflicts within state bodies. It has also encouraged great diversity in individually held landholdings in terms of how regulations are applied or land is allocated. Under an extreme set of circumstances, a single family head may receive full land use rights for permanent agriculture. The agricultural land use may be allocated by the cooperative, and land use titles may come from the district cadastral unit. He or she may also receive land titles but have restricted rights for a small parcel of production forest nearby. He or she may be contracted by a forest enterprise to harvest bamboo on one plot and plant forest trees on another, and may receive a small plot of protected forest from a watershed management board with the sole rights and duties to protect this land. These kinds of multiple allocations and activities created fragmented territories at the scale of the village or commune. It is also typical of a pyramidal organization of land rights, where each category of land has its own pyramid of users.

This situation was aggravated by the lack of legal recognition of communities with regard to land management. Before the 2003 land law was passed, only individuals and households were recognized as being able to receive land use rights; basic units of social organization, such as villages, were not considered. This situation is common in post-socialist countries and partly explains the persistence of cooperatives in some places (Sikor 2006, 619). Under the 2003 land law, villages and similar organizations were allowed to control land use and access to resources. But the necessary conditions and procedures for this are so numerous and complicated that few villages can fulfill the requirements to do so (Mellac 2006b).

To conclude, the "official" post-socialist land tenure regime has an apparent paradox. On the one hand, priority is given to individuals who benefit from extensive (and exclusive) land use rights, and recent laws have simplified land tenure in accordance with many international standards. But on the other hand, the marketization of land is still legally restricted, and there continue to be various layers of control of land. Unsurprisingly, this has led to an unclear situation that can be interpreted in different ways at the local level.

Implementing Land Reform in Tai-Speaking Localities: Diversity and Resistance

Let's now examine in more detail the specific aspects of land allocation in the two case studies, showing the shape that local reactions to the new land legislation took (see also Mellac 2004). These case studies also show how agency is at play in local responses to national regulations, with a strong influence from local history and customary rights among villagers.

The "Cooperative Paddy Land"

In Bản Lượt village (Figure 7.4), Than Uyên district, Lai Châu province (formerly in Lào Cai province), a predominantly Thái settlement, the history of paddy-land distribution is long and complicated (Mellac, 2006a). The process started in 1981 after the contract 100, but by 2002 it was still not officially completed. At this time, not all land was recorded in the Red Book, the official record of land use titles. Allocating (or reallocating) land to villagers was not, however, the major problem for the village. There were three major allocations after 1981. The first, from 1988 to 1989, followed the first land law and the implementation of contract 10. The second, in 1994, followed the second land law. The third, in 1997, was carried out to compensate land losses after catastrophic floods in 1996 and to anticipate the land titling campaign scheduled to start in 1998.

Each land allocation was organized by different people: the first was organized by the last chief of the cooperative, the final two by the successive village heads. According to villagers, each allocation followed procedures aiming to guarantee equal access to land for all villagers, including non-Tai speakers – approximately three hundred square metres of paddy land per worker (for the 1997 allocation).

If the first three land allocations were carried out in accordance with national decisions, the last allocation, in 1997, did not correspond to any official event, and the titling of rice fields was particularly late and slow. In addition, between each large-scale allocation, village heads carried out additional allocations in order to acknowledge demographic changes (births, deaths, and newly married couples). Consequently, many households had land that was allocated, and then modified, on several occasions. Therefore, land allocation was not inspired solely by national legislation; it was mainly determined by village heads.

Figure 7.4 An upper view of Ban Luot village, Than Uyên district.
Photo by Mellac 2000

Bản Lượt villagers distinguish clearly between two main categories of paddy land. The first category, called "cooperative paddy land" *(na hợp tác xã)*, is composed of sections that were attached to the village cooperative at its creation, plus a few others that were cleared under the supervision of the cooperative. Plots allocated to villagers belong to this category. The second category, called *na tí* (or *na tí hon*), refers to small plots cleared by the households after 1986, when households were officially authorized to open new plots for their own use. Such sections are mostly terraced and are located on marginal slopes. However, they tend to be cultivated twice a year. These newly opened plots were never taken into account by the successive distributions. None of them is registered in the official land use titles and, consequently, is not allocated by state decree. In addition to these two fundamental categories, there is another subcategory, besides the plots being allocated to villagers, within cooperative paddy land. Some plots are allocated as a form of salary to villagers holding one of three official positions: the village head, the chief of the forest protection, and the head of security. This land is withdrawn when they stop holding these positions. However, this very local category does not match any legal category and apparently does not exist in any other region of Vietnam. In fact, this allocation seems similar to the allocation of land to the local elite of the pre-collectivist period, such as noblemen or commoners holding important positions.

The different categories of rice fields have many similarities with categories that existed in the village during the colonial period. Rice fields at this time were also divided into two main categories: *na tí hon* and *na bản na muong* (village and *muong* rice fields).[9] The first category designated fields recently cleared by households. These new plots were directly managed by their creators without compensation for five to ten years before being added to the second category. The second category was considered to represent the village's collective rice fields. They could not be appropriated by individuals and were allocated by the village head to all the households in the village. In return, villagers were liable for taxes and corvées, that is, collective labour to maintain the local irrigation network and cultivate specific sections, such as those belonging to the village head and other elite. This work duty is no longer expected.

In short, today, land tenure in Bản Lượt village is still based on former land regulations and categories that jointly organize agricultural territory and village society. However, former land regulations are reactivated only on ancient paddy land. Three-quarters of Bản Lượt households are ignorant of official regulations and hold ideas on their rights that may be contrary to state definitions. They believe, for example, that transactions (sale, purchase, inheritance) are not authorized on allocated land (that is, the cooperative paddy land) but that transactions are permitted on non-allocated land *(na ti)*. This is consistent with the position of the village head, who defined the cooperative paddy land as the common property of the village, managed by the village, and indicates that villagers are totally free to manage the recently opened fields.

Bản Lượt demonstrates an apparent paradox. Officially allocated paddy land is managed by old customary regulations, but non-allocated land is managed in accordance with current regulations for allocated land. However, the only land allocated by the early 2000s was cooperative paddy land, which excluded, in addition to the *na ti*, non-irrigated slope cultivation, including subsidized perennial plantations (for example, tea and official forest land, even if the land of the latter had no trees and was used for agriculture).

The Return to the Ancestral Land
Chợ Đồn district (Figure 7.5), Bắc Kạn province, a predominantly Tày area where I conducted my doctoral fieldwork, appears at first to be the opposite

Figure 7.5 Phong Huan commune, Cho Don district. *Photo by Mellac 1997*

of the Bản Lượt case. Land was divided fast and early, without consideration of equal access to land for villagers.

Individual paddy land use titling was completed in the district in 1994, only a year after the 1993 land law came into effect. This rapid progress occurred because most of the cooperatives had long authorized households to cultivate individual plots on a long-term basis. Indeed, in some communes, most of the plots recorded in households' Red Books (land use titles) in 1994 had already been cultivated by them since the early 1980s.

Despite this progress, land division did not follow government procedures of allocating land to individuals on a new, equal basis. Tày households re-appropriated paddy plots cultivated by their ascendants before collectivization. Former customary rules and principles, such as the right of first occupancy, the principle of continuity of use, and transfer rights, were re-activated. In addition, they kept the use of the land they had individually cleared since contract 100. Accordingly, it is inaccurate to speak about land distribution or allocation in Chợ Đồn district; rather, it is more a return to the ancestral land-use principles.

This "return" has created important differences in land tenure among the population. These differences involve the amount of land ancestors used to hold and the location of the village or commune. It is obvious in Chợ Đồn that the creation of the cooperatives (and the control over the population) had created a different distribution of people around paddy land than what had developed previously when local populations could relocate as a response to land scarcity. As a result, there were now strong differences in the scarcity of paddy land. Moreover, some cooperatives responded by increasing the extent of paddy or the annual yield (by enlarging irrigation networks and modifying local topography), whereas others did not. In the first cases, farmers were more reluctant to "return to the ancestral land," as this might mean losing access to land that had been created or improved.

If the "return" generated land inequalities among the Tày, even stronger differences appeared between other ethnic groups. During the socialist regime, the Kinh had participated in migratory movements organized by the state, and the upland Yao had been resettled to valley bottoms. As a result of the "return to ancestral land," many of these people lost access to paddy land because most of the collective land had belonged to Tày households before collectivization. Non-Tày groups had no solution other than to buy plots, clear new plots, or give up irrigated rice cultivation. In this location, the non-Tày groups accepted the "return" without notable conflict.

The lack of conflict can be partly explained by the temporary permission for both Tày and non-Tày people to open large areas of swiddens as a form of compensation for land changes. This situation gradually changed when forest land began to be individually allocated, starting in 1992.[10] From then on, the ban on swiddens was progressively reactivated, and most agricultural land on slopes was reclassified as forest land. But in some cases, the government specifically allocated new land on slopes, at both national and local (district) levels, in order to compensate some groups for the loss of paddy land and to acknowledge the historical dependency on forest land. In Chợ Đồn, these acts impacted positively on land ownership for swiddeners such as the Yao. But it had limited impacts on the poorer households among the Tày.

Analyzing the Differences

Figure 7.6 summarizes the findings in the two cases of Chợ Đồn and Bản Lượt. The differences between these two districts can be explained by similar, if not identical, processes.

A factual description of Chợ Đồn and Bản Lượt puts too much emphasis on their differences. Differences are interesting because they reveal the wiggle room temporarily granted to the localities by the central power, and sometimes obtained by the localities. But there are also quite similar processes occurring in the two localities that involve local agency and history. An

Chợ Đồn	Bản Lượt
Two apparently opposite cases	
• no "organized" paddy land allocation	• four successive paddy land allocations organized at the village level
• official titling completed in 1994 for all paddy land	• official titling still not achieved in 2001 and affecting only one category of paddy land
• unequal access to paddy land	• equal access to the land for all villagers (300m²/person)
• "forest land" allocation started in 1992 and rapidly achieved	• no "forest land" allocation (in 2001)
Generated by similar processes	
"Traditional" (pre-collectivist) customary land rules and mobilization of institutions	
The "return to the ancestral land"	Paddy land categories: • collective management of the *na hop tac xa* • individual management of *na ti*
In the continuity of collectivization	
The "return to the ancestral land" was better accepted and less problematic in communes and villages where cooperatives were passive	Collectivization reinforced the collective appropriation of the land
A progressive implementation of the national legislation	
100 percent land titling	Land titling in progress
Land law enforcement	Emergence of local competition putting forward the national legislation

Figure 7.6 Behind the differences: two apparently opposite cases generated by similar processes.

in-depth analysis of the cases shows that traditional customary land rules were mobilized by farmers when reacting to decollectivization and the new land institutions. In both cases, the local responses to decollectivization reflected the historical nature of land tenure within non-Kinh societies.

In Bản Lượt, the social and political implications of using customary rules become visible in light of the multiple purposes of paddy land categories. These categories do not simply use the vocabulary of the past. Similarly, they are not directed by hydraulic matters. Indeed, the "traditional" categories are now largely part of more complex irrigation systems, involving multiple and independent units. The size and level of the irrigation networks no longer correspond with the extent and level of land management. Reactivating customary rules, therefore, must arise from social and political causes. In Chợ Đồn, the "return to the ancestral land" is similarly not motivated by hydraulic considerations: individual tenure is rendering water management much more problematic than did collective management. Many Tày have paddy land shortages. Accordingly, the "return" also cannot be understood as an individualistic Tày strategy to safeguard their rights on paddy land.

In Chợ Đồn, as in Bản Lượt, the traditional land-based institutions regulated the population as much as the land. This is particularly clear in Bản Lượt, where land categories structured local social groups in parallel to agricultural work. For instance, the former collective category *(na ban na muong)* was divided into subcategories that corresponded to functional social classes, with specific roles in redistributing resources. The use of two main land categories also played a role in social dynamics. Ancient *na tí* land was especially useful to newcomers in the village. Later, new *na tí* land gave households the potential to escape the collective constraints of cooperative paddy land.

Land institutions have also, in some localities, been linked to water institutions. For example, in Bản Lượt, the division of land gives each villager a minimum access to irrigated paddy land. In Chợ Đồn, however, access is not as secure or egalitarian. Instead, access to land is guaranteed as long as water conditions have been fulfilled, and access to water is assured as long as local collective work is performed under the supervision of the local "founders" (and their descendants) of the hydraulic units.

Such social regulations on access to land and water are possible only if some aspects of the cooperatives' management have remained constant. Or, to put it another way, the continuation of old systems of hierarchies have occurred most often where cooperatives had the least impact on pre-existing social practices. As Sikor (2006) notes, the collectivist process often reinforced, much more than destroyed, the collective appropriation of land within Thái villages. Decollectivization, in that sense, constitutes a potentially dramatic change in land management and social organization. And it is not surprising to observe today a clear and even idealized affirmation of collective principles. For example, the village head of Bản Lượt stated that land cannot be sold or bought. All land movements must be carried out under his supervision, on a purely free basis, and must take place within the strict limits of the village community. The village head is therefore reinforcing his position as the guarantor of fair (and equal) access to land for villagers. He still organizes collective work and allocates land to households.

In addition, villagers in Bản Lượt wish to adopt collective management (of the customary type, not the socialist type) of the cooperative paddy land because it facilitates a collective and localized identity, symbolized by the village (referred to as the *"bản"* in Tai). In Tai-speaking societies, the *bản* was the smallest socio-political unit, and it had a large degree of autonomy. Yet, under successive reforms by colonial and socialist regimes, the *bản* lost this autonomy, and *bản* and villages do not have any social or administrative meaning in today's Vietnam. In Bản Lượt, however, a permanent and recurrent reference is still made to the *bản*. Indeed, villagers still refer to the cooperative as an authority to designate the decollectivized plots, and view cooperative paddy land as a link between the village community and a very symbolic part of the village resources. As such, the *bản* might be called an "inspiring myth" (Di Meo and Buleon 2005), both in the pre-collectivist Tai socio-political system and today. The village is a place where a collective identity can emerge in the context of a still very centralized state. Emerging forms of land tenure in Bản Lượt may also be considered forms of "resistance" according to Scott's terms (1985), because they allow local people a sense of identity and continuity under imposed changes.

Land Tenure Reforms and Changes in Identity

After laying out these multiple foci and levels of agency, we turn to the question, how are land reforms connected to changes in ethnicity and identity? Under collectivization, ethnic minorities from lands at a higher altitude have been integrated into the midland majority Tai speakers' and former feudal lords' land system in many ways. Even representatives of the lowland Kinh majority have been integrated. In Bản Lượt, for example, the few Hmong and Kinh households that settled in the village under the cooperatives were perfectly integrated into the collective land regime. Most Kinh settled early in the village and immediately joined the cooperatives. They were party members who voluntarily moved from the Red River delta to reinforce the collectivization process; some worked as teachers or nurses. The Hmong in the region settled afterward, during the 1970s, and some were employed in the district police. These households, following the usual custom, were allocated land in cooperatives on an average basis and were required to conduct collective work. This situation was described as normal by both sides and did not create any apparent dispute. This was not the case for the *na ti*, nor was it for all plots that had been individually cleared and managed. The main problems that arose concerned plots dedicated to industrial crops, which were implicated in disputes when the Thái complained about land cleared by both the Hmong and Kinh, and by some Thái. It was considered illegitimate for non-Thái people to open large plots within the village community. There were also conflicts between neighbouring Thái villages. As a response, physical demarcations were erected in all disputed areas. Conflicts did occur with neighbouring Sa (Khmu) people. The Sa complained when Thái households opened swiddens near their village and let their buffaloes graze freely. On the other side, the Thái accused the Sa of stealing cattle. As a result, villagers defined green strips – strips of land approximately eight metres wide managed by forest protection units in order to fight erosion – clearly under the supervision of the district forest protection unit around Sa villages.

In Chợ Đồn, as discussed above, Kinh and Yao people lost most of the land they harvested in cooperatives during the "return to the ancestral land." However, paddy land disputes remained very rare and the return was not an important concern for these groups. But near Tày villages, Yao households opened large swiddens. In one commune (Tan Lap), for example, the Yao comprise about one-third of the population. Their villages are distinct from Tày settlements despite being adjacent. A few years after the Yao were voluntarily resettled to this valley bottom, the cooperative split into two monoethnic cooperatives, each one cultivating its own paddy land and dry crops on sloping land. At this time, the two cooperatives had common hydraulic activities and were closely related. When the "return to the ancestral land" occurred, the Yao lost paddy land and responded by clearing large swiddens in the immediate vicinity of the villages. This act openly contradicted the customary land rules of the Tày, which stated that swiddens should be remote and not close to villages or watershed areas. The Yao justified their initial decision to clear the land by saying they are no longer allowed to move.

Ethnic minorities were also given advantages during the process of forest land allocation. In the southeastern communes of Chợ Đồn, where access to paddy land remained relatively easy, non-Tày households (mainly Kinh) did not receive more forest than the Tày. In the northern communes, where access to paddy land was more difficult, the Kinh and the Yao insisted on receiving larger areas of forest land. In the commune of Tan Lap, for instance, plots were situated in the communal watershed area, in a location not typically cultivated by Yao people in ancient times. This situation exasperated some Tày people and raised concerns about ethnic divisions, land tenure, and forest protection.

There was surprisingly little protest over paddy land in both case studies. This can be partially explained by the application of customary rules on paddy land. In Bản Lượt, no difference was made between ethnicities in the allocation of collective rice land as long as they inhabited the village and participated in collective work. Land was allocated according to households' residential areas. This was an assertion of inclusive rights. In Chợ Đồn, the reactivation of ancestral rules excluded de facto households having no ancestral paddy land. But land access was not restricted to Tai groups. Kinh and Yao had the opportunity to buy land and were free to open new sections of land as long as they respected water regulations. There were also no theoretical constraints on the exchange of land between ethnic groups.

In both cases, the reactivation of customary rules on paddy land resulted more or less in the integration of non-Tai households into Tai society. In Chợ Đồn, for instance, the Kinh were more likely to be integrated into Tày villages (to settle or marry) when they were few in number or when they held a good political position in the area, such as being village leaders. In Bản Lượt, Hmong people benefited from a large amount of land within the village. They may have lived in marginal hamlets, but they played an important role in the district police.

The last point to consider is the willingness in both locations to offer compensation to ethnic minorities that temporarily lost access to paddy land. In Chợ Đồn, people were given extra access to swidden during the time of forest land allocation. In Bản Lượt, the Thái contested Khmu claims on forest land but made no special complaint about claims to paddy fields. This situation suggests that the Tai speakers in both cases were able to offer minimum living conditions to all groups. In turn, this indicates a willingness of people to implement the spirit of land reforms as a means of access to livelihoods (Sikor 2006). In addition, it signals a desire to use forest land as a means to offset problems experienced on paddy land.

Conclusion: Commodification of Land and Homogenization of Identities?

This chapter reviews evidence from upland northern Vietnam concerning the relationship of ethnic identity and land reform. I have argued here that different ethnic groups have held onto customary means of organizing access to land despite the changes to collectivization under socialism and toward individual land ownership and exchange afterward. Different communities of the majority Tai-speaking people (and their Tày and Thái subgroups) have also related to small ethnic groups, such as the Yao, Hmong, and – paradoxically – Kinh, in different ways, but these groups have become integrated when they shared other cultural practices. This flexibility strongly indicates that for these populations, ethnicity is not perceived as being above all essential but can be adapted strategically according to circumstances and various other criteria. But do these changes mean that land is now increasingly becoming commoditized, and peoples homogenized?

One important question is whether it is now possible for old ethnic identities to persist if the land management linked to them is changing. As Godelier (1984) argues, territorial ownership shapes, and is shaped by, relationships to nature and the relationships between humans. Regulation and land allocation also concern societies as a whole. Registration, for instance, is not merely a technical intervention but involves political-economic and cultural processes. It is about who gets what and why, and about how each society sees nature. Land reform that dramatically changes the terms of access to land may therefore impact ethnic identities, or produce a deterritorialization of ethnicity – that is, a downplaying of the primordial aspect of ethnicity. Is this happening in highland northern Vietnam? Or do ethnic groups there demonstrate an ability to meet change in creative ways?

In Vietnam, the state has sought to impose a uniform land tenure system based on individual rights, a geometrical conception of space. Its legitimacy is rooted at the national level with exclusive means of land ownership. But, as this chapter shows, the actual situation on the ground is far from homogeneous. This is not surprising. The colonial project was resisted in various ways, and socialism has come and gone; why should the new state automatically be more effective? Instead, there are various barriers against the implementation of a new dominant system of land tenure, calling into play the agency of local societies.

There are now various incentives toward globalization and investment in land. Vietnamese peasants cannot yet be called "mass consumers," but market relations are increasing. Land reforms also make land easier to buy and sell. State agents and organizations play an important role in this process by using their pre-emptive rights to expropriate rural land users abusively and to allocate (or sell) land to building industries, who, in turn, can sell on. Such dynamics have so far affected only small rural towns, but the general conditions for commoditization of all rural land and resources already exist.

A further factor here is the growth and influence of exogenous economic and political actors who favour land marketization in Vietnam. Such actors range from the World Bank to building enterprises and Chinese micro-traders crossing the border every day, all of them favouring a land market. The World Bank, for instance, repetitively insists on the necessity for all Southeast Asian countries, including Vietnam, to liberalize land markets and to allocate and deliver land titles (Grard 2004). As noted earlier, the 2003 land law legalized the role of some newcomers by recognizing land use rights for private enterprises, overseas Vietnamese, and foreigners. Such actors are particularly numerous and active in urban and suburban areas but are also more and more present in rural zones, as are lowland Kinh investors. As Scott (1998, 8) states, "Today, global capitalism is perhaps the most powerful force for homogenization, whereas the state may in some instances be the defender of local differences and variety."

Together, these factors suggest that the liberal land market may result in the commoditization of land, with implications for ethnic identities in rural zones. Indeed, the loss of legitimacy of the Communist Party after the introduction of individual land use rights might suggest that the state may not be a defender of local differences, as Scott proposes.

But the evidence put forth in this chapter suggests that the trends toward commoditization and homogenization may not be occurring as quickly as that. One of the most important findings in Chợ Đồn and Bản Lượt is that traditional means of land tenure and access are enduring and have enabled ethnic groups to cope with socio-economic and political change over the years. Even collectives reflected pre-existing social structures, and the means of allocating land were influenced by local customs of exchange and hierarchy. There has already been a long and active cohabitation of different ethnic groups into identical social unities. This trend suggests that wall-to-wall new land rules may still allow the coexistence of different ethnic groups, and that groups will find ways to overcome risks to livelihoods and access to agricultural land that might result from uniform land rules.

In addition, new land rules may not be implemented without some form of negotiation, or even delaying tactics, by local agents. Under socialism, there were no clearly recognized intermediate layers of control between the state and landholders, and this favoured individual behaviour and the ability of local communities to act with greater agency to implement land rules as they wished. The 2003 land law legalized one layer of intermediate control by establishing so-called population communities, which provided rural people with the opportunity to orient local land relations toward local priorities and to negotiate flexible access to land within the law. Within these arrangements are the ability for local actors to use pre-existing systems of social organization to provide land to local people rather than adopting the uniform market-driven and individualistic land system.

Notes

1 In this chapter, "Tai" refers to any speaker of the Tai branch of the larger Tai-Kadai language family, which includes all speakers of one form or another of that vast cluster of languages, be they located in Guangxi, Guizhou, Yunnan, Burma, Assam, Vietnam, Laos, or indeed Thailand, where most of them dwell. The Thái of Vietnam are not to be confused with the Thai of Thailand.
2 Data were collected by surveys in 1995-98 (Chợ Đồn), and in 2001-2 (Bản Lượt). In Chợ Đồn, in-depth surveys were conducted in three communes: Tân Lập, Bằng Lãng, and Phong Huân.
3 As Humphrey (1983, quoted in Sikor 2006, 623) has shown, this system matched the model of the Soviet state farms:

> The state farms had been allocated land by the district authorities. The state farm leadership, in turn, assigned estates of administration to several brigades. The series of allocation continued, with the brigade leaders allocating estates of production to production units. The local series of allocation therefore included the district authorities, the state farm, the brigades, and the production units, creating a hierarchy of overlapping claims on land. These series of allocations referred to geographically separate plots of land as well as shares in the total harvest of jointly farmed land.

4 In some cases, for instance, village heads still succeeded each other by way of patrilineal inheritance. The founding households still controlled water management, and cooperative members cultivated their own segments of land. Most cooperatives, and the brigades working for cooperatives, were based on pre-existing social groups.
5 These two contracts were defined by two successive directives, CT/TU/100 in 1981 and CT/TW/10 in 1988. The first encouraged the cooperative to divide the land between households and permitted them to keep the surplus production exceeding a fixed norm. The second specified and extended the duration of land allocation to households, which increased land tenure security. A nationwide land allocation followed this directive.

6 Articles 1 and 3, Land Law of Vietnam 1993 (National Political Publisher 1997).
7 Unlike the 1993 land law, the 2003 land law concentrates on urban and industrial land and does not introduce significant change for agricultural and forestry land management. Rights of private enterprises, overseas Vietnamese, and foreigners are found in art. 9, Luat Dat Dai 2003 – Land Law 2003 (National Political Publisher 1997).
8 Forest land is divided into three categories, with an increasing degree of protection: production forest, protected forest, and special-use forest.
9 The *muong* (or *muang*) were one of the basic Tai socio-political units through feudal times.
10 The process was, however, very slow until 1996.

References
Abadie, M. 1924. *Les races du Haut Tonkin de Phong Tho à Lang Son*. Sociétés d'Éditions Géographiques. Paris: Société d'Editions Géographiques Maritimes et Coloniales.
Bergeret, P. 1995. Land Policy in Vietnam. *Vietnamese Studies* 45(115): 31-45.
–. 2002. *Paysans, Etat et marchés au Vietnam: Dix ans de coopération agricole dans le bassin du Fleuve Rouge*. Paris: Gret/Karthala.
Câm Trong. 1978. *Nguoi Thái o Tây Bac Viêt Nam* [The Thái in Northwestern Viêt Nam]. Hanoi: Nha Xuât Ban Khoa Hoc Xa Hôi.
Di Meo, G., and P. Buleon. 2005. *L'espace social, lecture géographique des sociétés*. Paris: Armand Colin.
Godelier, M. 1984. *L'idéel et le matériel*. Paris: Le Livre de Poche (coll. Biblio Essai).
Grard, A. 2004. Les réformes foncières au Vietnam: Etude des marchés fonciers périurbains de deux pôles secondaires du Nord Vietnam. DESS dissertation, French Institute of Urban Studies, University of Paris.
Kerkvliet, B.J.T. 1997. *Land Struggles and Land Regimes in the Philippines and Vietnam during the Twentieth Century*. The Wertheim Lecture 1997, Centre for Asian Studies Amsterdam, Amsterdam.
Lavigne Delville, P. 1998. Avant-propos. In *Quelles politiques foncièères pour l'Afrique rurale? Réconcilier pratiques, légitimité et légalité*, ed. P. Lavigne Delville, 7-13. Paris: Karthala.
Lemoine, J., 1997. Féodalité Taï chez les Lue des Sipsong Panna et les Taï Blancs, Noirs et Rouges du Nord Ouest du Viêt Nam. *Péninsule*, n 35.
Mellac, M. 2000. Des forêts sans partage: Dynamique de l'espace et utilisation des ressources dans un district de montagne au Nord Viêt Nam. PhD diss., Université Michel de Montaigne Bordeaux 3.
–. 2004. Des politiques foncièères aux logiques locales: Exemple du foncier rizicole chez les Tai du Viêt Nam septentrional. *Annales de la Fondation Fyssen* 18: 93-108.
–. 2006a. Des "rizièères du muong" aux "rizièères de la coopérative": Réflexion sur l'évolution des catégories cognitives mobilisées par les Tai du nord-ouest du Viêt Nam dans le domaine foncier. Proceedings of the international symposium "Aux frontièères du foncier, enchâssement social des droits et politiques publiques," Montpellier, 17-19 May 2005.
–. 2006b. Gestion décentralisée des ressources forestières et jeux d'acteurs au Vietnam. Workshop "Les biens environnementaux: Biens publics, biens communs, quelles gestions décentralisées durables," Aménagement, Développement, Environnement, Santé, et Sociétés (UMR ADES), 6 January 2006. http://halshs.archives-ouvertes.fr/halshs-00335652/fr/.
–. 2009. Territorial construction and ethnic relations in the context of collectivisation: A case study from a mountain area in northern Vietnam. In *Inter-Ethnic Dynamics in Asia*, ed. C. Culas and F. Robinne F., 123-39. London and New York: Routledge, Contemporary Asia Series.
National Political Publisher. 1997. *Land Law of Vietnam 1993*. Unofficial English translation by the national political publisher. Hanoi: Luat Dat Dai, National Political Publisher. http://coombs.anu.edu.au.
Nguyen Ngoc Dien, and C.E. Leroy. 2005. *Pluralité des approches juridiques de la pluriculturalité au regard de la conception du patrimoine en droit vietnamien*, http://fr.jurispedia.org/.
Pillot, D., and F. Yvon. 1995. Technical development of an economy in transition. *Vietnamese Studies*, New series 45(115): 46-64.

Quang Canh. 1968. Economic transformation of mountain regions. *Vietnamese Studies* 15: 89-108.
SRV (Socialist Republic of Vietnam). 2003. *The Constitutions of Vietnam 1946-1959-1980-1992*. Hanoi: Thê Gioi Publishers. RSV (République Socialiste du Viêt Nam). 1995. *Les constitutions du Vietnam 1946-1959-1980-1992*. Hanoi: Éditions The Gioi.
Scott, J.C., 1985. *Weapons of the Weak: Everyday Forms of Peasant Resistance*. New Haven, CT: Yale University Press.
–. 1998. *Seeing Like a State*. New Haven, CT: Yale University Press.
Sikor, T. 2006. Politics of rural land registration in post-socialist societies: Contested titling in villages of northwest Vietnam. *Land Use Policy* 23: 617-28.
Spencer, J.E. 1966. *Shifting Cultivation in Southeastern Asia*. University of California Publications in Geography, vol. 19. Berkley: University of California Press.
Tessier, O. 2003. Le pays natal est un carambole sucré: Ancrage social et mobilité spatiale; Essai de définition d'un espace social local au nord du Vietnam. PhD diss., Université de Provence Aix-Marseille 1.
World Bank. 2007. *Country Partnership Strategy with the Socialist Republic of Vietnam for the Period 2007-2011*. World Bank, http://siteresources.worldbank.org/INTVIETNAM/Resources/387318-1127303447927/vn_CAS_2007_2011.pdf.

8
Commoditized Ethnicity for Tourism Development in Yunnan
Margaret Byrne Swain

Yunnan tourism development in the early twenty-first century relies heavily on selling ethnic diversity as a local renewable resource. To quote from the Yunnan Province Department of Commerce's website (2006): "The tourism resources of Yunnan, formed on the background of complex geographical environment, abundant bio-resources and diversity of ethnic cultures, are characterized by diversity, peculiarity and excellent combination of multiple scenic resorts."

Ethnic minorities comprise about one-third of Yunnan's population, while the majority are Han Chinese. There are twenty-four officially recognized minorities, with additional subdivisions, in this most southern province of China. They live in extraordinarily varied landscapes and cultural systems, in cities as well as in remote villages and valleys. Many live in extreme poverty. Tourism development might bring new livelihood opportunities, depending on who controls resources. State and private tourism development tend to commoditize the identity of these groups by presenting homogenizing images and marketable experiences while fostering the lure of authentic ethnic diversity.

This chapter looks at the contexts in which Yunnan tourism has emerged under late or post-socialism, and the consequences of ethnic tourism development for local identities and livelihoods. Some ethnic minority or indigenous people working in tourism seem to derive empowerment from commoditized identity, the marketing of identity traits as commodities for sale, by utilizing clever livelihood strategies. Results, however, are mixed and depend on many factors, as we see from research on individual tourism entrepreneurs among the Sani Yi people in Shilin (Stone Forest), with some comparison with the Bai people in Dali, the Naxi in Lijiang, Mosuo in Luguhu, Dai in Xishuangbanna, and the recently "created" Tibetan site of Shangri-La. I am interested in how the producers of ethnic tourism commoditize their identity resources through livelihood strategies. My discussion draws from the literature on authenticity and emerging debates on indigeneity and cosmopolitan aspects of identity. Both identity and livelihoods analyses are needed to examine the potential for equitable ethnic tourism development based on intersecting ethnic, class, and gender identity processes and local stakeholder agency.

Authenticity, Indigeneity, and Cosmopolitanism in Ethnic Tourism

Authenticity is a primary value in cultural tourism and is applied to everything from the ephemeral landscape to personhood to performance or artefact. Epistemologically, what is really authentic may be relationally constructed between the tourist and the toured, dictated by market forces, or defined by dominant cultural tropes and reactions to them. Complementary concepts of staged authenticity (MacCannell 1973) and cultural commoditization (Greenwood 1977) have shaped international study of cultural tourism for decades. Any marketing of cultural commodities as authentic tourist experience raises basic questions about identity and agency of the producers, particularly in ethnic tourism based on selling a minority group's culture. A protectionist perspective approves of staged performances, goods, and sites that purportedly keep tourism out of the backstage areas where ethnic minority people actually live. An essentialist bemoans the lack of authenticity encountered by the tourist, whereas a critical analysis may raise questions of agency by asking whose heritage is being packaged and by whom. In-between perspectives focus on articulations of commoditization, authentic cultural meaning, agency, and control, seeing both the positive and negative aspects of all ethnic tourism development.

Recent work in China illustrates these variations in value and construction of authenticity. Ning Wang's study (2001) of home-stay tourism shows that tourists and hosts coproduce "interactive authenticity" based on how each produce and consume processes and practices in authentification. Beth Notar (2006a, 65) argues that tourists visiting Chinese theme parks or ethnic villages embrace mimetics (imitation representing the authentic), not caring if a site is fake or real but, rather, enjoying the "journey to these fantasized places." Tim Oakes (2006, 172) uses the very Chinese concept "authentic replica" (*zhenshi zaixian*) and explains that authenticity in village theme parks both marks the originality of a place and replicates it, thus capturing "a 'real' distant world of modern prosperity and national prestige." Nyiri (2006, 183) argues against any Westernized construct of the postmodern in such tourism encounters and urges an inherently Chinese concept of the authentic.

Authenticity is also related to distance from important influences such as the market. Ateljevic and Doorne (2005, 4) maintain that the "context of authenticity is built upon all actors willing to suspend the reality of the marketplace, or at least acknowledge carefully constructed degrees of commercial engagement." They discuss a "series of stages constructed by individual entrepreneurs that function as places for both producers and consumers to engage with mythical realities of the 'exotic other' ... These dialectic relations undermine traditional arguments of cultural producers as passive victims commodified by the globalized tourism complex" (14).

This understanding of commoditization complements Notar's argument (2006a, 79) that we "should place authentification within a global process of commoditization." In a similar vein, Walsh (2005, 481) comments that authentic Mosuo identity "is lived and created in this context of representations, negotiations, encounters, and shifting identity." Even backstage, people continue to perform identity for one another, negotiating their many differences. Evoking James Scott (1992), in contrast to front-stage and public transcripts, these backstage strategies are the hidden transcripts that marginalized people might adopt to express their identity and agency despite the pressures of wider political or economic changes.

Within ethnic tourism, a subtype of indigenous tourism has evolved that emphasizes both ethnic and ecological resources. It is based on an indigenous group's cultural identity and land, and is controlled somewhat from within by the group, buffering direct incorporation into national or global markets (Swain 1989b, 85). Indigeneity refers to a global post-colonial identity of native or aboriginal peoples who claim some self-determination. Paradoxically, the more indigenous people mobilize for cultural survival, the more they may be perceived as inauthentic, but it is a false dichotomy to assume that there must be a choice between authenticity and political participation (Levi and Dean 2003, 3). Political solidarity and engagement in minority rights move an indigenous group to also function as an ethnic group with symbolic and strategic goals. Although there is no consensus in China or internationally that some Chinese ethnic minorities are indigenous, there is a rising consciousness among specific groups. A model of indigenous tourism development fits these groups well, given their histories and partial but real control over their resources.

Indigeneity reflects tensions between ideas of cultural fluidity and autochthonous claims to being the original people of a place, while cosmopolitanism means a consciousness of and engagement with the world outside one's home community. In Appiah's perspective (Appiah 2006), cosmopolitanism can be distinguished from competing universalisms by engagement with plurality, or difference. Indigeneity might be contrasted to cosmopolitanism in a series of binaries: local/global; rooted/mobile; timeless/contemporary; tradition/modernity. But it would be a mistake to think of these concepts as oppositional rather than complementary, or to deny the possibility of indigenous cosmopolitans.

The early twenty-first century is a historical moment, a global transformation of modernity, which some scholars have begun to map as the "cosmopolitan condition" (Vertovec and Cohen 2002, 9; Beck and Sznaider 2006).

This condition connects human mobilities, information webs, and commodity flows in ways that can be celebrated for challenging various racialized, ethnocentric, sexist, national narratives, but critiqued for associated global rootless hybrid cultural forms, standardized mass commodities, images, and practices (Swain 2009). Within this condition, a kind of cosmopolitan citizenship or connoisseurship of people, places, and cultures may develop into intellectual and aesthetic orientations toward cultural and geographic difference. Szerzynski and Urry (2006, 114-15) envision cosmopolitan practice as involving some or all of the following:

- mobility – bodily (travel), imaginatively (television), virtually (communication between people through paper mail, email, mobile calls, instant messaging, and so on), plus the right and means to do so
- consumption – capacity to consume places and environments (and people)
- curiosity
- risk-taking in encounters with the Other
- map-making of one's own society onto different sites, reflected aesthetically
- semiotic skill to interpret
- openness to appreciating the Other's culture. These factors arise within local ethnic groups' responses to the challenges of tourism.

Cosmopolitan theory focuses on the relationship between its political and cultural dimensions in people, their practice, and world society. Yet, little work to date has been done on its articulation with tourism, a global industry commoditizing exotic difference within the homogenizing forces of transnational capitalism. My work questions how people combine mobility with cultural exchange in tourism by looking at the cosmopolitan condition as an embodied phenomenon (Swain 2009). This "embodied cosmopolitanism" construct also takes a feminist approach to the tensions between the dualities of universal human rights and cultural diversity. Ethnic, indigenous tourism development is an environment ripe for cosmopolitan analysis and action. Analyzing individuals involved in ethnic tourism will indicate how these intersecting identities affect their day-to-day life, even as indigenous cosmopolitans.

Yunnan's Ethnic Tourism Stakeholders
In China, ethnic tourism has changed dramatically as the nation has moved from a centrally planned economy to a free market economy within a single-party Communist state. Yunnan province operates in a fairly post-socialist way (Zhang 2001) because it has long been removed from central authority, and its inclusion as the only Chinese member of the Greater Mekong Subregion creates an environment of transnational collaboration. Yunnan's government is an active partner in various ethnic tourism development

schemes offering economic development and revitalized cultures for impoverished, often rural minorities. These efforts connect governmental with non-governmental agencies at translocal, provincial, national, and transnational scales, such as different levels of Yunnan's government, the United Nation's World Tourism Organization and UNESCO World Heritage and geopark designations, the government of China, the transnational Greater Mekong Delta development agreement, and international organizations such as The Nature Conservancy (TNC) and the Ford Foundation. The Chinese national government is particularly involved through the Go West *(xijin)* initiative (see Forsyth and Michaud; Sturgeon; McKinnon; and Gros, this volume), which has involved various state-led initiatives for transport, resettlement of villages, and reforestation.

The Go West program, coded in a modernist assimilationist state-oriented discourse, seeks to incorporate the west, with its diverse culture and scenery, into the rest of China. Intergovernmental agencies have different suggestions. The World Tourism Organization's evaluation of Yunnan tourism (conducted with the National Tourism Administration of China and the Yunnan Provincial Tourism Administration) takes a stakeholder approach that provides a nuanced perspective. It urges "close coordination between the tourism industry and cultural heritage authorities to work in partnership with host communities and other key stakeholders in planning and managing cultural heritage assets as sustainable tourist attractions" (World Tourism Organization 2001, 10). One means to this end is "legislation adopted to protect and maintain tangible and intangible cultural heritage assets that are of particular significance to ethnic communities in accordance with their core values and traditions" (ibid.). The phrase "intangible cultural heritage" is a powerful affirmation of cultural diversity, if operationalized. But so far, legislative change and forms of sustainable tourism have been uneven at best (Dong 2005).

The state-led elements of the Go West campaign and the Greater Mekong Delta projects are actually not new. Throughout the post-Mao reforms of the 1980s, scenic areas and minority cultures became important exploitable resources. Party leader Deng embraced the free market and promoted entrepreneurialism, captured in a popular phrase often attributed to him, that to be rich is glorious. Marketing scenic and ethnic heritage to both domestic and international tourists is now a significant enterprise (Sofield and Li 1998). The Greater Mekong Delta has assisted tourism by completing the Kunming-Bangkok and Kunming-Hanoi roads. Well before the Go West campaign, the Yunnan provincial government focused on tourism as a primary pillar of development for some targeted areas, including Shilin, Dali, and Xishuangbanna. Income generated by international visitors to Yunnan rose from US$16 million in 1990 to US$350 million in 1999 (Yunnan Statistical Yearbook 2000, 393). There were also nearly 37 million domestic tourists in 1999, an increase of 32 percent from 1998, generating some $17.5 billion yuan (US$2.2 billion), largely because of the World Horticultural Fair *(Shibohui)* held near Kunming in 1999. The Kunming municipal district, which incorporated Shilin (Stone Forest) National Park within its boundaries, had the highest levels of tourists and income in the province (China Tourism Yearbook 2000, 334-36). Stone Forest features distinctive formations of weathered limestone and is a convenient daytrip from the provincial capital of Kunming. The World Tourism Organization report's (2001) regional forecast for 2010 was for 52.6 million tourists, bringing in $40 billion yuan.

Have these efforts reduced poverty? According to Donaldson (2007), tourism has raised provincial gross domestic product in Yunnan to more than that of neighbouring province Guizhou, but Guizhou has reduced rural poverty more than Yunnan. This disparity is the result of the volume, structure, and, most critically, the distribution of tourism development in Yunnan. Donaldson (2007, 338) notes that most of Yunnan's famous tourist sites are "located in rural areas designated as non-poor in 1986, the first year that China's State Council classified all China's counties as poor or non-poor." Tourism development after this period contributed to economic growth but not significantly to poverty reduction. Furthermore, "the province focused many of its other development efforts outside tourism, including transportation infrastructure and health care into these limited, non-poor regions" (340). The Go West campaign has also failed to invest in basic health and educational needs where they are most needed, despite plans to do so (Xia 2005). The Yunnan state has financed huge projects, rather than small-scale, local programs administered by communities themselves, especially by rural ethnic minorities.

Livelihoods and Indigenous Ethnicities

The original four major ethnic tourism sites promoted by the state – Shilin, Dali, Xishuangbanna, and Lijiang – have been joined by Luguhu and Zhongdian (now Shangri-La or Xianggelila). These new sites in northwest Yunnan are part of The Nature Conservancy's Three Rivers watershed project. Our tour starts with Shilin Sani tourism development.

The Sani from Shilin

The Sani, one of twenty-eight officially state-recognized branches of the Yi minority nationality, settled centuries ago in the limestone karst topography of southeast Yunnan within and around what is now the Shilin tourism district. Sani society has dealt with at least three major waves of globalization that have moved into their region over the past century, each with their own translocal civilizing project. French Catholicism was brought to the Sani in 1887 by missionary Paul Vial, who then spent the next thirty years documenting Sani life and language, and building his version of a modern society with schools, churches, and a model agricultural estate. His conversion efforts led to Catholic communities that were served by indigenous clergy, as well as by missionaries, until 1949 and the beginning of the Communist civilizing project. Communism brought a new world vision and global social organization that created a new kind of communal citizen. Ideological convulsions wracked the nation, especially the Great Leap Forward and the Cultural Revolution, with disastrous local results. Post-Mao reforms leading to a free market economy opened China to a new world of global capitalism in the 1980s that translated into tourism development within numerous indigenous ethnic minority homelands. Each of these globalizing contexts had associated livelihood consequences. The French Catholics' mission literally was to produce a new kind of Sani identity, with Sani pursuing new livelihood strategies ranging from religious work to modernized agriculture. Under Chinese Communists, Sani livelihoods reflected the national collective. Under free market reforms, state policies restructured livelihoods first under the household responsibility system and then under development programs partnering with international agencies.

Shilin (formerly Lunan) Yi Nationality Autonomous County identified tourism within long-term development plans in 1987. Han managers with ties to Kunming dominated the leadership of Shilin's tourism bureau, whereas local Sani usually controlled the county government. Tourism marketing has focused on Shilin's impressive limestone landscape and a commoditized form of Sani ethnic identity. The region is branded as "Ashima's home town," based on the Sani lore about the golden girl who turned to stone (Swain 2005).

During the 1990s, per capita income and employment in private sector and informal tourism grew rapidly (Shi 2000). Sani and Han have opened guesthouses, hotels, restaurants, and souvenir shops outside the park and were employed in various jobs within the park. Local researcher Shi Junchao (ibid.) reports that 2 million tourists (1.9 million being domestic) visited Shilin during 1999, up from about 1.5 million tourists in 1995. The Shilin Tourism Bureau's income alone grew to 107.3 million yuan (US$13.4 million) in 1999, when 30 percent of Shilin County tax income was from tourism (compared with the Chinese national average of 4.5 percent and a worldwide average rate of 10 percent) (ibid., 232). In 2004, Shilin National Park became a UNESCO geopark site, and the designation was instantly added to park marketing. Local marketers call the park "world class," though domestic tourism remains much more important than international tourism.

Tourism has dramatically improved overall livelihoods for many rural villages, with better roads, water supplies, health clinics, and schools. A negative factor, however, is the migrant magnet effect, or an influx of people from the countryside and beyond, especially Sichuan, which increases competition for jobs (Dong 2005). Often national or transnational investors redirect profits from one tourist site to others.

But there are ongoing efforts to organize piecework – where individuals are paid a fixed price for each unit made – for Sani-owned garment factories and for migrant garment workers (Sofield 1999). These workers buy Sani handiwork wholesale and then produce finished items to sell on to Sani peddlers and merchants. Missionary or other international organizations are also in the business of marketing Sani handicrafts, with a stated goal of improving women's lives.

In the early 1980s, small groups of Sani Yi women engaged in the tourist trade before large-scale government or entrepreneurial efforts began, by selling handicrafts and changing money in the provincial capital of Kunming. Since then, their numbers have varied from more than one hundred to fewer than ten, depending on seasonal, political, and economic climates. These entrepreneurs migrate from their homes in rural Shilin County, a two- to three-hour bus ride from Kunming, and often bring babies but rarely are accompanied by men. They wear vivid "ethnic uniforms" of indigenous clothing, often over street clothes, to mark their difference. On streets or around Shilin Park, women peddlers yell: "Hello! Sani bag?" and other phrases in English, Japanese, or Chinese to greet foreigners. Their easy banter also marks Sani women as confident Others in Han Chinese society.

These women's differences among themselves shape their livelihood strategies: some are young unmarried girls, some grandmothers; some are blood relatives, others are strangers; some cooperate, others compete; some are illiterate, others are high school graduates. Some women live full time in Kunming City, whereas some travel from rural homes for short periods; some are farmers, others are housewives. Some are poor, and some are from salaried households. Some are Roman Catholic, and some are Chinese Communist Party members. They reflect the complexity of contemporary Sani society.

Sani women, rather than men, predominate in this particular tourism livelihood strategy for reasons of Sani ethnohistory and cultural ideology, as well as the touristic cult of Ashima. Sani women are well known to pursue their own economic activities within kin and community networks, conducting activities that reflect Sani cultural and gender values. Sani women are the producers, wholesalers, and retailers of the commodities they sell and managers of the money they earn. Sani women's activities and appearance also marks Shilin as Ashima's place for tourists.

Bi's Story

A biography of one Sani woman and her family working in tourism animates abstract stakeholder livelihood strategies (see Évrard, this volume, for an analysis of biography as a guide to livelihoods).

Bi Meili is one of those Sani women who have responded to global tourism capitalism as an opportunity for change. I met her for the first time in 1987 when staying near Green Lake in Kunming. Bi was among many Sani women peddling handcrafts and changing money for tourists. This was often dangerous work, and the women had to deal both with police and their "boss," usually a Han man who paid his agents a percentage. Craft peddlers also faced city fines if caught selling without a licence.

Many tourists engaged in some limited pantomime and conversation as they bargained for goods and exchange rates. I was drawn to this scene and was soon sitting out on the street daily, talking in my rudimentary Chinese in a just slightly expanded tourist role. Bi was then in her in mid-thirties, an illiterate farmer and mother of three who travelled to Kunming from Shilin regularly in order to make a living *(zuo shengyi)*.

We met again in 1990 near Shilin Park. Curiously, it was like meeting an old friend, and Bi invited my students and me to visit her extended family. Bi's brother, Dage, was a salaried mid-level bureaucrat in the county tourism bureau. He had recently built a large two-storey house on the outskirts of Wukeshu village, overlooking community fields. His wife made tourism handicrafts, their younger children were in school, and his oldest son worked at home. Bi's other brother, Erge, lived in the old Sani-style rammed-earth family compound in the centre of the village. Goats and pigs were kept inside buildings, next to the small room where Bi's mother lived. The main building housed Erge, his wife, and children. Like her sisters-in-law, Erge's wife sewed and embroidered handicrafts for sale. Most of the farming was done by Erge and their children, some of whom were still in school. Erge was worried about the park's increasing encroachment on villagers' lands, but, as an ardent follower of Deng Xiaoping, understood that economic change could be necessary. Still, he expected to continue his life as a full-time subsistence farmer, earning a little cash on the side.

Bi invited my group to stay in her old, rented Han-style house in Ganlongtang (Dry Dragon Pool), a village some distance from tourism activity, reachable only by foot. While there, Bi demonstrated her rural life of fetching water, spinning pine needles for fuel, cooking, farming, sewing, and caring for animals, and introduced us to family and neighbours. Her farmer husband had never been to Kunming and knew little of life outside the township. He managed their crops and raised their youngest daughter, who was still at the local primary school. Their eldest daughter, disabled by illness that had left her partially blind, was living in town, and their son was in a district school. Meanwhile in Kunming, life was very different for Bi, as she bunked in a boarding-house room with seven other Sani women and earned the cash to fuel her dream of building a new house in Ganlongtang.

In early 1992-93, I spent considerable time with Bi. She refused payment for her time, but I was expected to buy handicrafts. We explored the villages surrounding Shilin and visited Bi's younger sister's home, an opulent house perched on the outskirts of the tourism district. This sister had married into a wealthy family but also participated in the Kunming tourist trade. We all celebrated New Year together, travelling to wrestling matches in rural villages using Dage's mini tour bus. The bus both earned money and was an outrageous marker of wealth and prestige. Dage's oldest son was the driver and provided occasional transportation to Kunming. Bi had turned her tourism profits into a stockpile of building supplies that she used to build a house near Ganlongtang. She was worried, however, that her eldest daughter was living a precarious existence, possibly as a prostitute in Kunming, and her son had dropped out of school to work in a tourist restaurant in Shilin. Over her husband's objections, their youngest daughter moved to live with Bi's mother to attend Shilin elementary school, so that she would have a chance of going on to junior high.

By the mid-1990s, Bi's eldest daughter was in a stable relationship, the son was farming in Ganlongtang, and the youngest worked in a Shilin souvenir shop after her father forbade her to continue in school. But in 1995, Bi's husband suddenly died. Bi returned to farming, but soon her twenty-year-old son beat her and kicked her out of "his house." Destitute, she ran not to her mother, brothers, or sister but to friends in the township of Lumeiyi, and started over. She married a Sani Catholic bachelor and had a fourth child in 1998. They lived in a tiny house, strewn with sewing work, farming implements, and food supplies. When I asked, she said she did not mind the picture of the Virgin Mary on the wall because it belonged to her new husband, who was a good man; she, however, did not become Catholic. Forging new family ties like this showed Bi's flexibility as well as the coexistence of complementary systems, a kind of cosmopolitanism, going back to the missionary Vial's day.

Bi returned to seasonal migration and tourism in Kunming, her new baby proving a valuable marketing tool. She and her baby stayed with her oldest daughter, who had married a Han urban transportation worker with an impressive apartment provided by his company. The apartment, and her son-in-law's work connections, allowed Bi to feel part of the emergent middle class. She moved easily between farmhouse and husband in Shilin, the streets of Kunming, and her eldest daughter's universe of modern Chinese-ness, phones, bathrooms, and fancy furniture. This daughter gave birth to a girl, and Bi's son married, having left the family farm to become a labourer in the county town.

But Bi became distraught in 1999 when her third child – then twenty-one years old – died just before getting married. As the years went by, Bi's life reflected the multiple influences of her family, world view, and circumstances of being a woman, as well as being a Chinese national, an entrepreneur, and Sani. She worried that her youngest child was not getting good enough schooling. She took down the picture of the Virgin Mary with her husband's permission, and began to study as a Sani shaman *(shima)*. Bi's desire to call ancient Sani spirits for guidance while living a modern life illustrates how grassroots cosmopolitanism works. Bi was comfortable negotiating the worlds of foreigners and living as a member of the urban modern Chinese middle class. Yet, her background as a rural farmer and entrepreneur reinscribed her Sani-ness to a much deeper level than most.

One of my favourite memories of Bi's indigenous cosmopolitanism has to do with her arranging my journey to the Kunming airport in 2002, where she translated freely across multiple cultures. Drawing on networks, technologies, time schedules, and entrepreneurial skills, Bi got six people gathered together, then transported them from the university guesthouse to the airport terminal gate. The details involved Sani friends, fictive and real kin relations, a cellphone, and Bi's son-in-law's car. When we arrived at the airport's departure lounge, Bi in full Sani dress drew a great deal of attention from the foreign tourists there. We waved goodbye as Bi encouraged her daughter to talk to the tourists in Japanese, who tipped for the privilege and took photos of Bi with her granddaughter. The tourists were pleased to have one more chance to capture the archaic image of a native Sani woman, of Ashima.

By 2004, Bi was more settled as a *shima* in villages but still travelling to Kunming to sell handicrafts. Her oldest daughter and family had fallen on hard times, losing their apartment, which forced the husband to become an illegal freelance taxi driver and the daughter into sewing and selling handicrafts. Out in Shilin, Dage had retired from the tourism bureau, and Erge was working as a cleaner in the park. Village farmland was almost entirely incorporated into the park. Wukeshu village had negotiated with the tourism bureau to allow villagers concessions within the park for a cultural show, photo stands, handicraft sales, and a range of maintenance and service jobs, including as park guides.

The diversity of economic and educational circumstances in Bi's family continues to play out against the family's articulations with tourism livelihoods. In 2006, Bi's house had hardly changed: no sanitation, a water tap nearby, and garden vegetables growing up the exterior walls. In Kunming, Bi's eldest daughter lived in shabby rooms in a former office building, with combined living and cooking spaces, shared with other renters. Here, Bi presented a ritualized showing of innumerable Sani goods. She made an extravagant gift of Sani outfits for my two adult daughters, which we negotiated down to my accepting just the hats, while I offered gifts and made purchases. Our very complicated relationship varied under these conditions of friendship and co-researcher role, and the vicissitudes of ethnic tourism as a livelihood.

Other Entrepreneurs and Sites
Bi's Sani-ness allowed her the visible identity and access to engage as a tourism entrepreneur. Her support network – the sustainability of this livelihood – was also based on a diverse family, her own ingenuity and agency, and the

ability to change identity in different circumstances. This combination of individual agency in response to new forms of capitalism under tourism has expanded the potential for cosmopolitan livelihoods and identities.

Case studies of other grassroots tourism entrepreneurs substantiate creative tensions between livelihood and identity strategies. For example, two clothing factory owners, Ms. Li in Shilin and Ms. Linda in Dali, have commonalities: they both design their wares using local indigenous aesthetics, goods, and motifs, produce by local workers, and have had successful businesses (Swain and Ateljevic 2006). But, from here, they diverge. Ms. Li is Sani and an intellectual invested in promoting indigenous knowledge and arts as a performer, writer, and costumer. She designs for local entertainers and tourist guides, and an emergent Sani elite. She produces a modern Sani style consumed by both locals and visiting tourists. Ms. Linda, on the other hand, is not indigenous but a migrant from Sichuan who works closely with Bai women producers, using Bai tie-dye fabrics in her designs, which she wholesales to international buyers on the Internet. She also sells locally to international backpackers and urban Chinese domestic tourists looking for something evocative of tradition and nostalgia.

Bai women street peddlers are common in Dali and, like the Sani in Shilin, have sold to tourists since the mid-1980s. Adept at reading international and domestic tourists' desires for authenticity, they sell an inventory of tie-dye fabric goods and "genuine" artifacts. Beth Notar (2006a, 2006b) describes how successful Bai women entrepreneurs have prospered. However, she notes that tourism development has also led to a litany of problems, from new roads that literally divided households, to the uneasiness of people seeking aspirations that cannot be met, to the discontent of local intellectuals grappling with the meanings of stereotypes and indigenous knowledge.

Similar issues can be seen in Lijiang, a northern mountain city, now a UNESCO World Heritage site, and locale of the Naxi minority, and in Xishuangbanna, a semi-tropical southern region dominated by the Dai minority, where tourism also developed during the 1990s. Access to these more remote sites burgeoned with the opening of direct flights from Kunming, negating the need for torturously long bus travel. Donaldson (2007, 339) documents the growth of tourism in these regions, noting that neither county was considered poor. My notebooks from 1987 indicate how, even then, images of Sani, Bai, Naxi, and Dai were iconic brands of Yunnan's ethnic diversity for domestic and international tourism, and how some factoids were used to market tourism. Shilin has fantastic rock forms and the mythic Yi heroine Ashima; Dali has tie-dye fabric, marble, and the mysterious Bai; Xishuangbanna is a Buddhist region, and its water-splashing festival is a must for seeing beautiful Dai girls; Lijiang is dominated by a majestic mountain and Naxi market women in distinctive costumes. Later,

Luguhu, a community of the matrilineal Na or Mosuo near Lijiang, joined these primary sites (Walsh and Swain 2004).

Walsh (2005, 468-69) has described how a Mosuo woman called Soma adroitly performed in the "back stage" of her kitchen for Walsh and some visiting Australian feminists staying in the "front stage" of her guest house. Soma projected a matrilocal idyll and introduced other women working there as her sisters. Several days later, one of the sisters approached Walsh, eager to explain that she was really an employee and distant cousin from a village that does not receive tourists. Previously, this woman's family supported Soma's family during hard times, but now they had an unequal business relationship as her service workers in this changing ethnic tourism economy where livelihood strategies can reshape identities.

Erasure of indigenous people living in tourist sites can range from loss of family identities to renaming whole groups or landscapes. For example, in 1997, a state tourism branding strategy renamed the county where Shilin Park is located from "Lunan" (a Chinese approximation of the regional name in Sani language) to "Shilin," despite considerable objections from local Sani and Han people. In Yunnan's northwest, the Diqing prefecture's local Tibetan government renamed Zhongdian County "Shangri-La" in 2002 (Kolas 2004) to promote tourism development tied to the famous 1933 western orientalist fantasy novel *Lost Horizon*, by James Hilton. This renaming signalled the region's claim to a cosmopolitan identity, meaningful to domestic and international tourists, as well as local residents. Shangri-La also denotes a favourable image of Tibetan-ness as utopian, in contrast to negative Chinese ideas of Tibetans as feudal and superstitious. The region includes poor counties qualifying for government aid (Litzinger 2004; Donaldson 2007) being used to build a premier tourism destination.

Close ties between ethnic tourism and ecotourism are evident in Shangri-La development. Even urbanized Shilin has a section, called Naigu, that is presented as more natural and less packaged than the main park. In the early 1990s, rural Lijiang attracted a Ford Foundation project on sustainable trekking tourism (Swope et al. 1997) that was later completed by the Yunnan Academy of Social Sciences. A village-based tourism cooperative was set up in 2004, promoting tourist hikes and horse rides up mountain slopes. Some local people have complained about its management, but most villagers participate, and the village receives more than thirty-three thousand visitors a year (Perng 2007). A Kunming-based NGO, the Center for Biodiversity and Indigenous Knowledge (CBIK), also works with local communities to develop eco/ethnic tourism. One project is in Gongshan Autonomous County, Nujiang Prefecture (see Gros, this volume), and another is in Shangri-La County, Diqing Prefecture (Perng 2007). CBIK's mission statement is "[to enable] local groups to strengthen their evolving cultural traditions and generate innovative ways to improve their livelihoods and enhance biodiversity." But the influence of regional hydrological projects, logging, and the tensions among groups arising from historic conflicts make this work slow going.

Interpolated Authenticity?

In 2001, I surveyed various tour companies' representations of Yunnan ethnic minorities on the Internet. A second survey in 2007 found little difference in representations but new players. The Visit-Mekong site (http://www.visit-mekong.com) was particularly striking. This company offers tours within the entire Greater Mekong Delta, Cambodia, Vietnam, Laos, Thailand, Myanmar, and Yunnan. Its tours go to all the Yunnanese regions mentioned in this chapter. The website briefly discusses Bai, Dai, Naxi, and Tibetan culture but names the Sani only once, as denizens of Shilin, one of the most commonly visited locations renowned for its Chinese-named rocks. This is a curious, almost total, erasure of a highland minority.

The images of any ethnic minority I encountered on these sites were often truncated, flattened, and limited by both the form and the intent of the messages. Advertisements for tours take on the nature of "windshield ethnography" – looking out the window of a tour bus or hearing the rote words of a tour guide presents very little about another culture. Encapsulated in the brief phrases of Internet-speak are interpolated identities of these minority natives. By using the word "interpolated," I intend to indicate partial impressions meant to misconstrue somehow or provide unauthorized interpretations. Subtexts denote that they are pre-modern, natural, and, as in the Sani case, part of an exotic limestone landscape to be looked at and consumed. Or they are tour guides and handicraft peddlers very involved in the business of selling their identity. These media carry mixed messages of cultural diversity and denigration, development, and backwardness. Tourism entrepreneurial sites are meant to seduce, draw in the reader, and stimulate a drive to consume someone else's culture. They are often written from an assimilation model – to present a predictable "generic exotic" subject distinct from the tourist.

Internet information on Yunnan's ethnic tourism presents the typical ethnic as a singing and dancing minority, as crafty traders to be bargained with, as folkloric heroes, or as heathens in need of evangelization. Their interpolated identities are parts of a whole system of identification creating "ethnic minority" or indigeneity. How might these dissonant contradictory images be resolved to negotiate an understanding of what constitutes ethnic identities for indigenous highland minority people and their beholders over time? A constant in this analysis is my own subjective outsider gaze as well. In the Internet data we are missing the "authentic" ethnic minority voice, which can be represented in part by the ethnography of indigenous intellectuals and other researchers. Cyber materials can be seen as discourses on cultural sameness and differences that emanate from paradigms of authenticity, indigeneity, and cosmopolitanism perspectives.

Empowering Stakeholders

Internet discourse refracts back onto real-life efforts of minority ethnic groups to claim greater agency in tourism development. Based on my understanding of the Sani experience in Shilin during the late 1980s, long before the Go West campaign, I devised a conceptual model of indigenous/ethnic tourism development (Swain 1989a). The units of analysis (stakeholders) were the nation-state, the tourism industry, and the ethnic group. The issues addressed were each unit's distinct political economy agendas or characteristics, the paradoxes they encountered, and proposed resolutions leading to sustainable development.

Despite the regrettable omissions of tourist consumers, non-state agents, and individual group members as stakeholders, and the room for many other improvements, the model's basic concepts still hold. In terms of agendas, the state regulates the access and autonomy of ethnic groups, the industry markets ethnic resources, and indigenous ethnic groups try to resist these moves to ensure some degree of autonomy. These intersecting agendas raise dilemmas: Is the state's promotion of ethnic cultures problematic, or does it assist ethnic group rights? The industry paradoxically promotes predictable, standardized packaged deals for tourists that often "museumize" ethnic subjects as quaintly non-modern, while the very presence of tourism transforms ethnic communities. The indigenous/ethnic group fights to maintain cultural diversity (pluralism) while also becoming more integrated (or even assimilated) into national and global culture. My model proposes that a strong ethnic identity might resolve these tensions. The cultural imperative to "stay ethnic" presented a valuable resource for the ethnic group to exert control and claim agency in relationships with government and industry.

Trevor Sofield's case study (1999) of Shilin applied the concept of empowerment to this model and argued that the devolution of power from the state to the minority group encourages cooperation in tourism development that promotes sustainable ethnic identity, indigenous rights, economic independence, and cultural diversity. Philip Feifan Xie (2001) applied another variation of my model to ethnic tourism on Hainan Island, off the south coast of China. He assessed the stakeholders' positions, the paradoxes they encountered, and tensions around issues of authenticity, which Xie concluded were understood relative to various stakeholders' interest.

Clearly, ideas of authenticity are flexible, partial, and expressed through interpolated identities in ethnic tourism marketing. Yang and Wall (2008) used Xie's work (2001) to contrast Han commodification of minority culture in Xishuangbanna, promoting ambiguous concepts of authenticity, with the potential of local ethnic minority control of tourism commoditization to revitalize evolving ethnic authenticity. We can use this model to think in terms of contexts (development schemes) and consequences (identities and livelihoods), weighing stakeholders' strategic uses of ethnic tourism development in our current era of globalization. There are no easy predictions. In the conclusion to his article on The Nature Conservancy's developments in northwest Yunnan, Litzinger (2004, 504) argues that local people should be empowered by participating in conservation planning. Yet, this is in sharp contrast to his general pronouncement that "neo-liberal dreams of regional and global markets as a panacea for the increased problems of poverty and inequality will continue to disempower ethnic minority populations [when] ... their cultures and worth as citizens of the [People's Republic of China] is seen only through the logic of commodity form" (ibid.).

He is right on both accounts.

Conclusion

If China's Go West campaign is to succeed with ethnic tourism as a vehicle for economic development, inclusive planning empowering individuals within indigenous minority ethnic groups must occur. By definition, touristic landscapes, including many indigenous ethnic minority groups, are places of integral meaning that are seen in various ways by both insiders and outsiders. Equitable tourism development must therefore consider these different viewpoints and avoid overlooking how interaction between hosts and guests contribute to images of authenticity (Cartier 2005). As a response to this, I argue for viewing identity issues in ethnic tourism development through the tropes of authenticity, indigeneity, and cosmopolitanism, while acknowledging stakeholders' political power and control issues that determine access to resources within development.

The World Tourism Organization (2001, 55) statement on Go West tourism concludes that there is a need to engage communities more strongly in order to achieve sustainable cultural heritage management. This means allowing local people to control their tangible and intangible cultural assets. This chapter presents examples of ethnic tourism that illustrate partial stakeholder development. Interpolated identities and livelihood strategies have actually driven commoditization of ethnic culture. The state and the tourism industry have contributed to the commoditization of ethnic identity, but these have been matched to varying degrees by the agency of local people themselves.

Some planners and analysts of ethnic tourism have argued that providing an inauthentic false front (or image) of ethnicity might protect the communities behind it (MacCannell 1973). But worldwide experience in many local ethnic tourism sites has shown that there is little distinction between the "staged" outside appearance and the "authentic" internal communal life (Cohen 2001, 22). Tourism becomes part of the local society and culture.

Is there really a distinction to be made between touristic and ethnographic representations, when indigenous ethnic minorities have embraced the "song and dance" and moved on? Cohen (2001, 23) notes that as ethnic communities become more involved in tourism, they intensify their concern with identity and self-representation, sometimes openly resisting the tourism media presented by the industry and the state. If members of an ethnic group have agency, or some base of control over their day-to-day life, then they might be able to adopt cosmopolitan strategies to incorporate interpolated indigenous identities as a means of control for both their identity and their livelihood.

In their study of cosmopolitanism in a touristed region of rural England, Szerzynski and Urry (2006, 126) asked groups of professional and working-class residents to talk about their perceptions of local landscapes. The professional group took a "citizen" approach, seeing place from afar, abstract and mobile. The working-class women took a "denizen" approach, seeing place from within, practical and known. This approach might seem far from ethnic minority communities in highland China, but it has similarities with non-local migrants moving into tourist sites with their local "denizens." Szerzynski and Urry (2006, 127) do not suggest that cosmopolitan openness is incompatible with living in specific places but conclude that we need to explore alternative kinds of cosmopolitanism that can include particularity.

I have taken up these questions in Yunnan, a place long acknowledged as a transnational crossroads witnessing the comings and going of numerous groups of people over the millennium, with strong links to the south (Swain 2002; Michaud 2006). Cosmopolitan theory helps us understand how stakeholders interpret the grand narratives of the state and global capitalism in ethnic tourism into their own narratives, driving embodied performances of authenticity and indigeneity. For example, we can see Linda as a citizen-cosmopolitan agent, bridging ethnicities marketing local traditions abroad on the Internet, whereas Ms. Li maintains a citizen-denizen identity, embedded in a local trade while promoting a modern, cosmopolitan understanding of fashion. Both factory owners create an imaginary flexible authentic ethnic dress. Like the grassroots entrepreneurs in Dali and Luguhu, Bi exhibits a denizen cosmopolitanism from below, rooted and also responsive to changing ideas of authenticity.

How is ethnic performance located in ideas about authenticity and indigeneity in this cosmopolitan age of the translocal, the transnational, and the global? Traditions, as foundational sources of meaning, provide frameworks for argument and exploration that change as conditions change (Hall 2002, 28). Tourism producers see "tradition" as part of their modern lives, while they actively engage change. Performance of ethnicity and the production of indigenity are expressed through strategically embracing economic opportunities, when attainable.

As we have seen in Yunnan, international governing bodies are one source of opportunities, for example, UNESCO World Heritage and geopark agencies that establish global standards for sites in terms of cosmopolitan cultural and environmental ethics. Transnational social movements, international NGOs such as The Nature Conservancy and the Ford Foundation, and local NGOs such as the Center for Biodiversity and Indigenous Knowledge promote a form of multiculturalism. But this multiculturalism complements a cosmopolitan preference for permeable boundaries between cultural units that are open to choice, dialogue, and critique. There are also barriers to inclusive tourism in the indifference of many tourists, government mismanagement, and corporate neglect. The state (both Yunnan and China) and transnational tourism corporations have sometimes adapted cosmopolitan goals when it is good business to go green, protect workers' rights, and conserve cultural landscapes. Achieving equitable ethnic tourism that can provide positive livelihoods for Yunnan's highland ethnic minorities depends on how far stakeholders with different ideological conditions, or philosophical positions, can develop approaches that promote minorities' equality and rights to resources.

References
Appiah, K. 2006. The case for contamination: No to purity; No to tribalism; No to cultural protectionism; Toward a new cosmopolitanism. *New York Times Magazine*, 1 January: 31-38, 52.
Ateljevic, I., and S. Doorne. 2005. Dialectics of authentication: Performing "exotic Otherness" in a backpacker enclave of Dali, China. *Journal of Tourism and Cultural Change* 3(1): 1-17.
Beck, U., and N. Sznaider. 2006. Unpacking cosmopolitanism for the social sciences: A research agenda. *British Journal of Sociology* 57(1): 1-23.
Cartier, C. 2005. Introduction: Touristed landscapes and seductions of place. In *Seductions of Place*, ed. C. Cartier and A. Lew, 1-19. London: Routledge.
China Tourism Yearbook *[Zhongguo Luyou Nianjian]*. 2000. Beijing: Zhongguo Luyou Chubanshe.
Cohen, E. 2001. Ethnic tourism in Southeast Asia. In *Tourism, Anthropology, and China: In Memory of Professor Wang Zhusheng*, ed. C.-B. Tan, S. Cheung, and H. Yang, 1-26. Bangkok: White Lotus Press.
Donaldson, J. 2007. Tourism, development and poverty reduction in Guizhou and Yunnan. *China Quarterly* 190: 333-51.
Dong, E. 2005. Regulations of the environmental management of tourism development in Yunnan province, China. Proceedings of the 2004 Northeastern Recreation Research Symposium, 192-99. http://www.fs.fed.us/ne/newtown_square/publications/technical_reports/pdfs/2005/326papers/dong326.pdf.
Greenwood, D. 1977. Culture by the pound: An anthropological perspective on tourism as cultural commoditization. In *Hosts and Guests*, ed. V. Smith, 129-38. Philadelphia: University of Pennsylvania Press.
Hall, S. 2002. Political belongings in a world of multiple identities. In *Conceiving Cosmopolitanism*, ed. S. Vertovec and R. Cohen, 25-31. Oxford: Oxford University Press.
Kolas, A. 2004. Tourism and the making of place in Shangri-La. *Tourism Geographies* 6(4): 262-78.

Levi, J., and B. Dean. 2003. Introduction. In *At the Risk of Being Heard: Identity, Indigenous Rights and Postcolonial States,* ed. B. Dean and J. Levi, 2-30. Ann Arbor: University of Michigan Press.
Litzinger, R. 2004. The mobilization of "nature": Perspectives from north-west Yunnan. *China Quarterly* 178: 488-504.
MacCannell, D. 1973. Staged authenticity: Arrangements of social spaces in tourist settings. *American Journal of Sociology* 79(3): 589-603.
Michaud, J. 2006. *Historical Dictionary of the Peoples of the Southeast Asian Massif.* Lanham, MD: Scarecrow Press.
Notar, B. 2006a. Authenticity, anxiety, and counterfeit confidence. *Modern China* 32(1): 64-98.
—. 2006b. *Displacing Desire: Travel and Popular Culture in China.* Honolulu: University of Hawai'i Press.
Nyiri, P. 2006. *Scenic Spots: Chinese Tourism, the State, and Cultural Authority.* Seattle: University of Washington Press.
Oakes, T. 2006. The village as theme park: Mimesis and authenticity in Chinese tourism. In *Translocal China: Linkages, Identities and the Reimagining of Space,* ed. T. Oakes and L. Schein, 166-92. New York: Routledge.
Perng, J. 2007. Eco-tourism: Snapshots from four villages. *China Development Brief.* http://www.chinadevelopmentbrief.com.
Shi, J.C. 2000. *Ashima: Yongheng de meili yu xiaoying-Shilin xian da luyou xiandai de wenhua gainian* [Ashima: Effects of eternal charm-modern notions in Shilin County tourism]. In *Shilin Yizu* [Shilin Yi People], ed. He Yaohua and Ang Zhiling, 231-44. Kunming: Yunnan Jiaoyu Chubanshe.
Sofield, T. 1999. The Yi nationality of Shilin Stone Forest, Yunnan province, China: A case study in indigenous tourism. http://www.sustainability.murdoc.edu.au.
Sofield, T., and S. Li. 1998. Tourism development and cultural policies in China. *Annals of Tourism Research* 25(2): 362-92.
Swain, M. 1989a. Developing ethnic tourism in Yunnan, China: Shilin Sani. *Tourism Recreation Research* 14(1): 33-40.
—. 1989b. Gender roles in indigenous tourism: Kuna Mola, Kuna Yala, and cultural survival. In *Hosts and Guests II,* ed. V. Smith, 83-104. Philadelphia: University of Pennsylvania Press.
—. 2002. Looking south: Local identities and transnational linkages in Yunnan. In *Rethinking China's Provinces,* ed. J. Fitzgerald, 179-220. London: Routledge.
—. 2005. Desiring Ashima: Sexing landscape in China's Stone Forest. In *Seductions of Place: Geographical Perspectives on Globalization and Touristed Landscapes,* ed. C. Cartier and A. Lew, 245-59. London: Routledge.
—. 2009. The Cosmopolitan Hope of Tourism. *Tourism Geographies* 11(4): 505-25.
Swain, M., and I. Ateljevic. 2006. Cosmopolitanism and gender performance among Sani and Bai women in Yunnan's ethnic tourism. Paper presented at the annual meeting of the Association of Asian Studies, San Francisco, 8 April.
Swope, L., M. Swain, F.Q. Yang, and J. Ives. 1997. Uncommon property rights in southwest China: Trees and tourism. In *Life and Death Matters,* ed. B. Johnston, 43-60. Walnut Creek, CA: AltaMira Press.
Szerzynski, T., and J. Urry. 2006. Visuality, mobility and the cosmopolitan: Inhabiting the world from afar. *British Journal of Sociology* 57(1): 113-31.
Vertovec, S., and R. Cohen. 2002. Introduction: Conceiving cosmopolitanism. In *Conceiving Cosmopolitanism,* ed. S. Vertovec and R. Cohen, 1-24. Oxford: Oxford University Press.
Walsh, E. 2005. From Nü Guo to Nü'er Guo: Negotiating desire in the land of the Mosuo. *Modern China* 31(4): 448-86.
Walsh, E., and M. Swain. 2004. Creating modernity by touring paradise: Domestic ethnic tourism in Yunnan, China. *Tourism Recreation Research* 29(2): 59-68.
Wang, N. 2001. On interactive authenticity in tourism: An illustration from hospitality tourism. Paper presented at the International Academy for the Study of Tourism, Macau, 20 July.

World Tourism Organization. 2001. *Yunnan Province Tourism Development Master Plan.* Executive summary. Madrid: WTO.

Xia, R. 2005. Asphalt net covers China's west. Asia Times Online. http://www.atimes.com.

Xie, P.F. 2001. Authenticating cultural tourism: Folk villages in Hainan. PhD diss., University of Waterloo.

Yang, L., and G. Wall. 2008. Ethnic tourism and entrepreneurship: Xishuangbanna, Yunnan, China. *Tourism Geographies* 10(4): 522-44.

Yunnan Province Department of Commerce. 2006. Tourism industry in Yunnan. http://eng.bofcom.gov.

Yunnan Statistical Yearbook *[Yunnan Tongji Nianjian].* 2000. Beijing: Zhongguo Tongji Chubanshe.

Zhang, L. 2001. Migration and privatization of space and power in late socialist China. *American Ethnologist* 28(1): 179-205.

9
Rubber Transformations: Post-Socialist Livelihoods and Identities for Akha and Tai Lue Farmers in Xishuangbanna, China

Janet C. Sturgeon

In Xishuangbanna, Akha and Tai Lue farmers, long featured in the national imagination as backward minority nationalities with subsistence livelihoods, are getting rich on rubber.[1] Through rubber trees planted on their own lands and on fields rented or share-cropped from others, in a response to government programs to encourage rubber cropping, these farmers have incomes that exceed those of state farm workers on state rubber plantations. Beyond the sheer extent of their rubber holdings, in recent years, Akha and Tai Lue farming households have forged flexible arrangements for land, labour, and capital, as well as cross-border ties in neighbouring Laos, using tactics and agility that mimic post-Fordist production models. Farmers' achievements are especially surprising in a prefecture dominated for decades by state rubber farms boasting world-class rubber production. To explain the farmers' unanticipated success, this chapter focuses on the governance of the environment and development, which includes cash crops in Xishuangbanna. This governance approach helps illuminate what "post-socialist" might mean in this context. In this locale, multiple forms of governance are at work simultaneously, including the developmental state, neo-liberal trends, and campaigns that hearken back to the Maoist era. Here I explore how these multiple and overlapping modes of governance inadvertently produced minority nationality farmers as neo-liberal subjects, comfortable with what we might call a neo-liberal political economy.

Located in the very south of Yunnan province, Xishuangbanna is a tiny tropical prefecture bordering on Burma and Laos (see Figures 9.1 and 9.2). Historically, it was known as Sipsongpanna, a Buddhist Southeast Asian principality ruled by Tai Lue lords related to the Shan in Burma, the Lao, and the northern Thai. China incorporated Sipsongpanna following the 1949 revolution, changing its name to Xishuangbanna, a transliteration of "Sipsongpanna" in Chinese. In addition to Tai Lue people in the lowlands, called "Dai" in Chinese, Xishuangbanna was inhabited by an array of upland

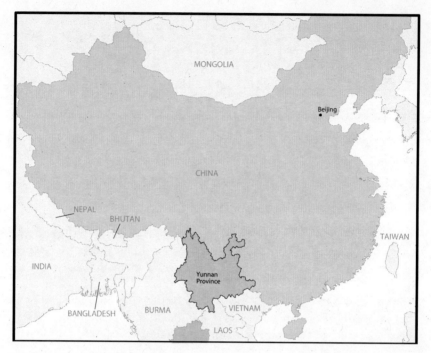

Figure 9.1 Yunnan province, China.

groups, including Akha, Jinuo, Lahu, Bulang, Yi, and Yao. The new government of the People's Republic of China regarded Xishuangbanna as a border region peopled by non-Han groups with dubious loyalty to the new regime. These groups were embraced into the Chinese nation through an official process of ethnic identification in the 1950s *(minzu shibie)* that categorized ethnic minority peoples into official minority nationalities (Harrell 1995). Once identified, each minority nationality was ranked according to its progression in the modes of production, from primitive to slave, feudal, capitalist, and socialist modes. Most minority nationalities nationwide, with the exception of Koreans, Manchus, and Muslims, fell behind the Han in production mode and level of social development. These identifications drew on long-held social hierarchies that for centuries had located the Han at the acme of civilization and culture, in contrast to the primitive peoples on China's southwest frontier (Harrell 1995; Hostetler 2001).

In China, the state has allocated roles and, in fact, identities to rural farmers since 1949, though these roles have changed at moments of major transformation in state plans. With the founding of agricultural communes in the late 1950s, rural citizens, including minority nationality farmers, became labourers producing grain for the state. In the early 1980s, the dismantling of communes and distribution of commune land to households

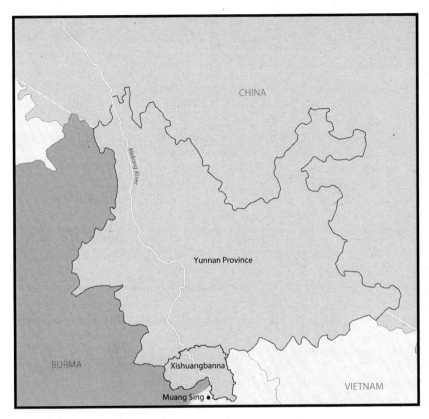

Figure 9.2 Xishuangbanna, Yunnan province and Muang Sing, in Laos.

reconstituted farmers from labourers for the state to entrepreneurs for the household. With China's 2001 entry into the World Trade Organization (WTO), the state-allocated role for minority nationality farmers may be yet in the making. During the past decade or so, Akha and Tai Lue farmers, like Chinese citizens elsewhere, have become increasingly linked to national and international markets. Their livelihoods and identities are again in flux as China enters the global arena.

To prepare for the WTO, in 2000, the Chinese government launched the Go West project, one of several regional projects to gear up for inclusion in the global economy. An explicit goal of Go West was to enclose the poorer western region of China (including Yunnan), home to the bulk of minority peoples, more completely into the People's Republic. Go West has entailed the development of infrastructure to attract foreign and domestic business investments, as well as major forest policies to plant more trees and regreen the environment (Goodman 2001, 2004; Economy 2002). As David Goodman notes (2001), Go West combines a focus on equality (poverty alleviation), nation building (national development), and colonization (making minority nationalities more like the Han), all held uneasily together under the rubric of "Great Western Development" *(xibu da kaifa)* (see also both Gros and McKinnon, this volume). The goals of Go West reflect different projects under multiple ministries with competing missions.

What I'm after here goes beyond Go West, however, in considering ethnic minority farmers' own lived experience of "development" in relation to land use, labour arrangements, and cross-border ties, all in concert with multiple modes of governance. From their own histories and emerging opportunities, Akha and Tai Lue farmers' practices have kept escaping settled understandings in China of "backward" and "stagnant" minority nationalities. At the same time, farmers' notions of what constitutes "modern," "developed," and "patriotic" clearly draw on ideas circulating in both urban and rural locales. Farmers are not creating autonomous spaces and practices but, rather, cobbling together livelihoods in the interstices of government development projects, state retreat from social services, and farmers' own links with minority peoples in neighbouring Laos. The outcomes presented here are contingent and perhaps transitory, but worthy of investigation as the unanticipated products of fractured governance and farmers' agency.

Modes of Governance

The mission of the developmental state is to bring economic development to its citizens, and the state in turn derives its legitimacy from economic success. In developmental states in East Asia, especially Japan and Korea, central state investment in industry produced seemingly miraculous economic growth (Wade 1990; Evans 1995). With respect to China, Shue and Blecher (1996) have argued that since communes were disbanded in the reform era, local governments have become more sophisticated and competent in promoting economic development. Walder (1995), by contrast, characterizes the local state in China as predatory, extracting taxes and fees from the local population to invest in industries owned by state officials. My purpose here is not to engage in this debate but, rather, to highlight that, from its founding in 1949, the People's Republic has featured itself as a developmental state aiming to transform China into a socialist nation that would "catch up" with the West (Unger 2002, 220). In the period of economic reforms beginning in 1978, even as the Chinese government began to allow markets rather than central planning to channel the exchange of goods, Deng Xiaoping, the top leader at the time, made the state's role as provider of economic growth even more explicit. In 1992, Deng famously declared that "to get rich is glorious," through what he called a "socialist market economy" (Anagnost 1997, 203; Sigley 2006, 487). Indeed, the very legitimacy of the Communist Party and the government has rested on helping citizens achieve the enticing goal of becoming gloriously rich (Sigley 2006, 498).

In terms of neo-liberalism, David Harvey asserts that China has participated in the global trend toward neo-liberalism through what he describes as "neoliberal elements interdigitated with authoritarian centralized control" (Harvey 2005, 120). Sigley characterizes neo-liberalism in China not as a retreat of the state but as a regrouping to govern by new means, to "combine neoliberal and socialist strategies" (Sigley 2006, 502). Harvey defines the neo-liberal trend (in general and in China) as the opening of markets; the devolution of political-economic power to localities, including land contracts to households; and an increasing engagement in foreign trade and investment. Although all of these things have happened in China, including in Xishuangbanna, more useful for my purposes is the notion that in rural China, the discourse of "quality" *(suzhi)*, which accompanied the retreat of the state from providing free education and medical care in rural areas (a neo-liberal move), transferred responsibility for development from the state to the individual (Murphy 2004). Rural people must improve their own "quality" to benefit from and contribute to "modernization," and they are also responsible for any failure to progress.

The emphasis on quality derives from the 1979 one-child policy to limit population growth. Couples were encouraged to have fewer children of higher quality, and under Deng Xiaoping, raising population quality became a key policy goal (Anagnost 1997, 203). A high-quality population was needed to achieve the four modernizations in agriculture, industry, science and technology, and the military. High-quality people would be educated, scientific, and rational, and as the socialist market economy deepened, they would also be entrepreneurial (Anagnost 2004; Greenhalgh and Winckler 2005, 42-43). During the transition from Maoism to the era of Deng Xiaoping, raising population quality in fact became the basis of political authority (Anagnost 1997; Murphy 2004; Bakken 2000). Initially, then, the developmental state was to improve population quality so that individuals and the country could become rich. As the discourse of "quality" rendered rural populations responsible for their own development, farmers needed to raise their own quality (Murphy 2004).

Through the notion of quality *(suzhi)*, which circulates widely in popular social discourse, members of China's population would "recognize their positions within the social order" (Anagnost 2004, 192). In addition, one effect of the *suzhi* discourse was the "reinforcement of related systems of valuation" (Murphy 2004, 3), such as urban/rural, modern/backward, progressive/stagnant, and, in this case, Han/minority nationality. These categories conform to Foucault's understanding of dividing practices through which populations are separated into binary pairs as a means of governing them (Foucault 1990, 1995).[2] Although public attention was focused on raising population quality to become rich, the binary opposite – "low-quality" people such as rural farmers – were thought to have personal characteristics that prevented them from improving and as a result, remained poor. Although all rural people had "lower quality" than urban citizens, minority nationality groups, which had been ranked below the Han at ethnic identification, were believed to fall even further behind on the national value scale. Minority nationalities were generally mapped onto the backward, irrational, and stagnant side of social binaries, identifying them as the most backward members of the nation, passively awaiting help.

As for campaigns, I focus here on the campaign mentality that infuses each wave of state cash crop extension. Under Mao Zedong, the core of socialist governance was the mass line. Through a top-down and bottom-up process, the mass line required local cadres to both indoctrinate the masses and respond to their needs. The mass line has also been used to mobilize the population for various national political campaigns, such as the Cultural Revolution (1966-76) (Sigley 2006, 506). To this day, the mass line is invoked to launch national campaigns, such as fighting corruption. Following the national style, government agencies in Xishuangbanna frequently use campaigns to introduce state programs, such as new cash crops. Periodic campaigns, which are manifestations of the developmental state, mobilize farmers to transform landscapes in the march to economic development. If a cash crop fails, however, the blame tends to fall on farmers for their "low quality," rather than on the state agents who promoted it.

Combining notions of the developmental state with the requirement that farmers raise their own "quality" reflects the fractured nature of governance, at once assuming that rural citizens must be mobilized and transformed, and that in the struggle for development, farmers are on their own.[3] At the same time, the dynamics of the developmental state, with the government as the dispenser of economic growth, produces and reproduces the state as the active, guiding agent for passive farmers who are childlike recipients of state beneficence.

In what follows, I explore how the developmental state, neo-liberal practices and values, and campaigns for successive cash crops have transformed Akha and Tai Lue livelihoods and identities in ways that neither state officials nor the farmers themselves would have foreseen a decade ago.[4] The pace of change in Xishuangbanna and in China as a whole is astonishing and, in itself, constitutes a key characteristic of Chinese post-socialism. At issue here is how people adjust to and take advantage of rapid transformations.

Cash Crops in Xishuangbanna

In Xishuangbanna, a prefecture where virtually all farmers are ethnic minority, state-led plans for development or environment are made as if farmers do not know anything. Whether to improve farmers' incomes or to control their use of forests, these plans set out to improve and control farmers' land use, with the understanding that minority nationality farmers are all *xiangdang luohou* (extremely backward). One of the striking features of state economic development plans for Xishuangbanna farmers since the early 1990s has been a series of cash crop campaigns. Since I first started going to Xishuangbanna in 1994, the featured miracle crop has jumped from pineapple to passion fruit to coffee to sugar cane. Starting about three years ago, the touted crops changed again to tea in the uplands and rubber in the lowlands. Like Maoist political campaigns, each new cash crop campaign erases the last one, relegating it to the trash heap of history. Sandra Hyde, a medical anthropologist who works in Xishuangbanna, argues that the campaign mentality suffuses each new plan for health care as well.[5] As a result, state agencies are not building up a stock of knowledge that would lead to incremental health care improvements. In the case of cash crops, state extension agents are not accumulating experience in how to select and extend them. With each new campaign, knowledge gets created *de novo*, again based on the assumption that farmers do not know anything. But the campaign mentality ensures that state agents are the ones who do not learn much about the elements required for market success. Each campaign is just supposed to work spontaneously, without benefit of a market analysis or a plan for transporting and processing the crop. Without growing expertise, extension agents do not select crops based on their lasting value for farmers, and when each campaign fails, the need for the next cash crop campaign is unwittingly assured.

I argue here that through these cash crop campaigns, farmers have learned what kinds of crops are associated with soil erosion; what happens when there is no infrastructure to transport, process, and market a crop; and who loses out when a crop sells for an unexpectedly low price. They have also learned, willy-nilly, how to replace one crop very quickly with another. With each crop failure, state agents may admit some mistakes but ultimately tend to blame failure on farmers' lack of knowledge and quality – their quality (*suzhi*) is very low.[6] In this version of the developmental state, the state claims any successes, but farmers are responsible for any failure to progress.[7] Farmers, meanwhile, have developed a keen sense of which crops are worth investing in. In an unintended fashion, then, the campaigns for state-sponsored cash crops have helped prepare farmers for the neo-liberal retreat of the state and the opening up of new marketing possibilities as Xishuangbanna has joined international markets.

In preparation for entry into the WTO in 2001, the government had gradually reduced the subsidized price of rubber during the 1990s so that adjusting to the world price, which was then lower, would not be a shock for producers in Hainan and Xishuangbanna, the tropical parts of China suitable for rubber. In Xishuangbanna in 2003, state rubber farms were hived off into private companies, a neo-liberal trend that responded to central state efforts to reduce its financial burden, as well as to WTO requirements to curtail state subsidies to industry (Holbig 2004, 342, 344). In principle, these rubber companies now had to compete in the market, and, as private enterprises, they also were allowed to extend operations outside China. Since production of natural rubber in China meets only about one-third of national demand, the newly formed companies were eager to open large-scale rubber concessions in neighbouring Burma and Laos.[8]

As a poverty alleviation measure, the national government revoked the agricultural tax beginning in 2003. Removing the tax was WTO-neutral, and in poor areas collecting the tax cost more than the revenue.[9] In Xishuangbanna, the elimination of the agricultural tax, together with the removal of restrictions on selling crops across county and national borders, meant that farmers could both engage in cross-border trade and make more lucrative use of their paddy lands, since they no longer had to produce grain for taxes. Most farmers had rubber trees on their sloping lands, and they, too, could extend rubber to Laos. These changes at both national and prefecture scales represent the important neo-liberal trends that opened up possibilities for "globalization" in Xishuangbanna, or, if that is too glorious a term, at least out-sourcing rubber and other crops to Laos. Here I examine how the new rubber companies and minority rubber farmers fared under these new conditions and the kinds of livelihoods and identities that emerged in the process.

The Rubber Story

For Xishuangbanna, rubber is the master crop, the primary source of income, and the capital for most other endeavours – for state rubber farms, county and township governments, and farming households. Rubber was first introduced to Xishuangbanna in the 1950s through state rubber farms, physical manifestations of the new political regime following the 1949 revolution, as well as spatial emblems of modernity. Rubber was then thought to be a critical product needed for national military and industrial development, since the People's Republic initially faced an embargo from Western nations (Xu Jianchu 2006, 254). The state farms were staffed by Han Chinese whose factory-like management was thought to be scientific, rational, and efficient. Set up to produce goods and capital for the state rather than the market, the state rubber farms can nonetheless be understood as models of Fordist production, meaning they were large-scale entities with a skilled work force organized for the efficient production of a single product (Harvey 1990, 125-27).

From the late 1950s until the dismantling of communes, the state rubber farms were almost hermetically sealed operations, physically and administratively separate from minority nationality farmers around them, all of whom, in contrast to the state farms, were categorized as backward, unscientific, irrational, and stagnant – the opposite of "modern." This socio-spatial arrangement calls to mind James Scott's "legible landscapes," in which state agents regularize and quantify both property rights and human populations to make them "legible" or readable for taxation and efficient administration (Scott 1998). The rubber farms would surely have appeared more legible and modern to central state administrators than did minority farmers' cultivation methods. The social categories also conform to Foucault's dividing practices (Foucault 1990, 1995) as a means of governance, with the categorization itself understood to be a means of ordering and controlling populations and spaces. Here populations were divided into advanced Han and backward minorities, with each group linked to particular land uses – a spatial manifestation of social hierarchy, with Han people and spaces equated with the modern, and minority peoples and spaces designated as backward. Under this geography of inclusion and exclusion, the state farms produced rubber, while minority farmers produced others crops in what was thought to be a chaotic and unproductive manner – illegible landscapes that needed to be governed.

In the 1980s, the dissolution of communes and allocation of land to farmers and villages was accompanied by a new understanding in Xishuangbanna that the state should help minority nationality farmers achieve economic development – the combination of Harvey's neo-liberal devolution of power to localities with the developmental state acting as the provider of economic growth. Land had been contracted to households, with farmers, including minority nationalities, reconfigured as household entrepreneurs. In China, the development discourse is inseparable from state responsibilities and campaigns to bring about dramatic changes. This is the developmental state at work. Shortly after the division of land to households, state agents, including state rubber farm workers, extended rubber to minority smallholders to help raise farmers' incomes. Through this extension, rubber was leaking out of those hermetically sealed state spaces and into farmers' fields, with the potential to disrupt the neat division between "modern" and "backward" bodies and spaces.

During interviews in thirteen Akha and Tai Lue villages in 2005 and 2006, farmers recalled this first campaign, which lasted from 1985 to 1987, when many began to plant rubber in shifting cultivation fields below nine hundred metres, the maximum elevation for rubber. Although not all farmers understood rubber at the time, and indeed not all farmers planted rubber, for those who did, this campaign established the basis for farmers' wealth twenty years later, the time of my research. Although the rubber price was quite low in the late 1990s, since 2003, the price has risen to the highest level ever, creating unexpected riches for lowland farmers.

In 1994-95, the next major state development campaign targeted poverty alleviation for farmers by opening more sloping lands for rubber. This campaign enrolled so many farmers that the area under household rubber actually now exceeds the area on state farms.[10] In 2002, a third wave of rubber planting, one that is more surprising, emerged from the Grain for Green project. Grain for Green, part of the ecological construction under the Go West project, was intended to encourage farmers to plant trees on sloping lands to extend forest cover (Economy 2002). For planting trees that would come under forestry department control, farmers would receive payment in grain for a period of eight years – grain for green. The impulse to expand forests originated from the crisis environmentalism that engulfed China after the disastrous 1998 Yangtze River floods, when deforestation in the upper Yangtze watersheds was held responsible for the flooding (Litzinger 2004; Sturgeon 2007). In Xishuangbanna, however, when Grain for Green was introduced in 2002, the forestry department in some instances gave out Grain for Green certificates to farmers to plant rubber trees, merging Grain for Green with yet another state campaign to alleviate poverty. As the head of the poverty alleviation bureau in Jinghong expressed it, the goal was to "put reforestation and poverty alleviation together." The environmental concern had not disappeared, however, since rubber counts as an economic tree as well as forest cover, and as an administrator in the prefecture forestry department explained to me, "rubber prevents soil erosion better than grain does." This slippage of poverty alleviation into Grain for Green, or slippage of rubber into an environmental initiative, has enabled many farmers to plant rubber not only in their shifting cultivation lands but also across any remaining household woods and collective forests. In Xishuangbanna, on sloping lands below nine hundred metres (and sometimes above), rubber is now everywhere (see Figure 9.3).

On state rubber farms, in the forestry department, and in numerous other state offices across Xishuangbanna, I heard many complaints about farmers planting rubber "chaotically" *(hen luan)*, implying that farmers' practices are still not legible or governed. Since 1995, state rubber farms have not been allowed to extend their size because of provincial worries about deforestation. That concern plays into derogatory remarks about minority farmers "not knowing the value of trees" and "not understanding environmental conservation," but at the same time, state agents are unable, or perhaps even unwilling, to slow down farmers from planting rubber. In spite of complaints about forest loss, rubber is a critical industrial good, as well as a symbol of all that is modern, developed, and progressive – the thoroughly modern product. All this rubber is bringing unprecedented wealth to farmers in Xishuangbanna, except those at high elevations. State agents can wring their hands and complain, but the result, after all, is economic development – and evidence that the developmental state has succeeded. When it comes to rubber, environmental protection and the goals of the developmental state become fused and distorted.

Figure 9.3 Rubber plantations in Xishuangbanna. *Photo by author*

The state rubber farms, meanwhile, continue to dominate the landscape of the Xishuangbanna lowlands with their extensive plantations and other enterprises, such as brick-making factories and electricity-generation facilities. Visits to five of the eight state rubber farms in 2005 and 2006 yielded many high-level administrators' testimonies to their own state-of-the-art rubber production, with the "highest productivity in the world" under "scientific management" and "rational, modern production." The Tropical Crops Research Institute in Jinghong, the prefecture capital, is in fact devoted to research on rubber, and has been for almost fifty years. Since state farms are not allowed to expand in size, the current research features how to intensify production, a focus that has resulted in two new rubber varieties, 77-2 and 77-4, which can be planted at elevations above nine hundred metres. As numerous state administrators emphasized, although the area of rubber in farmers' fields now exceeds the rubber area on state farms, the state farms still produce much more rubber – they are the modern, scientific, productive entities that smallholder farmers can never match. Another common statement at state farms was that "the state rubber farms brought development to Xishuangbanna. We built the roads and bridges. We brought in electricity. Without the state farms, Xishuangbanna would still be backward." State farm officials say that lowland farmers, especially Tai Lue rubber farmers, are comfortably well off as a result of state actions. State farms see themselves as important arms of the developmental state, with minority farmers as passive recipients.

Rubber farm administrators complain that farmers who cultivate rubber are "lacking in culture" and "waste natural resources." Farmers' rubber management, they say, is too casual and free *(ziyouxingde)*. Farmers cut rubber trees after ten years, not understanding that trees can produce latex for forty years. Farmers need to "listen to and follow the government" because their "cultural quality is low" *(wenhua suzhi di)*. These statements reflect administrators positioning themselves as modern, scientific, rational, and (inevitably) Han managers of important rubber companies, articulating the dividing practices between them and backward farmers. The comments encapsulate the understanding of the developmental state, which is to bring development to minority farmers, and the difficulty of doing so when the gap between modern and backward is so great and people's "quality" is so low. The statements also reflect an implicit belief that the state's actions, such as cash crop campaigns, produce markets out of the benevolence and wisdom of the intentions. This understanding brings to light the subjectivities of state workers who grew up under state plans punctuated by periodic campaigns to transform production. For them, having a market plan, something that someone raised in the West (whether economist or not) would routinely do before planting any new crop, is not part of the consideration. Development results from "state plans" rather than market expansion.

Comparing the production models and degrees of success of rubber companies and smallholder rubber farmers, however, calls into question both the "scientific management" of the rubber farms and the "low quality" of farmers' methods. Anecdotal reports in 2005 and 2006 from high-level researchers in the Xishuangbanna Tropical Botanic Garden and in the Kunming Institute of Botany indicated that the rubber farms, as companies, may be going bankrupt. They are not agile and adaptive enough to grasp how rubber might indeed be extended to Burma and Laos. As monolithic state enterprises, state rubber farms exemplify a Fordist model of production as large-scale operations that enjoyed "secure grounding in materiality and technical-scientific rationality" (Harvey 1990, 339). They also benefited from state subsidies and protection for some forty years.

The experience of rubber farmers has been quite different. During the economic reform years, from the 1980s onward, the paternalistic, heavy-handed state as central planner of what crops to cultivate, through a succession of cash crop campaigns, has inadvertently helped farmers learn how to switch rapidly from one crop to the next, rework land and labour arrangements, and accumulate capital for their own ventures. Farmers have unwittingly achieved a kind of postmodern or post-Fordist production model, characterized by flexibility in production and labour arrangements and by sale to niche markets (ibid.). These arrangements are allowing farmers to excel in a moment of rapid land use transformation and the explosion of rubber across the border into Laos. Rubber enterprises are allowing ethnic minority farmers in China to capitalize on long-standing close relations with people in the Sing district of Laos. At a national level, the Chinese economy has been the world's fastest growing for over a dozen years. Even in Xishuangbanna, the prefecture economy is much stronger than the economy in Sing, meaning that entrepreneurs and farmers from China are pushing across the border to take advantage of that economic disparity.

Formal and Informal Connections with Laos

Xishuangbanna, formerly Sipsongpanna, has long been connected to the neighbouring Sing district of what is now Laos (see Figure 9.2). Some district maps from before the arrival of the French in Laos in fact show Sing as part of Sipsongpanna (Gabrowski 1999). Whether claimed by China or Laos, Tai Lue and Akha people in districts along the border have been linked by ethnicity, kinship, and labour exchange for a long time, and used to move back and forth freely between Sing and Sipsongpanna. Since the founding of the People's Republic of China (1949), farmers have sometimes moved across the border in response to major political events. The parents of the village headman in Mom, a Tai Lue village in Sing, were born in the Meng Yuan district of Xishuangbanna, but escaped to Sing in 1958 to avoid the cataclysmic Great Leap Forward in China (1958-60). In recent years, villagers from Meng Yuan have drawn farmers from Mom and neighbouring locales into the expansion of cash crops. On the Lao side, several hundred Hmong refugees who fled to Thailand in the 1970s, during civil war in northern Laos, were transferred by the United Nations High Commissioner for Refugees (UNHCR) to Xishuangbanna in 1982, where the refugees worked on state rubber farms. Between 1992 and 1996, the UNHCR repatriated about a hundred of the refugees to Sing district, where the Hmong organized a rubber cooperative in Hat Yao in a modified Chinese state farm model. The cooperative continues to invite state farm experts from China to help in extending rubber to nearby Lao farmers. For the Tai Lue in Mom village and the repatriated Hmong, personal and professional connections in China continue to influence their livelihood possibilities, as Lao farmers seek to mimic Chinese economic growth.

Beginning in the early 1990s, the Meng La and Meng Peng sugar factories in China established agreements with the Sing district government to extend sugar cane into Laos, an early attempt to outsource a cash crop. With state approval, the sugar factories contracted with farmers to buy and collect the sugar cane on a regular schedule. As of 2006, the Chinese companies collected sugar cane from about a thousand hectares of farmers' fields in Laos. To encourage this development, Tai Lue and Akha farmers in Meng Yuan district in Xishuangbanna persuaded their relatives in Laos to plant sugar cane and brought their tractors to Laos to help open land for the new crop. For this help, the farmers in Laos paid them in grain.

Since 2001, with China's WTO entry, informal cross-border exchanges among farmers along the China-Laos border have accelerated and deepened, with dramatic implications for livelihoods and identities of ethnic minority smallholders in both countries. These transformations have been particularly remarkable on the China side, which I explore here through narratives from several Akha and Tai Lue villages in Xishuangbanna, showing how recent changes have turned China's ethnic minority farmers into dynamic entrepreneurs.

Tai Lue and Akha Rubber Farmers

Stories from several Tai Lue and Akha villages in Meng La County in eastern Xishuangbanna along the Lao border exemplify the rapidity and ease of transformations in land, labour, and capital as farmers adjust to new possibilities emerging from rubber (see Figure 9.2). Ban Dok Douang is a Tai Lue village that moved to the present locale in 1994 when the old village was flooded out. Most farmers planted rubber immediately and have been tapping these trees since about 2000. Some households have sold younger rubber trees to bring in additional capital and meanwhile plan to plant new rubber trees on other parcels of land, giving them several tiers of income from rubber as the newer trees begin to produce latex. These complex arrangements for rubber, possibly arrived at spontaneously rather than devised over time, lie outside state farm managers' understanding of what farmers might be up to. Despite being accused of not knowing how long trees can produce rubber, farmers realize that rubber trees can produce multiple forms and stages of income.

Until recently, most farmers in Ban Dok Douang planted sugar cane; now the price of sugar is too low, and farmers quickly moved on to bananas. With the 2003 removal of the agricultural tax, which farmers had to pay at least partially in grain, in 2005, farmers began renting out their wet rice fields to entrepreneurs from Guangdong to plant bananas. In return, farmers received between five and eight hundred yuan per *mu* annually.[11] In place of growing wet rice, these Tai Lue were now buying grain from Laos, which was cheaper than Chinese grain.

Many of these Tai Lue farmers share-cropped rubber on their relatives' land in Laos, gaining access to land through kinship (compare with Berry 1993). The profits were commonly split 60-40 or 70-30, with the farmers in China getting the larger share, since they provided the investment and technical know-how. The farmers in Laos provided the land and labour, and in some cases would eventually inherit the trees. Until recently, the relatives in Laos were brought to China to prepare, weed, and harvest paddy lands, since the Lao farmers charged only fifteen yuan per day, whereas labourers on the China side charged thirty-five to forty yuan per day. At the same time, young men from these same Ban Dok Douang households in China engaged in day labour in town at rates much higher than forty yuan per day. In other words, these households had devised complicated and highly flexible arrangements for land, labour, and capital, enabling them to use the capital from rubber, which they managed in tiers of age groups, to invest in other operations, such as expanding rubber into Laos. They also shifted land uses around based on quickly changing crop prices and new opportunities, such as the chance to replace sugar cane with bananas. Farmers made use of the wage differential between China and Laos for agricultural tasks, and the differential between rural and urban wage labour for household income. From a neo-liberal perspective, these operations exemplify a post-Fordist or postmodern production model, or even a miniature form of globalization.

In the Akha village of Man Ba San, the deputy village head explained that the villagers used to live in the uplands right next to the Lao border, where they planted upland rice in shifting cultivation fields. They have lived in the present lowland location since 1981, when the government asked them to move down. During land allocation in 1982-83, in addition to other lands, households received shifting cultivation fields, on which most families planted rubber in the first rubber campaign, from 1985 to 1987. For these households, by the mid-2000s, the mature rubber trees were the basis of their wealth. Like the Tai Lue farmers discussed above, they also sharecropped rubber on relatives' land in Laos on a 60-40 basis, and in 2006, they had just begun to rent out their paddy lands for eight-year contracts to Guangdong entrepreneurs for bananas. The village head explained how farmers calculated which crop to plant. For one *mu* of grain, the household could make a net income of one hundred yuan. For one *mu* of sugar cane, the net income would be three hundred yuan. For one *mu* rented out for bananas, the net income was five hundred yuan. Farmers' assessments of the market value of crops could hardly be clearer, and their choice to switch to bananas seems anything but "chaotic."

One remarkable feature of this village is people's response to the neo-liberal retreat of the state. Farmers must now pay for education and health care, services the state once subsidized (Murphy 2004, 4). Somewhat similar to urban citizens depicted by Lisa Hoffman (2006), whose subjectivities were formed as both entrepreneurs and national patriots, these Akha villagers noted that "money is the most important thing; money makes everything else possible." "Everything else" now included sending their children through high school in Jinghong and, for some, on to university. It included buying insurance for retirement and health care. It also included a holiday in

Jinghong, which the entire village enjoyed together the previous year. These investments and expenditures are more common among middle-class urban residents responding to the state call for people to help themselves and the Chinese economy, what Hoffman calls "notions of self-development and enterprise" (ibid., 556). Farmers' response is also inflected with the discourse of "quality" in rural areas, as Akha rise to the challenge to fend for themselves when the state no longer pays for education and medical care. In other instances, in relation to the discourse of "quality," farmers are blamed for their own poverty, owing to their lack of *suzhi* (see Sturgeon 2007), but here the picture was reversed, as farmers took pride in their achievements. Farmers never received pension benefits in the past, but these Akha were comparing their situation with that of state farm workers, who did receive state benefits, including pensions, but who now told farmers that they regretted not having their own land for planting rubber and other crops. Indeed, some state farm workers approached farmers to see whether they could rent land. As the village head noted, "Those Akha working on the state farms would be rich now if they [had] planted their own rubber." Through complex arrangements for land and labour, and their contacts across the border, Man Ba San farmers were taking responsibility for their development, rather than relying on the developmental state. At the moment, their incomes were higher than those of state employees on rubber farms and, like urban citizen-entrepreneurs, Akha farmers also made their patriotic contribution to national economic growth.

The third example is another Akha village, Guo Fang, which also used to be located in the uplands, where villagers developed strong connections with a number of Akha villages in Laos. In the mountains, they used to plant upland rice in shifting cultivation fields and kept large numbers of livestock, mostly water buffalo and cattle. Under state pressure, Guo Fang moved downhill in 1958 and has been in the current lowland location ever since. At land allocation in 1982-83, in a process similar to that in most Tai Lue and Akha villages across Xishuangbanna, households received shifting cultivation lands and forest land for fuel wood; the village as a whole got an area of collective forest for house construction. All of these lands are now planted in household rubber. Many Guo Fang households now share-crop rubber in Laos on the fields of both relatives and those hired for day labour, in most cases, Akha people known over many years – connections from before 1958. Through these links, one household had reportedly planted 2,000 *mu* of rubber in Laos. As one informant noted, "People in Laos are improving; they now have tractors and motorbikes. Now they bathe every day and wear new clothes, not the customary Akha dress *[fuzhuang]* they used to wear." For Guo Fang residents, who could now afford large, modern houses and the latest model cars, the location of *luohou*, or backward, had moved across the border into Laos, while they themselves were rising into the category of modern. Such statements also clearly located Guo Fang Akha in China, the site of modern production and rapid economic growth.

The rubber farms, meanwhile, were looking more and more like socialist monolithic dinosaurs, still emblems of all that had symbolized modernity for decades – massive operations, scientific, rational, organized, and decidedly Han, especially in the top leadership levels.[12] The rubber farms as companies were looking for new forms of rubber production in Laos through government-to-government relations. Some rubber farms were trying to negotiate deals for large-scale rubber concessions in Laos. Others were angling for participation in Chinese foreign aid projects to Laos. The Chinese government funnelled money through Chinese rubber companies to do poverty alleviation projects with Lao farmers. As of 2006, the arrangements were still awkward and stymied, at least in the provinces of Luang Namtha and Phongsaly in northern Laos, adjacent to China. As forestry agents in Sing district of Luang Namtha explained in February 2006, they are now in the midst of land and forest allocation, a process similar to the allocation of land to households that took place in China in the early 1980s. Until land is allocated and registered, forestry agents are reluctant to give concessions to Chinese companies, or even to encourage Chinese to work with farmers whose land has not yet been mapped and categorized.

Meanwhile, under farmer-to-farmer arrangements among Akha and Tai Lue farmers, rubber was spilling rapidly across the border. Farmers were managing to outsource rubber to Laos on relatives' land that may or may not have been allocated by the forestry department. All that rubber was coming back to China to be processed and fed into the huge China market. Unlike the failures of other cash crop campaigns, the infrastructure for processing and marketing rubber had long been in place and now served farmers as well as rubber companies. Farmers' efforts can be viewed as a "mini-globalization" through flexible and creative production arrangements, certainly post-Fordist and, in Harvey's terms, also postmodern. At the same time, they had forged their own economic development, as "modern" urban citizens do.

A final village story encapsulates both the campaign mentality and the collision between the state belief that backward farmers need help and villagers' new-found wealth and entrepreneurial strength. On my visits to rubber farms and villages across Meng La County in 2006, I kept overlapping in the same towns with a state-led anti-corruption and government-for-the-masses campaign, this one a national campaign invoking the mass line. I was constantly squeezed out of hotels and local eateries by the boisterous anti-corruption teams. As I arrived in Guo Fang, one of the wealthy Akha villages, the anti-corruption team was already there, busily interviewing the village head. After the team left, I sat down with the aging village head to ask about Guo Fang history and current land uses. I was sitting in the compound of

Figure 9.4 Modern young Akha women in Xishuangbanna. *Photo by author*

his enormous, newly constructed home. Out in front, modern young Akha women leaned against his brand new car, parked next to a couple of shiny motorbikes (see Figure 9.4). As we concluded the conversation, he mentioned, unbidden, that "We Akha are *xiangdang luohou* [profoundly backward]. We don't have a written language. We need the government and the Party to come teach us." My eyes kept shifting between the huge, modern house behind us and this seemingly sincere village head. Backward? In need of the developmental state? His statement baffled me. On reflection, I think his words can be read in several ways. Perhaps he had just admitted some degree of corruption to the anti-corruption team and argued that, as a backward Akha, he should be treated leniently. Or perhaps he was reciting a well-known litany, also just repeated for the anti-corruption team, to bring a restitution of order – Akha know their place in Chinese society, in spite of their wealth. In the hierarchy of China, Akha are backward, passive recipients of the sage advice of the state. Social harmony had been re-established, and everyone could go on. Either way, the anti-corruption team had left, and the village head could get on with making money.

Conclusion

I've examined here the effects of a developmental state that promoted waves of cash crop campaigns through which farmers figured out which crops worked and how to shift quickly from one crop to the next. Extension agents, whether from the agricultural department or the state farms, seemed not to learn how markets work: the need to plan for transporting, processing, and selling the product; and the need to calculate whether farmers will make a profit. Although farmers have had to deal with markets since the early 1980s, state farm administrators and workers have had direct market experience for their own livelihoods only since 2003. Through the many failures of cropping campaigns, farmers have figured out how to be successful in the transformations wrought by WTO and border-spanning possibilities. Smallholder households have been flexible and creative in deploying land, labour, and capital in multiple new forms. The obvious wealth and cross-border success of minority nationality farmers in Xishuangbanna was challenging entrenched social hierarchies in China that embodied centuries-old notions about Han superiority to primitive others. Rich minority nationality farmers, especially ones who were faring better than Chinese rubber companies, transgressed the dividing practices that kept everyone in place. Ethnic minority farmers were meanwhile also "governed" by understandings of what it means to be modern, and how to respond to the state call for citizens to be patriotic entrepreneurs. Farmers were not defying the state or creating autonomous spaces but, rather, responding to the multiple possibilities and constraints before them. Having farmers who were wealthier than rubber farm workers may be a temporary phenomenon, but these Akha and Tai Lue were well positioned to adjust rapidly to opportunities. The combination of the developmental state, the neo-liberal retreat of the state, entry into the WTO, and waves of cash crop campaigns all contributed to giving minority farmers the advantage at the moment, and they had the momentum to run with it.

Even more surprising, perhaps, was the emerging subjectivity of minority farmers as modern citizens, able to take care of themselves in business, education, health care, and leisure activities – and able to move beyond the developmental state into neo-liberal realms that transcend not only their ascribed backward status but also their location on a rural periphery. They were locating themselves in the heart of China, in tune with national aspirations. Their concerns and accomplishments mimicked those of urban middle-class entrepreneurs, who demonstrated their loyalty to China through their ability to make money.

As for multiple modes of governance, it is clear that neo-liberal moves such as transferring the financial responsibility for education and medical care to rural residents do not represent a teleological pathway toward "retreat of the state" on all fronts and may reflect state regrouping rather than retreat. The developmental state implemented through periodic campaigns is not going away – witness Go West. State administrators at various scales launch campaigns to transform rural citizens, even as they are convinced that passive and backward minority nationality citizens will not progress much. Dividing practices have blinded state agents to the fact that Akha and Tai Lue farmers have already been "transformed," though not by the direct tutelage of the developmental state. The same lack of understanding may also cause state agents to put the brakes on farmers' rubber expansion, especially into nearby Laos, as government administrators interpret minority farmers' cross-border ventures as chaotic and backward. Although the future is anything but certain, the current conjunctures of fractured governance of environment and development, through their very failures, have produced Akha and Tai Lue as neo-liberal subjects and as active and savvy contributors to China's economic growth. These farmers draw on their own experience and cross-border links to enjoy the post-socialist Chinese goal of being patriotic citizens by getting rich.

Acknowledgments
The chapter is revised from Janet C. Sturgeon, "Governing minorities and development in Xishuangbanna, China: Akha and Dai rubber farmers as entrepreneurs," *Geoforum* 41 (2010): 318-28, copyright Elsevier, 2010.

Notes
1. In China, Akha are subsumed within the official Hani minority nationality and Tai Lue are called Dai. Akha and Tai Lue are the names these groups call themselves. As of 2000, out of a total Xishuangbanna population of 993,397, Tai Lue constituted about 30 percent (296,930) and Akha constituted just over 18 percent (186,067). Akha and Tai Lue are the prevalent rubber farmers along the China/Laos border.
2. Foucault's pairings were male/female, sane/insane, and normal/deviant, but other binary categories function in the same way.
3. Sigley (2006) notes the resurgence of the idea of the "survival of the fittest" in China with respect to markets, which are thought to produce high-quality, competitive citizens.
4. Much of this chapter is based on field work in Xishuangbanna in 2005 and 2006, including interviews in thirteen villages; five state rubber farms; the prefecture forestry, agriculture, and environmental protection departments; the Tropical Crops Institute; the Xishuangbanna Tropical Botanic Garden; and private rubber factories. In addition, I have done periodic research in an upland Akha village in Xishuangbanna for more than ten years.
5. Sandra Hyde, personal communication, March 15, 2005. Hyde, a medical anthropologist at McGill University, has done research in Xishuangbanna for over ten years.
6. Interviews at the Agricultural Science Institute in Jinghong in 2006 revealed that extension agents knew why each crop had failed – low price, no market, no collection, no road – but the prevailing story in the prefecture agriculture department was that crops failed because of farmers' "low quality."
7. For a similar dynamic, Tania Li remarks of development experts: "Trustees promising improvement must distance themselves from complicity in chaos and destruction. Their interventions are 'always the cure, never the cause'" (Li 2007, 21, quoting Timothy Mitchell, *Rule of Experts*).
8. The figure of one-third of national demand comes from the head of production at Dong Feng state rubber farm and from a senior researcher at the Tropical Crops Institute in Jinghong, Xishuangbanna.
9. Andrew Watson, personal communication, February 12, 2005. Watson, representative of the Ford Foundation in Beijing, is an agricultural economist specializing on China.
10. This statement was repeated at the Tropical Crops Institute and numerous state rubber farms, including Meng Peng State Farm, in February 2006.

11 7.56 yuan = US$1.00; 15 *mu* = one hectare.
12 Interviews at Meng Xing State Farm revealed that the directors of the state farm and the heads of each production team must be Han. State farm workers can be minorities, though for all state farms except Meng Peng and Meng Xing, those minority workers must come from outside Xishuangbanna.

References

Anagnost, A. 1997. *National Past-Times: Narrative, Representation, and Power in Modern China.* Durham, NC: Duke University Press.
—. 2004. The corporeal politics of quality *(Suzhi). Public Culture* 16(2): 189-208.
Bakken, B. 2000. *The Exemplary Society: Human Improvement, Social Control, and the Dangers of Modernity in China.* Oxford: Oxford University Press.
Berry, S. 1993. *No Condition Is Permanent.* Madison: University of Wisconsin Press.
Economy, E. 2002. *China's Go West Campaign: Ecological Construction or Ecological Exploitation?* China Environment Series, Issue 5. Environmental Change and Security Project, Woodrow Wilson Center.
Evans, P. 1995. *Embedded Autonomy: States and Industrial Transformation.* Princeton, NJ: Princeton University Press.
Foucault, M. 1995. *Discipline and Punish: The Birth of the Prison.* New York: Vintage Books.
—. 1990. *The History of Sexuality.* New York: Vintage Books.
Gabrowski, V. 1999. Introduction to the history of Muang Sing prior to French rule: The fate of Lü Principality. *Bulletin de l'École française d'Extrême-Orient* 86: 233-91.
Goodman, D.S.G. 2001. *The Politics of the West: Equality, Nation-Building and Colonization.* Sydney: Institute for International Studies, University of Technology.
—. 2004. The campaign to "open up the West": National provincial-level and local perspectives. *China Quarterly* 178: 317-34.
Greenhalgh, S., and E. Winkler, 2005. *Governing China's Population: From Leninist to Neoliberal Biopolitics.* Stanford: Stanford University Press.
Harrell, S. 1995. Introduction. In *Cultural Encounters on China's Ethnic Frontiers,* ed. S. Harrell, 3-36. Seattle: University of Washington Press.
Harvey, D. 1990. *The Condition of Postmodernity.* Cambridge, MA: Blackwell.
—. 2005. *A Brief History of Neoliberalism.* Oxford: Oxford University Press.
Hoffman, L. 2006. Autonomous choices and patriotic professionalism: On governmentality in late-socialist China. *Economy and Society* 35(4): 550-70.
Holbig, H. 2004. The emergence of the campaign to open up the West: Ideological formation, central decision-making and the role of the provinces. *China Quarterly* 178: 335-57.
Hostetler, L. 2001. *Qing Colonial Enterprise: Ethnography and Cartography in Early Modern China.* Chicago: University of Chicago Press.
Li, T. 2007. *The Will to Improve: Governmentality, Development, and the Practice of Politics.* Durham, NC: Duke University Press.
Litzinger, R. 2004. The mobilization of "nature": Perspectives from north-west Yunnan. *China Quarterly* 178: 488-504.
Murphy, R. 2004. Turning peasants into modern Chinese citizens: "Population quality" discourse, demographic transition and primary education. *China Quarterly* 177: 1-20.
Scott, J.C. 1998. *Seeing Like a State: How Certain Schemes to Improve the Human Condition Have Failed.* New Haven, CT: Yale University Press.
Shue, V., and M. Blecher. 1996. *Tethered Deer: Government and Economy in a Chinese County.* Stanford, CA: Stanford University Press.
Sigley, G. 2006. Chinese Governmentalities: Government, governance and the socialist market economy. *Economy and Society* 35(4): 487-508.
Sturgeon, J.C. 2007. Pathways of "indigenous knowledge" in Yunnan, China. *Alternatives: Global, Local, Political* 32(1): 129-53.
Unger, J. 2002. *The Transformation of Rural China.* London: M.E. Sharpe.
Wade, R. 1990. *Governing the Market: Economic Theory and the Role of Government in East Asian Industrialization.* Princeton, NJ: Princeton University Press.

Walder, A. 1995. The quiet revolution from within: Economic reform as a source of political decline. In *The Waning of the Communist State: Economic Origins of Political Decline in China and Hungary*, ed. A. Walder, 1-24. Berkeley, CA: University of California Press.

Xu Jianchu. 2006. The political, social, and ecological transformation of a landscape: The case of rubber in Xishuangbanna, China. *Mountain Research and Development* 26(3): 254-62.

10
Conclusion: Lesson for the Future
Jean Michaud

Many lessons can be learned from studies such as the ones in this volume about how, in the socialist portion of the Southeast Asian Massif, local populations interpret globalizing shifts in their livelihood choices and practices and how, in Sally Engle Merry's words (2006), they vernacularize modernity. The themes explored in this book are many, from migration, cross-border trade, relocation, and economic mobility to the importance of local history, identity maintenance, avoidance, and subordination. Attempting to summarize such findings would inevitably lessen the unique and rich contributions made by each of the case studies. It is precisely this uniqueness that matters because it has too often been downplayed within this region.

Nevertheless, all of the local groups about which we read in this volume are living within politically centralized, one-party socialist states that have recently opened up to liberal market economies. This constitutes a unique political combination in history and one that commands attention. I would like to illustrate this by briefly considering two dimensions that cut across all the case studies in this book, though not necessarily addressed directly by all the authors here; namely, the legacy of the implementation of modern state borders, and the politics of environmental issues in this highland space. Borders matter because their establishment has caused nation-states to deal with peoples on the frontiers in an entirely new way; the politics of environment are of consequence because highland livelihoods are intrinsically linked with nature, and the manner by which the state regulates nature (through environmental policies) has weighty consequences for highland peasants and their livelihoods.

First, the border question. The casting of modern and permanent borders has been a key factor in fragmenting and segregating highland societies between China, Vietnam, and Laos and turning these into national minorities (Michaud 2009). In the process, groups such as the Zhuang, the Dong, the Naxi, the Bai, and the Drung (Gros's chapter) have been nearly totally enclosed within one country, China, and have had to cope with the Han majority's definition of what national identity should look like. Other highland societies have instead been split between adjacent countries. This is the case for the Hmong (chapter by Tugault-Lafleur and Turner), the Yi (Swain), the Hani (Sturgeon, McKinnon), the Khmu (Évrard), the Tarieng (Daviau), and many more. As exposed in this volume, the long-term adaptation of these societies to their new political reality has varied from one group to the next not only because of diverse and often conflicting national agendas but also because of an array of factors such as cultural resilience, economic practices, and political organization, in addition to location, demographics, languages, religion, history, and cultural proximity to lowland majorities (McKinnon 1987; Schoenberger and Turner 2008). Factors of change that reflect new national decrees, laws, development programs, and so on, thus met local specifics.

In the domain of history, one element in particular has been of great significance. As explained in Chapter 1, a key distinction among the highland groups in the Massif can be made between two distinct categories. On the one hand, we have groups with a flexible social structure based primarily on kinship ties (lineage-based groups) and non-territorial social organization. Such groups, for whom primordial links with a given territory play a less fundamental role, include some groups from the Tibeto-Burman and Austro-Asiatic language families (Hani and Lolo outside China, as well as Khmu, Lisu, and Jingpo, for instance) and all of the Miao-Yao. These groups have been able to cope relatively well with political separation, in particular through cross-border mobility and migration. On the other hand, there are some profoundly territorial groups, including many Tibeto-Burmans (for instance, the Naxi, Yi, and Bai), and virtually all Austronesian (Rhade, Raglai, Jarai, and Churu) and Tai speakers (Dong, Dai, Buyi, Zhuang, Nùng, Thái, and Tày, to name a few), for whom the land they inhabit is intrinsically part of their core identity. For many among these latter groups, a territorial fragmentation or the plain political disappearance of their customary domain has been, and for many still is, traumatic.

With the establishment of European colonial powers in Vietnam and Laos and the advent of Republican China, long-established feudal privileges were formally abolished. Private ownership of the land along capitalist lines was promoted until it reached even the highlands, albeit often with appreciable difficulty, but yet it altered customary land tenure systems there. This triggered a syncretic reaction. Local communities, when operating among themselves, would often continue to abide by the old rules (communal or feudal or a blend of both) privately, while publicly, in front of agents of the colonial/republican state, they would follow the newly introduced ones (Mellac 2000; Sikor 2002). When socialism and the subsequent collectivization took place in the second half of the twentieth century, most landowners were dispossessed and land was appropriated by the state (Brandt et al. 2002). Today, in these three countries, land is still nominally owned by the socialist state, but over the last twenty-five years or so, liberalization and decollectivization have allowed for local communities to take back local responsibility for the management of communal land and forests (Sikor 2001; Sturgeon 2005; McKinnon this volume).

For the ancient feudal groups in the Massif, territoriality has resulted in certain links to modernization. It appears that the more geographically rooted a group was, the more swiftly and efficiently it could adapt its land use practices and livelihoods to fit the market economy when modernity reached – be it through colonialism or socialism (or more recent liberalization practices). This, in all likelihood, can be explained by the fact that sedentarity and primordial links to the soil were key factors behind the integration of these groups into centrally controlled feudal systems. This in turn facilitated the move later on into the modern nation-state and, in turn, the liberal economy. As a result, such groups undertake a greater diversity of livelihood options today and are often far more integrated into the market economy than are those less territorially rooted.

Now to the second point, the environment. As several authors in this book have emphasized, over the past twenty years, despite their numbers being extremely small compared with the national majorities – with the exception of Laos, where minorities account for roughly half the population – highlanders in the socialist portion of the Southeast Asian Massif have been persistently blamed by their respective governments for deforestation, land erosion, and chemical poisoning of land and waterways that affect virtually every watershed. Highlanders' agricultural behaviour, especially swiddening, is publicly decried by state officials and many experts alike as highly detrimental to the environment (reviewed in Forsyth and Walker 2008). To discourage swiddening, isolated populations are relocated along national road networks and sedentarized, and crop substitution programs are implemented to enforce commercial agriculture and integration to the market (Colchester and Erni 1999). In several areas in the Massif nowadays, increased demography, decreased availability of forested land, and the spreading of cash cropping all contribute to reducing the duration of fallows beneath a threshold where natural regeneration becomes severely impaired. This is forcing the adoption of chemical additives and modified seeds that are often distributed and handled in ineffective or inappropriate ways. All these factors are in turn used in official rhetoric to blame environmental degradation on highland farmers, adding new challenges to an already fragile balance between people, their livelihoods, and the local environment.

In China, because of the country's sheer scale of nationwide industrial development (notoriously entailing significant pollution) and large-scale population movements, highland minorities are less directly accused by the state of having a harmful impact on the environment (Xu Yuan 2004). To be frank, the Chinese state does not really perceive ethnic minorities in southwestern China as actors of any significance on the national scene (MacKerras 1994, 2003). Yet, the provincial states in Yunnan or Guizhou, for instance, have to constantly remember that 15 and 13 million of their constituents, respectively, are from non-Han extraction. Thus, prudently, in such provinces, the official blame is not directly placed on "minority nationalities" but on "bad habits" or "backward" practices – which, indirectly and conveniently, are often linked to the highland "little brothers" in day-to-day dealings anyway.

In Vietnam, by contrast, for a number of years, the most hotly debated issues regarding the highlands have been linked to environmental degradation (Rambo et al. 1995). In the north, highlanders form a sizable portion of the population and, ironically in comparison to China, are systematically held responsible by the state for deforestation and its adverse consequences for the lowlands and the coastal plains. In the south, tensions over the environment are reaching dangerous levels. The massive migration to the Central Highlands of Kinh from the plains, officially launched in the late 1970s under the New Economic Zone scheme, spearheaded the penetration of the market and put immense additional pressure on highland natural resources and ecosystems there (De Koninck 1996, 1999). In addition, spontaneous economic migration from lowlands to these same highlands started to unfold at the end of the 1980s, thanks to Economic Renovation (Đổi Mới). This was encouraged by crop substitution schemes and extensive plantations such as coffee, tea, and rubber (Tan 2000, Hardy 2002). This policy persists today (and is gaining momentum in the northern highlands too). The pressure thus exerted on resources has generated social tensions, triggering severe social unrest (Tran Thi Thu Trang 2009).

Laos is a country of mountains. Thanks inadvertently to the growing impact of an international agenda of environmental protection channelled through large institutions such as the World Bank (Goudineau 1997), moving highlanders around can be officially legitimized by arguing that forest and watershed protection must be ensured. The widespread and allegedly unsustainable practices of both pioneering and rotational swiddening must, therefore, be put to an end (Ireson and Ireson 1991; Ovesen 2004; Rigg 2005). As both Daviau and Évrard (this volume) explain, scores of highland populations in upland Laos have thus been subject to authoritarian measures and moved out of the forested hills. They are brought down to new resettlement zones established as modern centres where new livelihoods can be developed. By the same token, this policy emphasizes the two themes that have dominated the state's strategy toward ethnic minorities in Laos since 1975: economic modernization and inclusion within a Lao nation-state (Daviau, Cottavoz, and Gonzales-Foester 2005). It has been estimated that by the year

2000, as many as one million peasants in Laos had been relocated, about one-fifth of the total population (Évrard and Goudineau 2004). Much as in Vietnam and China, local protests against this type of policy are swiftly gagged, and news of them still rarely reaches the outside world.

Lesson for the Future
With this picture in mind, and at the closing stages of this particular journey, what lesson can be learned from the socialist parts of the Southeast Asian Massif on how ethnicity and livelihoods correlate?

As a starting point, I would like to recall briefly a key argument made in Chapter 1. There we suggested that the ways local populations on the margins of centralized states make a living while preserving and re-working their identities are shaped not only by external forces (an underlying assumption often made by outside agents) but also by their own culturally embedded agency. The focus of this book was to examine the creative ways by which people on the margins use this agency to retain control over their lives when faced with powerful external normalizing factors. The eight case studies, each in its own way, have shown this assertion to be demonstrable on the ground. Time and again, through highly varied circumstances, ethnically rooted agency appears as a key factor in the local interpretations and translations of global commands and engagements. This is a key factor that has seldom been given adequate space in livelihood studies to date.

Moreover, as discussed above, nation-state building and environmental disputes play directly into local livelihood decision-making processes. It is therefore of interest to note that if we go back to the definitions of sustainable livelihoods in Chapter 1, such specific elements are often ignored in development practitioners' approaches to livelihood studies (Scoones 2009). Livelihood studies are frequently situated within the physical and political limits of the nation-state, and the environment is merely (albeit not always) reduced to "natural capital" within the livelihood asset pentagon (see Conway et al. 2002 and Toner 2003, for critiques of the "asset pentagon").

So, how could livelihood and development research and policy making factor into these key dimensions more constructively? Toward the end of Chapter 1, three suggestions were made: (1) to study and understand ethnicity and culture in order to assist highland peoples in achieving effective livelihood strategies; (2) to realize how ethnicity influences livelihood strategies and vice versa; and (3) to operationalize these lessons for livelihood practices, especially through understanding the role of local agency.

This collection's case studies in (post-)socialist contexts are culturally distant from each other, yet, they highlight the need to be creative in learning about the place ethnicity could be given in livelihood studies. In a nutshell, the message is: local actors have their own ways of doing things, ways attuned to their particular cultures; as a consequence, this implies necessarily that livelihoods are embedded in local identity and ethnicity. Therefore, livelihoods can only be understood and, eventually, successfully changed, when studied comprehensively within discrete cultural contexts that are acknowledged to be fluid and open to change. Beyond paraphrasing Karl Polanyi's assertion (1957) that the economy is always embedded in culture, this statement has far-reaching implications that have been richly illustrated in each of the situations we have just seen. These implications have often been ignored, passively or energetically, by outside agents whose gazes are narrowly focused on swiftly elevating the level of economic performance among "poor" peasants in a given country. This lack of awareness is visible more than ever in socialist Asia, where the enduring Marxist dogma of social evolutionism still thrives, hardened over the last two decades by the equally evolutionist take on economic progress that is typical of neo-liberal agendas (Escobar 1995, Michaud 2009).

Culture as Agency

In China, Vietnam, and Laos, locally embedded traditions distinct from those of the dominant majorities have been labelled "backward" by national majority actors, actors who are often not entirely aware of their own ethnic footprint. This unawareness of their hegemonic character has rendered these actors prone to ethnocentrism and a normalizing polity (MacKerras 1994; van de Walle and Gunewardena 2001; McElwee 2004; Ovesen 2004; Sowerwine 2004; more broadly, see also Scott 1998, Acheson 2006). What the case studies in this volume have demonstrated is that we – and more importantly the subjects of our development schemes – would benefit greatly from a rethinking of these normalizing processes and the prescriptive approaches to livelihood studies they entail. We need a shift from the theoretical and institutional designs of livelihoods based on mechanistic models (Forsyth 2003) to recognizing ethnic networks and culture as core, vital elements.

For modernist thinkers still highly influential within many mainstream approaches to the international development agenda (Leys 2005), ethnic particularity among national minorities is a remnant from an obsolete past, a pre-modern feature in need of "straightening up" – of *redressement*, in Michel Foucault's language. For these thinkers, the ethnic factor is not an asset but an obstacle to the effective implementation of modern (that is, rational and effective) development programs (Ferguson 1997). Ethnic distinction has been reduced to a superfluous artefact that has to be downplayed to allow the efficient implementation of dependable and economically sound solutions (Nederveen Pieterse 2001). In this way, elements of local cultures have been derided by state and development actors alike as superstitious, counter-productive, atavistic, based on ignorance, or just plain stupid. Examples include ritual expenditures, animal sacrifice, the symbolic value attached to certain entities and places, refusal to perform certain "logical" actions, time "wasted" propitiating the spirits, a lack of interest for accumulation, and so on (for instance, see Viet Chung 1968).

This derogatory interpretation on the part of many outside actors in the Massif (not all of them, of course, but still an unfortunately high number) is further compounded by a rampant will to ignore local and regional history and culture along with their implications for today's economics and politics. This will is often rationalized with arguments such as a lack of time, means, or easily accessible information. We also hear of the political and historical unimportance, in the broader scheme of things, of these marginal groups and their deficiency in written archives that could help attest to who they claim they are. As for their oral history, this is frequently brushed aside as unreliable. These "people without history" (Wolf 1982) – peasants around the world as much as in the Massif – have as such been craftily turned into "people without culture" (Scott 2009).

In all the case studies in this volume, it becomes clear to the watchful eye that the type of deep-seated analysis and multi-faceted conclusions reached by each author could be shaped only after a significant amount of time and energy spent working to understand the subjects' take on their own lives and their material and spiritual worlds. As a consequence of this challenging methodology and in place of pinpointing what should be changed among these societies to make them more socially "fit" and economically "competitive," each writer has instead opted for presenting the current reality in an historical perspective, factoring in how the subjects see themselves and how they grasp their current challenges. Proposed solutions, if any, are cautiously worded and come as a result of considering the situation from within and at length. By contrast, outside agents with the predefined aim to "develop the underprivileged" and "alleviate poverty" – an archetypal position within large development institutions and regional states alike – tend first to rely on macro-level measurements, such as national income per capita or flow of goods and capital, to make a general assessment. Then, on the ground, they contain their analyses to objective, rational, and quantifiable factors to underpin their actions: demographics, statistical pictures, agricultural yields, heads of cattle, land surface, formal education levels, the state of biodiversity, slope gradients, erosion rates, chemical inputs, transport costs, soil and forest regeneration cycles, and so on. Undoubtedly, taking such quantitative data into account to analyze a local situation can be useful and is not to blame in any way per se, it often highlights crucial patterns of economic or health demise. It is drawing definitive conclusions and planning action from this type of quantitative analysis *alone* that constitutes the real liability.

Standing at the opposite end of the spectrum, authors in this book have relied predominantly on qualitative factors: beliefs and spirituality, customary wisdom (or indigenous knowledge), social organization, fears, desires, and more. Across the board, their studies have benefited from long and recurring fieldwork periods, intense participant observation, life stories, oral histories, loosely structured and repeated interviews, and, perhaps most importantly, a marked empathy for their subjects, for their fate, and for their right to participate fully in deciding their own future. But equally clear is that qualitative research alone is not going to help highland peasants to determine which variety of crop to adopt to enhance yields, how best they can stop soil erosion, or what the cure is for that malign disease afflicting their livestock.

It was not the point of the authors here to make such assessments; but it rests on the shoulders of development practitioners and policy writers to be able to bring together these two approaches. Qualitative research alone, like quantitative research alone, is not sufficient to ensure long-term solutions and contentment. Both are needed. To achieve this, development practitioners and state officials have to accept that letting the subjects genuinely participate in their own development may require additional flexibility and time. But time is in short supply in most development schemes. Yet, is time the problem, or is it the schemes themselves? Rather than discarding the "take more time" option as impractical and idealistic (that is, more costly), the initiators of those schemes must come to terms with the implications of the simple fact that quick fixes for complex societies do not carry lasting results. And as the case studies in this volume have made patently clear, highland societies in the Southeast Asian Massif are truly complex.

Results-oriented development thinkers, state officials, and development practitioners also have to accept that inviting subjects to participate in their own progress carries the risk of a community not making the "optimal choice" because of a lack of understanding of global forces, a restricted vision linked to a lack of information or formal education, or simply a rejection of the scheme (see McKinnon, this volume). However, we must ask: How total is a failure when it stems from a choice that is coherent with the cultural fabric and the endogenous decision-making processes of a given community? Is such an outcome any less acceptable than failure following the implementation of ill-conceived and ill-applied solutions after a too-short investigation in a poorly understood cultural and historical context? And, one might also ask, why is this latter type of failure so often spun into "a good solution" that was "not properly understood and implemented" by the local subjects, who are "lacking in will and awareness"?

Ethnicity and Resistance

What is it, then, that is not understood well enough about the recipients of development in this case – minority ethnic groups in the socialist portion of the Southeast Asian Massif?

Local groups translate outside demands into locally intelligible arrangements due to the distinctive impetus of their own vision of the world – their culture – and the resulting interpretations may differ significantly from the original intended meaning of the message sent by outside actors, such as state development programs and development practitioners. Putting to use the case studies in this collection, we can see, for instance, that the state's encouragement to increase trade may be objectively sensible for diversifying the livelihoods of the Hmong of Lào Cai province in Vietnam; however, these Hmong do not seem to want to fall in line entirely with the plan that promoters have designed for them and so come up with unexpected actions (see Tugault-Lafleur and Turner's chapter). In Yunnan, Dai, Hani, and Yi peasants, rubber planters, and entrepreneurs are turning their new economic activities into success stories that appear consistent with the principles of the government's Go West scheme; on the ground, however, customary principles are inserted into the equation, and the result sometimes bears only passing resemblance to the model of liberal rural entrepreneurship promoted by Beijing (see chapters by McKinnon, Sturgeon, and Swain). Tarieng and Khmu peasants in Laos may agree to relocate their hamlets as demanded by the Lao state and adjust their livelihoods accordingly, but when examined at closer range, the precise mechanisms of their movements show signs of a project that largely escapes the state's gaze (see chapters by Daviau and Évrard). And while Thái and Tày peasants in northern Vietnam do agree to play by the national rules of land tenure, ancient kinship networks and customary rights are nonetheless essential ingredients in their livelihood strategies (see Mellac's chapter). In all these situations, a degree of overt conformity meets a degree of covert defiance that remains under the radar – James C. Scott's very notion (1990) of infrapolitics – and it is the particular contours of customary social relations, local culture, and agency that decide the balance between the two.

And here the question of resistance arises. How far is resistance a form of livelihood strategy in the Massif, and what does this tell us about the politics of identity maintenance there? Does the notion of resistance allow us to adopt a more dynamic and relevant approach to understanding livelihood strategies locally? First, we have to realize that forms of resistance available to most minority groups in the highlands of China, Vietnam, and Laos, three politically rigid states with potent police forces and matching legal systems, are of the quiet type. Open defiance has long proved to be hazardous, sometimes plainly suicidal. This risk is not to be solely associated with socialist regimes; much the same applied to earlier colonial and imperial times, as the millions of victims from countless rebellions that beset southwest China and northern Indochina in the eighteenth and nineteenth centuries have demonstrated (Lombard-Salmon 1972; Jenks 1994; Culas and Michaud 2004). The lesson has been learned the hard way: a peasant without historical memory can promptly become a dead peasant. Civil society is the necessary condition for social movements to emerge, and in its absence, or in the absence of its most fundamental elements, no such movements can be successfully set in motion without running the high risk of the repressive arm of the state setting out to crush it mercilessly (Pickett 1996; Mittelman and Chin 2000). This is true of mainstream society in heavily populated lowlands, in industrialized settings, and in urban centres, as was manifest in the Tiananmen Square events of 1989. Extreme domination is even more potent on the rural and cultural margins of the state, where open defiance can carry a high price, as recent examples in Tibet, Xinjiang, Vietnam's Central Highlands, and the Xaysomboun Special Region of Laos reconfirm like clockwork.

Yet, I contend that resistance is at play in the ways that new livelihoods are adopted among minorities in the socialist Massif. Resistance, rooted in Scottian infrapolitics, especially its covert form – hidden transcripts – is activated as a custom-made response to disproportionate power exercised in conditions of intense domination. Scott's "everyday forms of peasant resistance" (1985, 2005), also convincingly developed within "everyday politics" by Benedict Tria Kerkvliet (2005, 2009), provide a simple yet powerful explanatory apparatus to decipher the invisible forces of disobedience and refusal at play behind the facade of compliance. The implications of this type of explanation for understanding the strategies of the "weak" in the Massif are palpable (Turner and Michaud 2009). Scott himself (2009) explores them at length in his latest book, *The Art of Not Being Governed: An Anarchist History of Upland Southeast Asia,* and makes a powerful case for reappraising the upland situation in this new light.

In the field of livelihoods, which sits at the core of this book, local peasants are not resisting modernization simply for the sake of refusing change – that would be the outdated homogenous model (Cancian 1989). All peasant societies are interested in change that can ease hardships and bring about a better life. But they also clearly see that new livelihood propositions that arrive from the outside carry cultural and political implications that will impact their social life and identity, in spite of these being "proven" and "objectively excellent" development schemes. Such implications, in themselves, can be enough to trigger resistance. Change, yes, but not at all costs, as this book documents powerfully.

Concluding Thoughts

Mechanistic models applied to livelihood strategies neglect the local role of culturally embedded forms of agency. Consequently, these models also overlook the role of locally rooted and structured micro-politics. The conceptual and methodological solutions proposed here require paying more and deeper attention to the subjects' ways of indigenizing modernity and fashioning infrapolitics, as well as to public and hidden transcripts. Ethnic minority peasants in the socialist part of the Southeast Asian Massif understand the difference between what can be expressed openly and what would better remain concealed. This is not necessarily a case of careful political strategizing but, instead, is played very pragmatically in terms of what represents a risk so big – be it economically, politically, or culturally – that it would be wiser not to run it.

This book aims at making a compelling statement that new livelihood strategies are, for the ethnic minority subjects in the Southeast Asian Massif but also elsewhere, not mere ways out of objective difficulties but also experiments in activating culturally rooted approaches that are geared toward finding solutions to, among other factors, the unyielding imperatives of physiological, social, and spiritual reproduction. In this regard, local communities are not just reactive; they constantly innovate.

In short, here, as in any other situation around the world involving ethnic minorities in modernizing states, the lesson is that culture, ethnicity, and agency play core roles in livelihood decision making, alongside local politics and history. Yet, these features are frequently ignored in livelihood approaches, especially those taken onboard by development practitioners. Bringing together approaches that can build on such locally rooted understandings of livelihoods, while being acceptable to the state, should be the aim. It is where the challenge lies for creating and supporting truly sustainable livelihoods and development and rewarding life strategies.

References

Acheson, J.M. 2006. Institutional Failure in Resource Management. *Annual Review of Anthropology* 35: 117-34.
Anonymous. 2002. Vietnam: *Indigenous Minority Groups in the Central Highlands*. UNHCR Centre for Documentation and Research, Writenet Paper no. 05/2001, 2002.
Brandt, L., J. Huang, G. Li, and S. Rozelle. 2002. Land rights in China: Facts, fictions and issues. *China Journal* 47: 67-100.
Cancian, F. 1989. Economic behavior in peasant communities. In *Economic Anthropology*, ed. S. Plattner, 127-70. Palo Alto, CA: Stanford University Press.
Colchester, M., and C. Erni, eds. 1999. *From Principles to Practice: Indigenous Peoples and Protected Areas in South and Southeast Asia*. 1st ed. IWGIA document no. 97. Copenhagen: International Work Group for Indigenous Affairs.
Conway, T., C. Moser, A. Norton, and J. Farrington. 2002. Rights and livelihoods approaches: Exploring policy dimensions. *Natural Resources Perspectives No. 78*. London: Overseas Development Institute.
Culas, C., and J. Michaud. 2004. A contribution to the study of Hmong (Miao) migrations and history. In *Hmong/Miao in Asia*, ed. N. Tapp, J. Michaud, C. Culas, and G.Y. Lee, 61-96. Chiang Mai: Silkworm Books.
Daviau, S., P. Cottavoz, and G. Gonzales-Foester. 2005. *Resettlement in Laos: Is Resettlement a Solution for Human Development?* Vientiane: Action contre la Faim.
de Haan, L., and A. Zoomers. 2005. Exploring the frontier of livelihoods research. *Development and Change* 36(1): 27-47.
De Koninck, R. 1996. The peasantry as the territorial spearhead of the state in Southeast Asia: The case of Vietnam. *Sojourn* 11(2): 231-58.
—. 1999. *Deforestation of Vietnam*. Ottawa: International Development Research Center.
Ellis, F. 2000. *Rural Livelihoods and Diversity in Developing Countries*. Oxford: Oxford University Press.

Escobar, A. 1995. *Encountering Development: The Making and Unmaking of the Third World.* Princeton: Princeton University Press.

Évrard, O., and Y. Goudineau. 2004. Planned resettlement, unexpected migrations and cultural trauma in Laos. *Development and Change* 35(5): 937-62.

Eyben, R. 2000. Development and anthropology: A view from inside the agency. *Critique of Anthropology* 20(1): 7-14.

Ferguson, J. 1997. Anthropology and its evil twin. In *International Development and the Social Sciences: Essays on the History and Politics of Knowledge,* ed. F. Cooper and R. Packard, 150-75. Berkeley: University of California Press.

Forsyth, T. 2003. *Critical Political Ecology.* London, UK: Routledge.

Forsyth, T., and A. Walker. 2008. *Forest Guardians, Forest Destroyers: The Politics of Environmental Knowledge in Northern Thailand.* Seattle: University of Washington Press.

Gardner, K., and D. Lewis. 1996. *Anthropology, Development and the Post-Modern Challenge.* London: Pluto.

Goudineau, Y., ed. 1997. *Resettlement and Social Characteristics of New Villages: Basic Needs for Resettled Communities in the Lao PDR.* 2 vol. Bangkok: UNESCO/United Nations Development Programme/Orstom.

Hardy, A. 2002. *Red Hills: Migrants and the State in the Highlands of Vietnam.* London: Curzon Press.

Holland, D., W. Lachicotte Jr., D. Skinner, and C. Cain. 2001. *Identity and Agency in Cultural Worlds.* Cambridge, MA: Harvard University Press.

Ireson, C.J., and W.R. Ireson. 1991. Ethnicity and development in Laos. *Asian Survey* 31(10): 920-37.

Jenks, R.D. 1994. *Insurgency and Social Disorder in Guizhou: The Miao Rebellion, 1854-1873.* Honolulu: University of Hawai'i Press.

Kanji, N., J. MacGregor, and C. Tacoli. 2005. *Understanding Market-Based Livelihoods in a Globalising World: Combining Approaches and Methods.* London: International Institute for Environment and Development.

Kerkvliet, B.J.T. 2005. *The Power of Everyday Politics: How Vietnamese Peasants Transformed National Policy.* Ithaca, NY: Cornell University Press.

—. 2009. Everyday politics in peasant societies (and ours). *Journal of Peasant Studies* 36(1): 227-43.

Leys, C. 2005. The rise and fall of development theory. In *The Anthropology of Development and Globalization: From Classical Political Economy to Contemporary Neoliberalism,* ed. M. Edelman and A. Haugerud, 109-25. Malden, Oxford and Carlton: Blackwell Publishing.

Lombard-Salmon, C. 1972. *Un exemple d'acculturation chinoise: La Province du Guizhou au XVIIIe siècle* [An example of Chinese acculturation: The Province of Guizhou in the eithteenth century]. Paris: École française d'Extrême-Orient.

MacKerras, C. 1994. *China's Minorities: Integration and Modernization in the Twentieth Century.* Hong Kong: Oxford University Press.

—. 2003. Ethnic minorities in China. In *Ethnicity in Asia,* ed. C. MacKerras, 16-47. London: RoutledgeCurzon.

McElwee, P. 2004. Becoming socialist or becoming Kinh? Government policies for ethnic minorities in the Socialist Republic of Vietnam. In *Civilizing the Margins: Southeast Asian Government Policies for the Development of Minorities,* ed. C.R. Duncan, 182-213. Ithaca, NY: Cornell University Press.

McKinnon, J. 1987. Convergence or divergence? Indigenous peoples on the borderlands of southwest China. *Asia Pacific Viewpoint* 38(2): 101-5.

Mellac, M. 2000. Des forêts sans partage: Dynamique de l'espace et utilisation des ressources dans un district de montagne au Nord Viêt Nam [Forests not for sharing: Space dynamics and resource use in a highland district of North Vietnam]. PhD diss., Université Michel de Montaigne Bordeaux 3.

Merry, S.E. 2006. Transnational human rights and local activism: Mapping the middle. *American Anthropologist* 108(1): 38-51.

Michaud, J. 2009. Handling mountain minorities in China, Vietnam, and Laos: From history to current issues. *Asian Ethnicity* 10(1): 25-49.

Mittelman, J.H., and C.B.N. Chin. 2000. Conceptualizing resistance to globalization. In *The Globalization Syndrome: Transformation and Resistance,* ed. J.H. Mittelman, 165-78. Princeton, NJ: Princeton University Press.

Nederveen Pieterse, J. 2001. *Development Theory: Deconstructions/Reconstructions.* London: SAGE Publications.

Ovesen, J. 2004. All Lao? Minorities in the Lao People's Democratic Republic. In *Civilizing the Margins: Southeast Asian Government Policies for the Development of Minorities,* ed. C.R. Duncan, 214-41. Ithaca, NY: Cornell University Press.

Pickett, B.L. 1996. Foucault and the politics of resistance. *Polity* 28(4): 445-66.

Polanyi, K. 1957. *The Great Transformation: The Political and Economic Origins of Our Time,* 2nd ed. Boston: Deacon Press.

Rambo, T., R.R. Reed, Trong Cuc Le, and M.R. DiGregorio, eds. 1995. *The Challenges of Highland Development in Vietnam.* Honolulu/Hanoi/Berkeley: East-West Center/Center for Natural Resources/Center for Southeast Asian Studies.

Rigg, J. 2005. *Living with Transition in Laos.* London: RoutledgeCurzon.

Schoenberger, L., and S. Turner. 2008. Negotiating remote borderland access: Small-scale trade on the Vietnam-China border. *Development and Change* 39(4): 665-93.

Scoones, I. 2009. Livelihoods perspectives and rural development. *Journal of Peasant Studies* 36 (1): 171-96.

Scott, J.C. 1985. *Weapons of the Weak: Everyday Forms of Peasant Resistance.* New Haven, CT: Yale University Press.

—. 1990. *Domination and the Arts of Resistance: Hidden Transcripts.* New Haven, CT: Yale University Press.

—. 1998. *Seeing Like a State: How Certain Schemes to Improve the Human Condition Have Failed.* New Haven, CT: Yale University Press.

—. 2005. Afterword to Moral economies, state spaces, and categorical violence. *American Anthropologist* 107(3): 395-402.

—. 2009. *The Art of Not Being Governed: An Anarchist History of Upland Southeast Asia.* New Haven, CT: Yale University Press.

Sikor, T. 2001. The allocation of forestry land in Vietnam: Did it cause the expansion of forests in the northwest? *Forest Policy and Economics* 2(2): 1-11.

Sikor, T., and Dao Minh Truong 2002. Agricultural policy and land use changes in black Thai villages of northern Vietnam, 1952-1997. *Mountain Research and Development* 22(3): 248-55.

Sowerwine, J. 2004. The political ecology of Dao (Yao) landscape transformations: Territory, gender and livelihood politics in highland Vietnam. PhD diss., University of California.

Sturgeon, J. 2005. *Border Landscapes: The Politics of Akha Land Use in China and Thailand.* Seattle: University of Washington Press.

Tan, S.B.-H. 2000. Coffee frontiers in the Central Highlands of Vietnam: Networks of connectivity. *Asia Pacific Viewpoint* 41(1): 51-67.

Toner, A. 2003. Exploring sustainable livelihoods: Approaches in relation to two interventions in Tanzania. *Journal of International Development* 15 (6): 771-81.

Tran Thi Thu Trang. 2009. State-society relations and the diversity of peasant resistance in Vietnam. In *Agrarian Angst and Rural Resistance in Contemporary Southeast Asia,* ed. S. Turner and D. Caouette, 159-79. London: Routledge.

Turner, S., and J. Michaud 2009. "Weapons of the week": Selective resistance and agency among the Hmong in northern Vietnam. In *Agrarian Angst and Rural Resistance in Contemporary Southeast Asia,* ed. S. Turner and D. Caouette, 45-60. London: Routledge.

van de Walle, D., and D. Gunewardena. 2001. Sources of ethnic inequality in Vietnam. *Journal of Development Economics* 65(1): 177-207.

Viet Chung. 1968. National minorities and national policy in the DRV. *Vietnamese Studies* 15: 3-23.

Wolf, E. 1982. *Europe and the People without History.* Berkeley: University of California Press.

Xu Yuan. 2004. Minority rights and national development in the People's Republic of China. *IIAS Newsletter* 35 (12).

Contributors

Steeve Daviau is a PhD candidate in Anthropology at Laval University, Québec, Canada and a consultant in Laos where he has been living for twelve years. He has recently published in *Ethnia* (2008) and *Indigenous Affairs* (2007) and co-edited with Sarah Turner a special issue of *Asia Pacific Viewpoint* (2010) entitled, "Challenges and Dilemmas: Fieldwork with Upland Minorities in Socialist Vietnam, Laos, and Southwest China." He also co-authored with Vanina Bouté, "International agencies and national policies: What development for rural societies? A case study in two Tibetan-Burmese communities in Phongsaly district, Northern Laos," in *Indigenous People under Command*, ed. P. Bourdier (White Lotus, 2009). Daviau has written several reports for multilateral, bilateral, and Non Governmental Organizations in Laos.

Olivier Évrard is an anthropologist and researcher at the Research Institute for Development (IRD) in France and is also Invited Researcher at the Center for Ethnic Studies and Development, at Chiang Mai University, Thailand. He has been conducting research in Laos since the mid-nineties and in Thailand since 2005. His work focuses on the cultural heritage of highland populations, especially Mon-Khmer linguistic groups, inter-ethnic relationships, and forms of mobility. His book, *Chroniques des Cendres: anthropologie des sociétés khmou et des dynamiques interethniques du nord Laos* [Anthropology of Khmu Societies and Interethnic Dynamics in Northern Laos] was published by IRD in 2006.

Tim Forsyth is Reader in the Development Studies Institute at the London School of Economics and Political Science, United Kingdom. He specializes in environment and development with special reference to environmental governance, climate-change policy, technology transfer and international investment, civil society, poverty and environment, scientific uncertainty, and expertise. He has conducted research in Thailand, Vietnam, the Philippines, Indonesia, Burma, Laos, China, and India. He co-authored, with Andrew Walker, *Forest Guardians, Forest Destroyers: The Politics of Environmental Knowledge in Northern Thailand* (University of Washington Press, 2008).

Stéphane Gros is an anthropologist and researcher at the Centre for Himalayan Studies, National Centre for Scientific Research (CNRS), France. He has been conducting anthropological research in the northwest of Yunnan province, China, since the mid-nineties, especially among the Drung (Dulong). He has published a number of articles on issues of interethnic relations, ethnic classification, representations of ethnic minorities, poverty, and categorization.

Terry McGee is Professor Emeritus in Asian Research and Geography at the University of British Columbia, Canada. Author of numerous articles and books over more than five decades, he has carried out research on urbanization in Southeast Asian and is currently researching the urbanization transition in Malaysia.

John McKinnon is Associate Professor (retired) in Geography at Victoria University of Wellington, New Zealand and a consultant. He does action research, enthnogeography of aid policy and practice, community development, and livelihood enhancement. His consulting work has focused on the challenge of participatory rural development (PLA/PRA) and development intervention to promote sustainable livelihoods, especially as it relates to the indigenous minority peoples in the central Massif of Mainland Southeast Asia.

Marie Mellac is Assistant Professor (Maître de conférences) in Geography attached to UMR ADES, Université de Bordeaux/CNRS, France. She specializes in development and the environment, as well as in the management of natural resources, in particular land tenure and forests. In Southeast Asia, she has worked in Vietnam and Laos and has recently published "Foncier et citoyenneté des Tai du nord-ouest Viêt Nam (1850-2000)," in *Politique de la terre et de l'appartenance*, ed. by J.-P. Jacob and P.Y. Le Meur (Karthala, 2010).

Jean Michaud is Professor of Anthropology at Université Laval in Quebec, Canada. His research examines the general processes by which transnational highland societies in upland Southeast Asia and Southwest China indigenize modernity. His recent publications include *"Incidental" Ethnographers: French Catholic Missions on the Tonkin-Yunnan Frontier, 1880-1930* (Brill, 2007); *The A to Z of the Peoples of the Southeast Asian Massif* (Scarecrow, 2009); and he guest edited the thematic issue "Zomia and Beyond" in the *Journal of Global History* (2010).

Janet C. Sturgeon received a doctorate from the Yale School of Forestry and Environmental Studies and teaches in the Geography Department at Simon Fraser University, Canada. Her work focuses on ethnic minority farmers in China, Laos, and Thailand, through rapid transformations in their property rights in natural resources, landscapes, and identities. Her book *Border Landscapes: the Politics of Akha Land Use in China and Thailand* was published by the University of Washington Press in 2005.

Margaret Byrne Swain is a feminist anthropologist at University of California at Davis, United States. She has been working on and off in Yunnan since 1987, focusing on ethnographies of indigenous groups' engagement with post-colonial/post-socialist states and globalization through ethnic tourism and religious conversion.

Claire Tugault-Lafleur has an MA in human geography from McGill University in Canada and is now a Research Assistant at the Center for Indigenous Nutrition and the Environment Department of Dietetics and Human Nutrition, McGill. She is currently finishing a diploma in Dietetics specializing in issues of food security, infant and maternal health, and the role of HIV in breastfeeding and dietary intake. She has co-published with Sarah Turner on cardamom commodity chains in northern Vietnam in the *Singapore Journal of Tropical Geography* (2009).

Sarah Turner is an associate professor in the Department of Geography, at McGill University, Canada. She is a development geographer who specializes in research on ethnic minority livelihoods in the Vietnam-China borderlands, as well as marketplace trade, small scale entrepreneurs, and urban livelihoods of people "on the margins" in Vietnam, southwest China, and Indonesia. She has recently co-edited the book *Agrarian Angst and Rural Resistance in Contemporary Southeast Asia* (Routledge, 2009).

Index

Note: "(f)" after a number indicates a figure

1996-2000 Rural Development Program in Laos, 60

Action contre la Faim, 73n1
agency, 2-3, 9-10, 15-22, 219-25; of the Drung, 45; of the Hani, 131-32, 141-43; of the Hmong, 116; of the Khmu 76-77; of minorities in Yunnan province, 174-75; of the Tarieng, 50, 65-66, 73; of the Thái and Tày, 159, 163-66, 169-70, 184, 187-89
agriculture, 1, 6-7, 41, 45, 64, 68-72, 86, 106, 130-34, 139, 179, 211; cooperative/communal, 146-53, 157-58, 194; subsistence, 11-14, 44, 62, 79, 100; swidden, 45, 69-72, 79, 100, 104, 108-16, 133, 154, 163, 166-68, 217-18; tax, 200, 206
Ailao and Wuliang Mountains, 126
Akha (people) 20, 22, 123-43, 193-212. *See also* Hani
Alak (people), 78, 104
alder *(Alnus nepalensis),* 144n11
Amo Jiang River, 126
Annam Range, 50, 51(f), 57-61, 72
Ashima, 179-84
Asian Development Bank (ADB), 89
Assam, 23n4, 170n1
Attapeu province (Laos), 50, 58, 73n1, 81
Austro-Asiatic language family, 148
Austronesian language family, 58, 216

Ba Be Lake, 148
Bac Kan province (Vietnam), 148-52
Bac Thái province (Vietnam), 5
Badong River, 136-43, 137(f), 138(f)
Bahnaric language subfamily, 58
Bai (people), 21, 173, 184, 186, 215, 216

Ban Dok Douang (Tai Lue), 206-7
Ban Huey Din Chee, 97n12
Ban Khoang commune (Vietnam), 108, 112, 115, 114(f)
Ban Konechan, 89
Ban Luot (Vietnam), 148, 153-55, 159-70
Ban Mokkoud, 79, 84, 87-88, 96n11
Ban Namtchang, 84
Ban Oudom (Laos), 81
Ban Saphut (Khmu), 80
Ban Vangli (Laos), 68
bananas, 207
black cardamom. *See* cardamom
Bokeo province (Laos), 84
Bolaven Plateau, 71
Bolikhamsay province (Laos), 97n22
borders, 1-10, 15, 19-21, 215-16; Laos-Thailand, 90-91, 92-93; Laos-Vietnam, 50-51, 58, 61-65, 72-73; Sino-Burmese, 35-36; Sino-Laotian, 193-96, 200-12; Sino-Vietnamese, 102-6, 169; of Yunnan province, 31, 33, 102
Brahmaputra River, 3
Bulang (people), 194
Buyi (people), 216

camphor oil, 43
cardamom, 20, 100, 107(f), 108, 112-17, 119, 135
Cat Cat (Vietnam), 108
Center for Biodiversity and Indigenous Knowledge (CBIK), 185
Central Highlands of Vietnam, 7, 119n6, 119n8, 218, 224
Champasak province (Laos), 71
Chavan village (Tarieng), 69
Chiang Hung, 83

232 Index

Chiang Khong (Thailand), 81-82, 91-94
Chiang Mai (Thailand), 91, 92, 123, 124
Chiang Rai (Thailand), 91, 92, 124
Chin (people), 6
Chinese fir, 141
Cho Don (Vietnam), 148, 153-55, 161-70
Churu (people), 216
Cultural Revolution in China, 130, 179, 198

Dai (people). *See* Tai Lue
Dak Lieng Loung (Laos), 71, 74n9
Dakang (people), 58
Dakcheung district (Laos), 58-61, 66, 70, 72, 73n1
Dali (Tali), 21, 173, 177-78, 184, 189
Danish East Asiatic Company (EAC), 91
Dao (people). *See* Yao
Daru (Daru Nung), 35-36
Daxing, 126
debt slavery, 33-34
Democratic Republic of Vietnam (North Vietnam), 6, 146, 153, 171
Deng Xiaoping, 177, 181, 196-97
Deutsche Gesellschaft für Technische Zusammenarbeit (GTZ), 90
development, 6-7, 9-16, 21-22, 216-25; developmentalism, xiii-xiv; among the Hani, 123-24, 141-43; among the Hmong, 101-2, 104, 106; among the Khmu, 76-80, 85, 87-90, 95; among the Tarieng, 50, 56-62, 65-66, 69, 73; in Xishuangbanna, 193-212; in Yunnan, 28, 41, 43-47, 173-90
Dien Bien Phu, 5
Diqing prefecture (China), 185
Doi Moi (Economic Renovation in Vietnam), 56, 101, 104, 116, 218
Dong (people), 215-16
Drung (people), 18-19, 28-47, 215
Drung Valley, 130
Dulong (people). *See* Drung

eco-tourism. *See* tourism
Emperor Bao Dai, ix
environment, harm to, 6, 11-12, 21, 215, 217-19; protection, 43, 56, 190, 193, 195, 202; in Yunnan, 29, 43, 123-43
Environment Protection Bureau (China), 140-43
European Union, 90

Five Million Hectares reforestation program, 105, 119
Ford Foundation, 177, 185, 190,
Foucault, Michel, 51, 57, 72, 197, 201, 220

Ganlongtang (China), 181-82
Giay (people), 103, 108, 117-18
Go West campaign, 7, 21, 143, 177-78, 187-88, 195-96, 202, 211, 223
Gongshan Autonomous County (China), 28-30, 40, 43, 185
Gourou, Pierre, xv
Grain for Green, 202
Great Leap Forward, 130, 179, 205
Great Rivers Project, 29
Great Western Development, 44, 47, 196
Green Lake (Kunming), 180
Guangdong province (China), 206-7
Guizhou province (China), 178, 218
Guo Fang village (Laos), 208-9

Hainan (China), 187, 199
Han (people), 3, 7, 35, 43, 134, 150, 173, 179-211
Hani (people), 18, 20-21, 22, 123-43, 216, 223. *See also* Akha
Hani-Lisu Honghe Institute for Minority Studies (China), 124, 140, 143
Hanoi, 80, 148, 149
Hat Yao district (Laos), 205
Highland Inter Mountain Peoples Education and Culture in Thailand Association, 124
Hmong (people), 18, 20, 83, 100-20, 148, 166-68, 205, 216
Ho Chi Minh Trail, 19, 50, 58
Hoa (people), 103
Hoang Lien National Park (Vietnam), 105, 110-12
Honghe Prefecture (China), 126, 134
Huangcaoling district, 134
Huaphan province (Laos), 84
Hueysay (Laos), 81-85, 90, 93-94

identity, xi-xii, 6, 8-10, 13-22, 124, 215-16, 220, 223-24; among the Drung, 28-46; among the Khmu, 77, 80; among the Tarieng, 73; in Vietnam, 156, 166, 168; in Yunnan, 173-75, 179, 183-90
Institut de Recherche pour le Développement (IRD), 123
Irrawaddy Valley, 33
Isthmus of Kra, 3

Jarai (people), 216
Jiache district (China), 134
Jinghong, 202-8
Jingpo/Jingpaw. *See* Kachin
Jinshajiang (Golden Sand River), 28
Jinuo (people), 194

Kachin (people), 6, 9, 35, 216
Kalum district, 60, 71-72
Kanha (Laos), 87
Karen (people), 8, 124
Katu (people), 84
Katuic language sub-family, 58
Kayson Phomvihane, 74n5
Khmer (people), 3
Khmu, 18, 20, 76-95, 148, 152, 155, 216, 223; Khmu Kwaen, 82-87, 92; Khmu Lue, 82, 86; Khmu Rok, 82-87, 92; Khmu Yuan, 82-87, 92; *tmoys* (subgroups), 82-83
Khumban Phathana. *See* Village Development Clusters
Kinh (people), ix, 3, 101-18, 148-69, 218
Kon Tum province (Vietnam), 50, 58
Konkoud (Laos), 84, 87-88
Kunming (China), 7, 28, 31, 142, 177-85
Kunming Institute of Botany, 204

Lahu (people), 83, 143n6, 194
Lai Chau province (Vietnam), 149, 159
Lamam district, 60, 71
Lamet (people), 81-83. *See also* Rmeet
Lampang (Thailand), 81-82, 90-94
Lamphun (Thailand), 91
Lancangjiang. *See* Mekong River
land reform: in Vietnam, 21; in Yunnan province, 130, 141, 146-70
Lao Aluminium Industry Company, 64
Lao Cai province (Vietnam), 20, 101-4, 112, 148-49, 152, 159, 223
Lao Chai commune (Vietnam), 114
Lao Front for National Construction, 54, 67
Lao Issara movement, 79
Lao Language, 52-54, 65, 73
Lao People's Revolutionary Party, 52, 65-66, 73
Lao Women's Union, 54, 67
Lao Youth Union, 54-55
lemon grass, 135-36, 139
"Liberation" (Chinese Communist Victory, 1949), 31, 37-41, 125, 129-30
Lijiang (China), 29, 173, 178, 184-85
lineage societies, 19, 50-73, 94
Lisu (people), 28-33, 216
Lolo (people), 216. *See also* Yi
Long March, 5
Long Shanli, 129
Luang Namtha province (Laos), 76-95, 209
Luang Prabang province (Laos), 78-79, 91
Luangnamtha town, 82-88
Lüchun County (China), 126-30

Lüchun Environmental Protection Bureau, 143
Luguhu/Lugu Lake (China), 173, 178, 184, 189
Lumeiyi town (China), 182
Luzi (people), 29, 36, 40

maize, 11, 41, 94, 100, 104, 106-8, 113-16, 126, 129, 136
Man Ba San town (Laos) 207-8
Mao Zedong, 37, 40, 43, 198
Maori (people), 8
marginalization, 28-47
Masai (people), 8
Mekong River, 28, 78-94, 176-77, 186, 195
Meng La County (China), 205-6; 209-10
Meng Xing State Farm, 213n13
Meng Yuan district (China), 205-6
Miao (people). *See* Hmong
Miao-Yao language family, 11, 102, 148, 216
Mien (people). *See* Yao
migration, 7, 14, 58, 76-95, 102, 148, 182, 215-18
minority policy, xi-xiv; in China, 5, 134; in Laos, 73, 218; in Vietnam, 6, 120
modernity/modernization, xii-xv, 3, 12, 45, 57, 92, 102, 130-32, 142, 147, 174-90, 196-97, 200-12, 217-20, 224-25
Mokachok, 92
Mom village (Laos), 205
Mon-Khmer language family, 50, 55, 78, 95, 96n3, 97n17
Moso. *See* Naxi
Mosuo (people), 173, 175, 185
Muang Beng, 82, 84
Muang Hun, 82, 84, 93
Muang Sing, 82, 83
Muong (people), 103

Na (people). *See* Mosuo
Nalae district (Laos), 68, 76-95
Nam Pha (Laos), 71
Nam Tha River, 76-95
Nan (Thailand), 83, 92
National Growth and Poverty Alleviation Strategy (Laos), 60
National Tourism Administration (China), 177
Naxi (people), 28, 29, 31, 33, 39, 42, 273, 184, 186, 215-16
nay roy (Khmu middlemen), 91-93
Neo Lao Hak Sat (NLHS, the Lao Patriotic Front). *See* Neo Lao Issara
Neo Lao Issara (Free Laos Front), 79

New Economic Mechanisms (NEM, Laos), 56
New Economic Zone scheme (NEZ, Vietnam), 218
New Socialist Man, 52-53
Ngkriang (people), 72
Nong Bu (Laos), 61
Nu (people). *See* Luzi
Nujiang Prefecture (China), 29
Nujiang River (Salween), 28, 33, 41
Nung (people), 28, 31, 33, 25-26, 216

opium, 12, 20, 100, 104, 105, 112, 116, 130, 135
oral history, xiv, 221
Oudomxay province (Laos), 78, 80-87

Pak Tha (Laos), 96n12
Paksong district (Laos), 71
panopticon, 8, 51, 57, 65, 72
Pathet Lao, 76, 81-85, 96n8
Pelzer, K.J., xv
Phongsaly province (Laos), 78, 80, 84, 91, 209
Phrae (Thailand), 91, 92
Phu Noy (people), 84
plantations, 7, 44, 73, 143, 161, 218; cassava, 62; coffee, 62, 71; rubber, 22, 90, 193, 203; teak, 91; tobacco, 91
poppy. *See* opium
post-socialism, 82, 85-95, 173, 198
Prince Phetsarath, 96n8
Prince Souphanouvong, 96n8
Prince Souvanna Phouma, 96n8
Pushan community, 128
Puyi, 128

Qing dynasty, 31, 33
Qiuzi. *See* Drung

Raglai (people), 216
Rawang (Rawang Nung), 36, 47n2
Red Guards, 131
reforestation, 7, 12, 40, 44, 56, 104-5, 119n6, 177, 202
relocation, 7, 11, 12, 19, 215, 217, 218; in Laos, 7, 56-73, 76-77, 81-90, 94, 219, 223; in Vietnam, 163, 167; in Yunnan, 44
resistance, xi, xiv-xv, 7-9, 17-22, 50, 65-67, 72-73, 77, 88, 147, 155, 159, 222-24
Rhade (people), 216
rice, 36-44, 68-94, 100-20, 161; biodiversity, 45, 70; dry (non-irrigated), 11, 129-30; High Yield Varieties (HYV), 107-16; wet (irrigated), 44, 136, 163, 206

Rmeet (people), 86, 94, 97n18
Rok. *See* Khmu
rubber, 22, 90, 193-212, 218, 223

Sa (people). *See* Khmu
Sa Pa district (Vietnam), 101-18
Sakaen (village), 84, 87
Salween River. *See* Nujiang River
Samneua province (Laos), 80
San Sa Ho commune (Vietnam), 109
Sang village (Laos), 72
Sani Yi (people) 173, 180
Sanmeng, 126
Sanxay district (Laos), 58, 71-73
Saravane province (Laos), 66, 81
Sedaka village (Malaysia), 16
sedentarization, 11, 20, 217; among the Hmong, 100; in Laos, 56, 60-65
Sekaman 3 hydropower project, 61-62
Sekong province (Laos), 50, 58, 60, 64, 84
Shan (people), 6, 193
Shangri-La, 29, 173, 178, 185
Shangshapu village, 126-43
Shilin (the Stone Forest, China), 21, 173, 177-87
Shilin Tourism Bureau, 179
Shilin Yi Nationality Autonomous County (China), 179
Sichuan province (China), 28, 179, 184
Sin Chai hamlet (Vietnam), 110
Sing district (Laos), 78, 205, 209
Sino-Vietnamese War, 104, 106
Sipsongpanna. *See* Xishuangbanna
socialism, xii, xv, 1, 2, 216-17; in China, 31, 123, 135; in Laos, 19, 20, 51, 56, 76-95; in Vietnam, 19, 116, 168-70. *See also* post-socialism
Song Da (Vietnam). *See* Amo Jiang River
South China Sea, 1
Southeast Asian Massif, ix-xiii, 1-22, 34, 102, 110, 215-25
Stalin, Joseph, 4-5
sugar, 135, 199, 205-8
Suharto, xv

Tai language sub-family, 23n4
Tai Lue, 22, 193-212; Dai, 18, 23n5, 173, 184, 186, 216, 223; Tai Dam, 81
Tan Lap commune (Vietnam), 167
Tarieng (people), 18-19, 50-73, 216, 243
Tay (people), 5, 18, 21, 103, 146-68, 216, 223
tea, 135-38, 161, 199, 218
teak, 91-92
Thai (people); Black Thai (Tai Dam), 148; White Thai, 148

Than Uyen district (Vietnam), 148-49, 159-60
Thateng district (Laos), 60, 71
The Nature Conservancy, 29, 177-78, 188, 190
Tibeto-Burman language family, 28, 31, 216
tourism, 19, 86, 100-16; eco-tourism, 28-29; in Yunnan, 21, 173-90
trade, 2, 11-12, 40, 197, 200, 215, 223; among the Drung, 33-34; among the Hmong, 100, 104, 106, 110-11, 115-18. *See also* World Trade Organization
transnationalism, xi, 2, 8, 15, 17-18, 57, 92, 102, 106, 176-79, 189-90, 193-212, 215-16
Tribal Research Centre (Chiang Mai, Thailand), 123
Triu (people), 58
Tropical Crops Research Institute (Jinghong, China), 203, 212
Tropical Forestry Action Plan of 1990 (Laos), 56
turpentine, 91

UNESCO World Heritage, 29, 177, 179, 184, 190
United Nations Development Programme (UNDP)
United Nations High Commissioner for Refugees (UNHCR), 205

Vial, Paul, 178
Vieng Kaen district (Thailand), 92, 94
Viengphukha town and plateau, 78(f), 82(f), 84, 87
Viet Minh, 5, 50, 66, 103
Village Development Clusters (VDC, Laos), 58-73

World Bank, 15, 89, 169, 218
World Tourism Organization (UN), 177-78, 188
World Trade Organization (WTO), 22, 195, 199-200, 206, 211
Wukeshu (China), 181, 183

Xay Phou Louang (Laos), 50
Xaysomboun Special Region (Laos), 8, 224
Xianggelila, 178. *See also* Shangri-La
Xiashapu, 126-43
Xibidong, 128
Xieng Louang (Laos), 59-61, 64, 69
Xiengkok, 82(f), 84
Xinjiang province (China), 224
Xishuangbanna, 22, 173, 177-78, 184, 193-212
Xishuangbanna Tropical Botanic Garden, 204, 212n4

Yangtze River, 3; floods of 1998, 202
Yao (people), 83, 103, 112, 117, 118n1, 148, 154-55, 163, 167-68, 194
Yeh (people), 58, 68
Yi (people), 5, 18, 21, 23n5, 178-90, 194, 216, 223. *See also* Lolo
Yuanyang county (China), 129, 134
Yunnan Academy of Social Sciences, 185
Yunnan province (China), x, 1-22, 83, 94, 170n1, 218, 223; northwest, 28-46; rubber in, 193-212; southeast, 123-43; tourism, 173-90
Yunnan Provincial Tourism Administration, 177

Zhongdian, 29, 185
Zhuang (people), 215, 216
Zomia, 2, 3n1

Printed and bound in Canada by Friesens
Set in Stone by Artegraphica Design Co. Ltd.
Copy editor: Judy Phillips
Proofreader: Dianne Tiefensee